LETTERS TO NIMROD

Edward Elgar to August Jaeger, 1897–1908

Elgar and his father

LETTERS TO NIMROD

Edward Elgar to August Jaeger

1897—1908

EDITED AND ANNOTATED BY

PERCY M. YOUNG

London : Dennis Dobson

First published in 1965 by Dobson Books Ltd
80 Kensington Church Street, London W.8

Printed in Great Britain
by Bookprint Limited
Kingswood, Surrey

CONTENTS

LIST OF ILLUSTRATIONS

ACKNOWLEDGEMENTS

I am grateful to the following for helping to elucidate details in Elgar's Letters: Dr. I. Kecskeméti (Budapest), Mr. John Littleton, Professor Dr. Paul Mies (Cologne), Professor Dr. P. Nuten (Antwerp), Dr. Konrad Sasse, and Mr. Günter Weise (Halle), Mr. Frieder Zschoch (Leipzig), the Deutsches Musikgeschichtliches Archiv (Kassel), and the Librarians of the *Guardian* and of the City or Municipal Libraries of Birmingham, Leeds, Liverpool, Manchester, Sheffield, and Worcester; to the family of the late Miss Rosa Burley for access to her records and for the use of the photograph of Llangranog facing p. 60; to Messrs. Boosey and Hawkes Ltd., for permission to reproduce the opening of the manuscript score of the second *Pomp and Circumstance* March; and to Mr. Herbert Rees, of Bookprint Limited, for his invaluable assistance.

P.M.Y.

PREFACE

August Johannes Jaeger (18 March 1860–18 May 1909) was a native of Düsseldorf. At the age of eighteen he came to England, first finding employment with a map-printing firm in the Strand. In 1890 he joined the publishing staff of Novello,[1] then controlled by Alfred Henry, and Augustus James, Littleton. In that year Edward Elgar placed a part-song (*My love dwelt in a northern land*) with the firm and during the next six years a number of other works, including the *Spanish Serenade*, *The Black Knight*, *Lux Christi*, and *King Olaf*, were accepted by them. These works, although considered by some to stand on the edge of obscure modernity, were welcomed by the English choral societies – then the main support of native music – and performances multiplied. By the time he was forty Elgar's name was by no means unfamiliar. There were, of course, other successful composers – for instance, Cowen, Mackenzie, Parry, Stanford, Sullivan: their names occur frequently in the following pages. It was, however, Elgar who struck the experienced and perceptive Jaeger as the one with the largest share of genuine talent. 'I am,' he wrote in the autumn of 1897, 'conceited enough to think that I can appreciate a good thing and see genius in musicians that are *not* yet dead . . .'

This was shortly after the extant exchange of letters between Elgar and Jaeger began. The letters begin on a business basis and continue, with a rapidly developing intimacy, until Jaeger's death in 1909. At their commencement Elgar, sustained by the enthusiasm of provincial choral singers, by his fellow-countrymen in and about Worcester, was about to make a major break-through. In April, the *Imperial March*, catching the national, euphoric mood of the times, was to enjoy an extraordinary favour, by which Elgar first claimed recognition as a Laureate composer. About success he was half-indifferent. As was the composer's situation then, success furnished no adequate standard of living. 'It's all very well,' he wrote as late as 1904, 'to talk to me about doing Sextetts & Symphonies & all the things I *want* to do, but tell me what & who is going to keep a roof over our heads? Nobody thinks of that.' Thus, his energies and ambitions gnawed by discontent, and his inherent anxiety-neurosis increased by the uncertainties that afflict every artist concerning the maintenance of his creative integrity, he looked for encouragement and moral support. He found both in Jaeger.

[1] Until 1906 Novello's were at 1 Berners Street, the Wardour Street premises being adopted in 1906. In 1898 the firm became a limited company.

The respect which Elgar maintained for Germany, based on the works of the great masters, a fortnight's visit to Leipzig in 1883, and envy of the social position enjoyed by the composer in that country, predisposed him to listen attentively to the German-born Jaeger; and a feature of this correspondence is the relationship established between Elgar and the leading musicians of Germany. That this became possible, and a main cause of Elgar's leap into the first rank of European composers at the turn of the century, was largely due to Jaeger, with his many contacts in the cities of his fatherland. During the nineteenth century German influences, indiscriminately accepted by many English composers, brought English music to a condition of near-atrophy. Elgar, studying in Germany for no more than a fortnight, was more selective, so that when his music was first heard in the Rhineland it impressed not because it revealed German traits but because it was original, and English. At this point the Germans took it to their hearts and elevated the composer to a high rank for the right reasons. 'I can't believe,' wrote Elgar in 1903, 'all those great Germans are doing my music: is it true? I think it is a dream.' Two World Wars and subsequent changes of musicological emphasis have obscured the great debt which England owes to Germany in this respect. A personal note obtrudes. – One day I had occasion to visit the engraving firm in Leipzig responsible for the publication of the new *Hallische-Händel-Ausgabe*. The head of the firm, the septuagenarian Herr Fritz M. Geidel, reminded me that his father, first introduced to English trade through the firm of Oppenheimer, had, long years ago, engraved music of the leading English composers for Messrs. Novello. Pride in having been connected with Edward Elgar still maintains. The hotel in which Elgar first stayed in Leipzig is now a block of flats: in one of them lives the harpist of the Gewandhaus Orchestra. That too, I feel, would please Elgar.

If one stresses the German connections it is because these run throughout these letters and, by comparison, underline the inferior place which Elgar felt himself, and English composers in general, to occupy in a society which, to say the least, was self-conscious in coming to terms with culture. In England composers were most often honoured when, to quote Jaeger again, they were 'Cathedral organists, or Directors of music in colleges for boys'. In the 1890s the Establishment was pretty powerful – and so remained for many years. Jaeger deplored this, particularly when called upon to assist in the publication of indifferent music distinguished only by its propriety, or when required – as he was – to moderate his critical asperities in *The Musical Times*. Elgar, the outsider, regarded the Establishment with perpetual displeasure. Although, both in a musical and social way, he conquered it he always remained aloof, remembering how, when *Gerontius* was in gestation he must undertake 'hack-work – orchestrating a comic opera for another chap'. He was always in sympathy with those of this kind of vocation.

The reader of these letters will discover how, in the course of time, Jaeger reflected Elgar, and Elgar Jaeger. These were poor men, rebellious about their poverty; they were more often than not reduced to physical and mental discomforts by their exertions – Jaeger increasingly also by the ravages of tuberculosis, which throws the last, diminishing, part of the correspondence into the field of tragedy; they were, on the other hand, imbued both by imaginative fervour and a vivid perception of the wryness of the human comedy. To each other they were generous, and bound by a warmth of affection that shows, perhaps, too nakedly on the printed page. Elgar, in particular, in moments of high emotion spilled himself without restraint. Jaeger, more and more, became the godfather of Elgar's compositions and in respect of one of them at least – the *Introduction and Allegro* – he could claim complete credit for its genesis.

This correspondence starts when Elgar is on the threshold of writing his major works – with the *'Enigma' Variations* a year away – and concludes with Jaeger's welcome to the first symphony, of which the long, chequered history runs like a *leitmotiv* through these pages. It covers the oratorios, *Cockaigne*, the *Introduction and Allegro*, *In the South*, the first four *Pomp and Circumstance* Marches, and many lesser works. Elgar reveals much of his compositional processes, many autobiographical minutiae, and also considerable psychological insight. His views on society, on the condition of music, on the harassments attendant on the production of new music, are exposed, as well as his assessment of various composers, some of whom are forgotten, some not. Taken together, Jaeger and Elgar provide an illuminating picture of a phase in British music that, in spite of Elgar's fame, has on the whole lacked detailed commentary.

Since the centenary of his birth Elgar has been mulled over by many and his reputation as a composer, a subject of special pleading, perhaps, in 1957, has greatly appreciated. What kind of man he was: here there is no finality, for he was too various to ever permit easy categorization; but these documents, in their spontaneity, add to our existing knowledge. No commentary is here needed, unless to draw attention to what might easily be forgotten, that on 20 August 1903 he wrote 'I feel I can only *non* say *sum dignus*': a sentiment that was always prevalent.

These letters have been preserved in the Elgar Archives, at Broadheath near Worcester; and all those of Elgar which are extant are reproduced, only excepting five already published in my *Letters of Edward Elgar*

(Bles 1956) to which there are cross-references, and twelve of uncertain date and minimal interest. The principles of editorship which were the basis of that volume have been applied to this. Elgar's orthography and punctuation remain as they were, often showing obvious signs of haste. Doubtful words or speculative replacements are given in square brackets. Dating has sometimes been difficult and here again editorial calculations or surmises are similarly shown. To have published the whole of Jaeger's side of the correspondence would have been physically impossible. I have, therefore, indicated those points that have direct reference to what Elgar writes, or observations on his music, and in some cases have included complete letters, which have been edited according to the principles outlined above.

Among other documents of the period to which I have had access are excerpts from letters by various German musicians, and some notes, preliminary to a projected book, made by Miss Rosa Burley. These have been quoted extensively to amplify the general scheme. Further useful information has been extracted from the files of contemporary newspapers and magazines. It will be seen how valuable some of these are – as, for example, the sketch of Elgar's personality as it appeared to the reporter of the *Sheffield Telegraph* in 1902 – and how much they reveal of the general musical scene and, indeed, the scale of values. Together with the letters of Elgar and Jaeger there have been preserved some which passed between Lady Elgar and Jaeger and Mrs. Jaeger. These increased towards the end of Jaeger's life when Elgar himself was more and more involved in affairs and with people: a circumstance that Jaeger viewed with misgiving in that he saw it as potentially disastrous to creative activity. Many of those musicians named in the correspondence will be unfamiliar, not always, indeed, mentioned in works of reference. I have, therefore, added a fairly complete Appendix with their *curricula vitae*. This provides evidence as to those who, at that time, were effective in English music. Some of those detailed were distinguished, some less so; but the debt owed to such as Benton, Coward, Gill, Read, Schöllhammer, and Wilson, is considerable, and Elgar would, I feel sure, have it acknowledged.

In his belief that music should be a general experience and amenity Elgar was, whatever his other attitudes, radical beyond his generation. In feeling, this is the character and quality of his music. The opposition resented the dethronement of a sectarian academic mystery by one who could wake one day to a flippant mood to describe himself as 'Gibbonsy, Croftish, Byrdlich, & foolish'; yet this approach, which holds its point today as yesterday, was, when allied to genius, the spur both to vigorous creation and to wide appreciation. What is music? In this book lies some part of the answer, the more compelling, perhaps, because Elgar was writing without care for his posthumous literary reputation, or for aesthetic theories, and only for the eyes of an intimate.

In encouraging me, in many ways, to continue my researches into her father's life and works Mrs. Elgar Blake is my principal creditor. If all descendants of the great were as generous and as devoted to the principles of scholarship, biographical studies would provide less cause for contention than often they do. For permission to issue the letters of Elgar I am indebted to Mrs. Elgar Blake and the Trustees of the Elgar Will; for the excerpts from Jaeger to Messrs. Novello & Co. Ltd, in the transaction of whose business and generally on whose note-paper the original letters were written. Other acknowledgements appear under a separate heading.

January 1965   P.M.Y.

1897

INTRODUCTORY

Elgar had been publishing music with various houses for more than a decade before this correspondence opens, at which point he may be seen as having achieved a major break-through. By now his works were readily making their way into print and were enjoying frequent performance. In the main they were acceptable to the more forward-looking provincial choral societies, in which the firm of Novello had a particular interest. Elgar had published with Novello's since 1890, in which year Jaeger had joined their staff, and the works so far on their list were: Froissart (*1890*), Spanish Serenade *and* The Black Knight (*1893*), *the two part-songs of Op. 26* (*1894*), *and* Lux Christi (*1896*). King Olaf *was also published in 1896, and in the early part of 1897 Novello's accepted the* Imperial March *and* The Banner of St. George.

Regarding the preliminaries to the performance of King Olaf *at the Crystal Palace on 3 April, Miss Rosa Burley, who maintained a private school, The Mount, at Malvern, left this record:*

'. . . I promised to take a party of four of his pupils to hear it, and we made a day of it. The girls very pleased & excited. We go to Paddington and then to Victoria. The train was very full of men all speaking with Yorkshire & Lancashire accents. They were very excited and they all seemed to have bottles of whiskey about them. I explained to the girls that the North Country people were very musical & most enthusiastic. They were a little bit rough but it was wonderful for them to make all that journey to hear Elgar's music. Before the train really stopped at the Palace they rolled out of the train and rushed along the platform. I began to think that perhaps we should have difficulty in getting to our seats, but when we arrived at the end of the long corridor they had all vanished and we got our seats quite easily, surrounded by many, nice and demure old ladies and the very quiet people who attended these concerts. It was only later in the day that I learned that these brave lads of the North Country had come to see the "Koop fahnel" (Cup-final) played off [*Aston Villa v. Everton, a famous match: Miss Burley's assignment of Aston to Yorkshire does no credit to her sense of geography*]. Edward shouted with laughter when I told him this afterwards.'

On 15 June Elgar had completed the score of his Te Deum *and Benedictus, which was to be given its first performance at the forthcoming Three Choirs Festival at Hereford, where G. R. Sinclair, to whom the work was dedicated, was organist. A letter from Jaeger was expected and while awaiting developments Elgar amused himself by flying kites and playing bowls. On 26 June Mrs. Elgar noted in her Diary:* 'E. heard from Novello re Te Deum & Benedictus. D.G.' *On 4 August there was a further reference, in which Jaeger is mentioned by name for the first time in the Diaries:* 'E. heard from Mr. Jaeger quite as enthusiastic as he should be over E's music for Hereford.' *Jaeger's letter, according to an annotation by him on Elgar's of 6 August, made some reference to the inadequacy of the payment for the* Te Deum.

Forli, Malvern.
Augt. 4 1897

Dear Mr Jaeger:

I send you my very sincere thanks for your kind and appreciative letter: I feel after reading it that I shd. like it to 'go on':

but cui bono?

You praise my new work too much – but you understand it; – when it is performed will anyone say *anything* different from what they wd. say over a commercial brutality like the 'Flag of England'[1] for instance: naturally no one will & the thing dies and so do I–

All the same hearty thanks for your sympathy: I told you that I wd never put pen to paper when I had finished this work: but shall I?

v sincerely yours
Edward Elgar

I should like to have a copy if you have a proof to spare: I only possess the corrected sheets.

Forli, Malvern.
Augt. 6: 1897

Dear Mr Jaeger,

I must send one line to thank you for your last letter which has put new heart into me!

As you wish, your writing is destroyed or I would take the whole

[1] A cantata, to words by Rudyard Kipling, by Sir Frederick Bridge. Published in 1897, *The Flag of England* proved very popular.

thing as a text: please do not think I am a disappointed person, either commercially or artistically[;] what I feel is the utter want of *sympathy* – they i.e. principally the critics, lump me with people I abhor – mechanics. Now my music, such as it is, is alive, you say it has heart – I always say to my wife (over any piece or passage of my work that pleases me): "if you cut that it would bleed!" *You* seem to see that but who else does?

Kind regards. I note all you say and will call when I am in town.

Vy sincerely yours

Edward Elgar.

Jaeger went to the performance of the Te Deum *and wrote to Elgar on 15 September. After saying that his anticipations regarding the quality of the work were fully realized he observed that the one combined rehearsal that had been possible (as in the case of the* King Olaf *performance at the Crystal Palace on 3 April) was quite inadequate, and that a really effective interpretation demanded a conductor of the rank of Richter. As for the critics, Joseph Bennett and Herbert Thompson – the latter already a confirmed Elgarian according to a reported conversation with Jaeger – were commended for their insight. As for himself, Jaeger said:* 'I am conceited enough to think that I can appreciate a good thing and see genius in musicians that are *not* yet dead, or even not yet well known, or Cathedral organists, or Directors of music in colleges for boys.'

Jaeger complained that when critics wrote of Elgar's works they failed sufficiently to emphasize 'the *feeling* in the music, the emotional qualities which *alone* make music *live*'. *He continued:* 'Our Editor and other good folk keep on saying very clever, *very* clever etc. etc. and I say hang your cleverness, *that* won't make *any* music great and "alive"....I am forever pushing and have pushed since I played through your *fine* Black Knight, Mr. Elgar's claim to attention.' *More reluctantly he was also being required to forward the claims of such composers as Parry and Harford Lloyd. About these then fashionable masters Jaeger was not complimentary, but for the young Coleridge Taylor,* 'the other coming man', *he had nothing but praise and opined that he would do great things.* 'Novellos published 5 Anthems of his while he was 16 or 17. Now he develops his individuality and strength they will take nothing of his. I have before me a Morning and Evening Church Service which I consider splendidly *fresh*, original, and simple and effective and devotional which "we" won't do because the Editor thinks it is not the English Church style (precious English Church style). He says that of your work! You see: to succeed always write as others did before you!'

An indication of Elgar's regard for Jaeger's judgement and of his own willingness to help younger composers lies in his recommendation of

Coleridge Taylor's Ballade in A minor[1] *to Herbert Brewer, who included this work in the programme of the Gloucester Festival of 1898.*

At this time steps were being taken to form the Worcestershire Philharmonic Society, and Elgar's involvement is described in the correspondence with Miss M. Hyde published on pp. 68-70 of Letters of Edward Elgar *(Bles 1956).*

Malvern
private
Oct 18: 1897

Dear Mr Jaeger:

Don't reply to this if you are busy.

They (the public) are trying to get up a large choral and orchl. Society for this County with the idea of offering the Conductorship to ME.

Now: it may come to something or it may not, – but if it does, I want you to tell me of any deserving works by people I don't know. Has Coleridge Taylor anything? If so, I would like to know. I shall call on the firm & see (in a few days) what is to be had, but Myles Foster, Somervell & several others are in no request. Do you know anything of Macpherson who wrote a Psalm[2] which has a good *look* about it. I don't mean the *advertising* Macpherson – I imagine the youth I mean must be quite a different person.

If this Society *does* go on there will be a chance to do something novel – in fact if they are not disposed to let young England whoop! I shall not take it on.

Yrs ever sincerely,
Edward Elgar.

I forgot if I told you I am appreciating your Wagner letters very much: go on. It is nice to be told I am a sheep – but after all a bell-wether *is*[3] something.

The following letter is in reply to one from Jaeger dated 18 October, in which he says that Novello's were in correspondence with more than a dozen

---

[1] played at Jaeger's Memorial Concert, see p. 279
[2] *Psalm 137*, conducted by Elgar at Worcestershire Philharmonic Society concert, 11 December 1902
[3] twice underlined

societies regarding projected performances of King Olaf. *A choral society in Torquay had promised to perform* The Black Knight, *and another performance was about to take place in Sligo. The Elgars were considering moving house, but for the time being didn't.*

Malvern.
private
very
Oct 19: 1897

Dear Mr Jaeger:

I had just posted a note to you on another matter when yours of yesterday arrived.

Many thanks for telling me of the performances of 'B.K.' & 'K.O.' All who have written to me asking about performing rights I have at once referred to the firm. Manchester & Bolton I have only heard of from vocalists (I forget whom) who said they were singing in K.O. at those places. Sheffield is arrgd because this morning I have a letter from the conductor, F. Schöllhammer,[1] asking about pronunciation, etc. He asked me long ago about the orch. *required.* Yes! I have some ideas: but am about taking a new house – *very noisy* close to the station where I *can't write* at all but will be more convenient for pupils (!) to come in – I have no intention of bothering myself with music.

Look here! in two years I have written

Lux Xti
King Olaf
Impl. March ★
S. George
Organ Sonata (big)
Te Deum
Recd £86.15. | Debtor £100

after paying my own expenses at two festivals I feel a d—d fool! (English expression) for thinking of music at all. No amount of 'kind encouragement' can blot out these simple figures.

Ever yours
Ed. Elgar.

★ [*marginal note*] Don't mention this to anyone

[1] see p. 288

[*postcard*]

Malvern

Monday [6 Dec. 1897]

Dear Mr Jaeger:

Many thanks for your card: the Concert is on Dec. 21: let me have any sort of copy this week if you can. Poor B.K.

Yours ever,

E.E.

On 10 December Jaeger, in view of the imminent reprint of The Black Knight, *asked for alteration of the words at one point in Scene II. At the passage* 'When he rode into the lists' (*vocal score, p. 20*) *the singers at Torquay could not* 'get the words in edgeways'. *Hearing that Elgar was busy with* Caractacus, *Jaeger offered some advice based on criticism of* King Olaf (*which he had lately heard at Camberwell[1]*) *with which he agreed. This work, he said, was marred* 'by the absence of a developed broadly melodious lyrical movement with the "fat" given to the chorus where the ear can *rest* and just drink in *quietly* moving strains of a broadly melodious type . . .' *Jaeger also drew attention to another setting of* Caractacus, *by a gentleman on the Stock Exchange named Read,[2] who was* 'what a certain unsuccessful musician I wot of called Dr. Parry [was] viz: a bl—— amateur'.

M'vern

Dec. 13 [1897]

Dear Mr Jaeger,

In the parcel with Read's 'Caractacus' & B.K. I return also the Analysis of *K. Olaf* – it is awfully incomplete still but would be better than nothing if the firm intend reproducing it – I promised to send Mr. Bennett a proof – otherwise it is to go thro' my hands for correc-

---

[1] 24 November, South London Choral Society, conducted by Leonard C. Venables

[2] John F. H. Read's *Caractacus*, a cantata with words by E. J. Stokes, was published by Novello in 1882. See p. 288.

tion – that is to say Mr B. tells me to do what I like & finally offer it
to him.

Yrs ever
Ed: Elgar.

*About this time Jaeger became engaged to Isabella Donkerley, formerly a
violin student at the Royal College of Music. At a later stage of the correspondence she will be discovered as putting her professional training to good use
by editing some of Elgar's string parts. On Christmas Day 1897 her mother
died, to which Elgar makes reference in his next letter.*

1898

Jan 3 [1898]
Dear Mr Jaeger:

Very many thanks for your cheery letter: I am grieved to hear of your fiancée's loss which must have cast a great gloom over you both: may it soon be dispelled.

As to the Analysis of K[*ing*]. O[*laf*].[1] it is of course 'all to pieces' at the end – why won't *you* offer to do it? You wd do it so much better than I could.

When are the str[in]g pts of 'Te Deum' to be issued and when shall I receive the Chanson de Nuit?[2] Don't trouble to reply: I hope to be in town in a day or two and may see you.

Yours ever,

Edward Elgar

P.S. I have, during the last week, reaped four scalps which I wear with pride (golf).

His 'own tunes' *referred to in the following letter were* Caractacus, *which was to occupy him until 21 August, and* The Dream of Gerontius. *The reference to the latter work* (Hora novissima) *is the first to be discovered in any extant document, although the* 'prayer theme' *was inscribed in G. R. Sinclair's Visitors' Book in April 1898 (see Elgar O.M., pp. 398–9). The published law reports of that period mention no libel action concerning music in England.*

Forli, Malvern

Private   Feb. 4 [1898]

My dear Mr Jaeger:

The B[*lack*]. K[*night*]. is retd. to you to-day – I have looked thro' the arranged wind pts – at the *more important* points – otherwise neither critically or vindictively and think it's all right and very well done.

[1] by Joseph Bennett
[2] Op. 15, no. 2; violin and piano, Novello 1897; orch. arr. 1899

I have not had time to read your letter yet. I want to see S. Christopher[1] soon but I must work and weep over my own tunes for a little.

Hora novissima contains more 'music' than any of your other englishmen have as yet managed to knock out including Parry Stanford Mackenzie – these great men seem to be busily employed in performing one another's works: nobody else will? By the way – in the report of *the* libel case it was said that "Dream of Jubal" had been done *20* times – now in the M.T. it says in a leaderette that it is the most popular and *most frequently performed* of any of Mackenzie's works! the publishers must not grumble at me after this admission.

Yours ever,

Ed. Elgar.

In a letter, dated 28 February, Jaeger referred to the simplified second edition of The Black Knight *and to the desirability of Elgar's drawing attention to its possible performance by 'small orchestra'. Taking up Elgar's comments on the then musical 'Establishment' he observed that he had lately written an adverse review of Parry's* Magnificat, *but had had to alter it. 'One has', he says, 'to write one's views to order when they concern a man who is a somebody. Now Parry of all men in England is the one who would not take offence at one's opinion if sincerely stated and without any insulting personal remarks à la Sat. Review. I know him too well and I would risk his displeasure with pleasure. I have done so already in writing about the R.C.M. performances and he is as friendly as ever and more.'*

Forli, Malvern.

March 1 [18]98

Dear Mr Jaeger:

Thanks for the B.K. title which is all right. I don't see how the thing is ever to go on 'at the price' but no matter.

I intended the work to be a sort of symphony in four divisions founded on the poem – different to anything, in structure, ever done before, where the 'picture' is fixable for a little time the words are repeated – in dramatic parts the words 'go on': it's not a proper cantata as the orch: is too important: but if the pretty little public want a small orchestra they must have it.

I will reply to your letter sometime soon.

Caractacus frightens me in places.

Yours ever,

Ed. Elgar.

Jaeger writes on 8 March urging Elgar not to hurry his magnum opus. *He concludes his letter thus:*

[1] see p. 75, f.n.1

'Tonight Bach Choir concert with Stanford's Requiem and Parry's Variations[1]. Won't you come and assist? I fear Stanford hates me by this time because I have called his performance at the R.C.M. bad names. But really one gets quite disgusted and wants to say something nasty when one sees those critic friends of composers and conductors use only eulogisms to describe whatever the latter do, good, bad, or worse than bad. Parry's Variations are very good, I think, but as usual badly scored. I heard them again last Saturday under Wood. The latter has put his foot in it with Russian music this season. He has played some dreadfully ugly or stupid stuff. Of course it is all well scored, but the subject matter and the "Faktur" cannot interest us Western fellows at all. Those old Russians, Moussorgsky, Balakirev, Glinka, Borodin, etc. are awful bores. I suppose there will be a chance for English composers some day at Queens Hall.'

M'vern,
Mar 9: 1898

Dear Mr Jaeger,

Many thanks. I enclose the note for B.K. & am *very* glad to have it in: I spoke about it to dear old Tours but he looked so sad and in those days I did not know Mr Littleton who was held up to poor shy(!) (really I was then) me as a sort of destroying angel instead of, as I now know him, a very white-winged one.

The par: is *wordy* and could begin with 'The work may be described etc' but I did it 'with malice aforethought' because it begins nobly 'This *Cantata*' which wd. not frighten the mildest conductor that ever misdirected vocal miscreants whereas the bold statement that it's not a cantata at all might lead to trouble.

No: I cannot stand Parry's orchestra: it's dead and is never more than an *organ part arranged*.

Nothing with chor. seems to have gone well with Wood – only the things are bearable which Randegger taught 'em. I do not understand much about music but I *should* like to know when I may write a passage like unto this: and then be paid for it, and see cultured people like you paid to hear it. Do tell me when I may?

Yours ever,
Ed. Elgar

(Choice excerpt enclosed) [*subsequently lost*]

As the result of Elgar's approach to Brewer, Coleridge-Taylor's Ballade *in A minor* was performed at the Three Choirs Festival at Gloucester in *1898.*

[1] *Symphonic Variations*, pub. 1897

Strictly private.   M'v'n
                                                 Ap 17 [1898]
Dear Mr Jaeger:
  I have been asked to furnish a short orchl work for Gloucester
Festival (Concert) & have refused as I have enough to do, but I have
strongly urged them to make the offer (alas! an honorary one) to
Coleridge-Taylor. I don't in the least know if they will do so but *if* it
shd come and he shd consult you, you had better advise him to
accept – nicht wahr?
  It is not a bad introduction and I should *dearly* like to see a clever
man get on and – upset the little coterie of '3-Choir-hacks.'
                              Yours ever,
                                    Ed. Elgar.

                                         Forli,
                                           Malvern.
                                         Ap. 20 [1898]
Dear Mr Jaeger:
  Many thanks: I *don't* think it wd. do any real good to send C.T's
things (such as chamber music etc) the Committee probably can't
read music. – I said very strongly what I thought – of course the
disgusting thing is that if two men at the top of the scaffold (I mean
tree but in their case it shd be gallows) said the word they shd say
the thing wd be done – but Somervell is the only person they are not
afraid of! in the way of honest rivalry.
  I don't want Bridge to see *early* proofs of Caractacus. I can't prevent
his seeing the thing when ready for the chorus: you are the best judge,
but if he didn't like it, his remarks, *altho' not unkind* might prejudice
me – for instance if he said (in Aug. or Sept) that it wd not do for the
Albert Hall everybody would hear of that and there would be ructions,
I leave it to you. I fear you won't find a romping movement just yet!
                              Yours ever,
                                    Ed. Elgar
Proofs?? You might send on that second scene.
  On 28 May J.H.G.B. wrote as follows in The Musical Standard (*edited
by Edward Baughan*): 'Edward Elgar's "Chanson de Nuit" . . . is
indubitably broad, rich, melodious and effective. But the tune in the
opening bars of the accompaniment is rather curiously more interesting
and telling than the tune there assigned to the violin. Doubtless the
violin part has the merit of being grateful to the player; but, as melody,
it strikes one as somewhat uninspired and unstriking. In other words,
"made up".'

Forli, Malvern
June 2 [1898]

My dear Mr Jaeger,

Your news about Coleridge-Taylor[1] gives me great joy & I am happy in thinking I may have had a *little* to do in bringing the invitation about. I hope he won't write anything *too* startling – that is founded on a too remote subject – of course he will want to show the critics what's in him but the easygoing agriculturists who support these things also want a tiny bit of consideration and, if he can please *them, without the slightest sacrifice of his own bent of course*[2], it would be well in view of future commissions. You had better not tell him this from me a stranger – or he will kick me if we ever meet, and – well I'm thin and bony and it might hurt.★

Yours ever,
Ed. Elgar

★ I don't know – I never have been kicked. Who is the ass who writes criticisms in "Mus. Standard" a vulgar-minded pig?

[*Worcestershire Philharmonic Society note-paper*]

Sunday, June 5 [1898]

My dear Mr Jaeger,

Alas! I had no idea you would want – for these early chorus copies (or to 'set out'), the duet – I left it till last & am 'doing it' *now*. Do send Sc. I and II anyhow this week, or they will be clamorous. I hope to send you the remainder in a few days the *arrgt*[3] for two hands is awful to me & covers me with perspiration outside and indigestion within – the *scoring* is nothing! I am likewise generally chilled and miserable – the weather. I sent the last scene yesterday and it wd be well to get it forward (with pro. tem. paging).

May I thank you for not saying *one word* about the work, either for or against, and *please don't yet*[4] or I shall surely die being on edge.

Many thanks for the poetic valses – I have only time to look and like what I see.

Yrs. ever
Ed. Elgar

P.S. Or could you send to the end of p. 94? The chorus have a few bars more in this sc: later though.

[1] 'that S.C.T. had been asked to write a work for the Gloucester Festival,' *pencil note by Jaeger.*
[2] *of course* twice underlined
[3] twice underlined
[4] *yet* twice underlined

According to Mrs. Elgar's Diary Elgar began to orchestrate Caractacus (*of which H. A. Acworth was the librettist*) *on 21 June. Most of this work was done at his country cottage, Birchwood, near Malvern.*

Forli, Malvern
June 21 [1898]

My dear Mr Jaeger:

Good! by all means will I ask Acworth to eliminate the truculent 'note' in the lines! any nation but ours is allowed to war-whoop as much as they like but I feel we are too strong to need it – I *did* suggest that we should dabble in patriotism in the Finale, when lo! the *worder* (that's good!) instead of merely paddling his feet goes and gets naked and wallows in it: now I don't think he meant by 'menial &c' Germany &c. more probably hill tribes and suchlike – jealous evidently, refers to anybody you like. Now 'pluck ye by the ear' if you feel aggrieved, I will bring my sword up & give you as pretty a fight as you can wish – in Berners St – but I warn you I am probably a better swordsman than you and I should be sorry for Miss D.! So my dear Jaeger, *we* won't fight after all.

I am sorry I troubled the firm about Spark's[1] telegram – I enclose it. You will see I of course thought it referred to the *first* batch – he explains (by another wire) that he wants *two more* scenes: – the first time I have had "scenes" ordered like barrels of beer!

As to the title page I don't really mind but leave out 'composed' – this word always brings up a vision of a man scratching the back of his head with a pen – if I *do* scratch (which heaven forbid!) its not for ideas.

As to Index – I suppose you want one and it bothers me: I enclose a *bit* of one. I have only tabulated the principal points – do you think it will do?

I hope you will get the whole thing off to Leeds as soon as possible.

In haste,
Yrs (belloque frementem) (Virgil)
Edward Elgar.

Malvern.
June 24 [1898]

My dear Mr Jaeger:

My good friend who 'reads' for me has discovered the enclosed small errors. I wired about a bad one in the *chorus* – these concern soloists.

[1] Frederick Spark, Secretary of the Leeds Festival, at which *Caractacus* was to be performed

Please alter p *114* – you need not send it me again – I quite forgot to give the poor wretches time to breathe! I suppose they want to

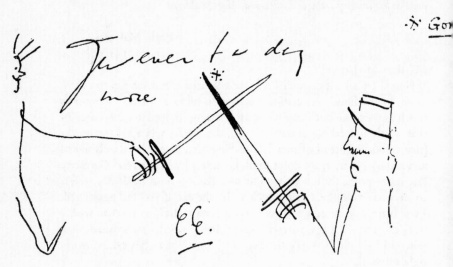

Birchwood Lodge
[June or early July 1898]

My dear Mr Jaeger:

Many thanks for all the bundle of corrections [for *Caractacus*].

    p. 60 *marcato* please

    p. 114 Could you send either to me or to Mad[ame] Henson &
        Mr Lloyd *two* copies of this p. & they could paste it in their
        books?

    p. 172 no proof with this old page – it doesn't in the least matter.

    p. 167. no corrections that I can see necy – no 'copy' recd.

Yours ever,
Ed. Elgar

P.S. I have Taylor's theme jigging in the vacuities of my head – have sent the book to Forli but the tune remains and I am trying to orchestrate! – I feel like Poins I would steep the cantata in sack and make him eat it! It's jolly good, but not exd. yet.

In a notice of the sixth Philharmonic Concert of the year, given on 9 June, a criticism of d'Albert's Symphony in F (Op. 4) observed that while the effects looked all right on paper they did not come off: 'such scoring will not do in these days of Richard Strauss, Rimsky Korsakow, Glazounow, and Edward Elgar' (Musical Times).

Birchwood,
July 7 [1898]

My dear Mr. Jaeger:

Many thanks: I think it would be far best to print that page (which includes a wrong note! as well as *menial*) & they (the Leeds people) could paste it in *over* the present page: that wd be least bother & could be done during the chorus recess.

I will tell 'em on Saturday – a day of dread for me. I can face any orchestra under the sun the players always enjoy new effects but a chorus looks so disgusted if they haven't a shouting four-pt yell from beginning to end.

Net bag: two snakes – a blind worm (so called) and a yaller one. neither of 'em critical – I mean poisonous.

I say – *who* put my name in the M.T.? I have just discovered it in the Phil: notice – that is the word that gave me most pleasure.

Yours ever,
Ed: Elgar

Saty. morning Queen's Hotel Leeds if you want anything desperate.

Elgar travelled to Leeds on 8 July for the first rehearsal of Caractacus *on the next day. Before returning to Worcestershire he went to Settle to visit his old friend Dr. C. W. Buck.*

[*W.P.S. paper*]

Malvern July 12 1898

My dear Mr Jaeger:

Many thanks for all yours. I am only just home and got on well: that *Invocation* has made me ill. Oh! the effect is curdling.

Now. business. Please send the copies of page 189 'menial' to Mr Spark who will have 'em pasted in. By this post I return the libretto for the last time.

I find to my sorrow that I wrongly transcribed my notes on p. 22. I enclose the page corrected. I should be glad if the semi-q's could be dropped in.

I find a memo: as to a Horn passage which I send on a separate sheet: I forgot it in the hurry of rushing away: your very able copyist can put it in the score and *don't* bother to send it back until you return it for revision. All or many slurs in Sc. V want curling round in the plate: they may be done now but do not appear very gay in my copy.

Thanks for news of the Index: next time you shall write the work and *I'll* make the Index.

I knew you wd laugh at my librettist's patriotism (& mine) never mind: England for the English is all I say – hands off! there's nothing apologetic about me. Now as to the wind – what do you mean by *lithographing* the parts – do you mean that obscene process by which the M.S. is, as 'twere, multiplied. I don't like the look of it but I suppose it's cheap – and – the other thing: if you are bent on it do let the *writist* put in no end of vocal cues & I might see a specimen, mightn't I?

A practical point: P. 190 bar before $\boxed{56}$ in the voc. pts they altered my rests: *here* (in the score) it doesn't matter but if the voc. pts are printed separately the rests should correspond with the accompanimt, because the conductor has, for orch., to beat out to the fourth crotcht. – the chorus are confused as the beat takes 'em on to the next bar, the rests, usefully, should stand thus

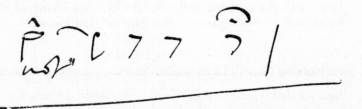

I 'queried' it & said put what is usual but it is *not*[1] right.

As to waiting till after the performance before duplicating the wind, I don't know – I never *have* had to alter anything but I am very dubious about myself when you suggest waiting: send me a specimen.

In great haste and with kindest regards,

Yours ever,
Edward Elgar.

There *are* 'pints' in Carac – *all* the IInd. scene.
[*in pencil*] please send these excerpts back anyhow. Shew 'em to Mr. L[ittleton].

[1] twice underlined

[*W.P.S. paper*]

> Birchwood (once more!)
> Wedy July 13 [1898]

My dear Mr Jaeger:

I think the *old* way will do: I only want to show that the passage in 6ths isn't as plain as a barn-door (or an organ loft) in the f. score – nobody will *play* it I suppose! I vote for the first attempt – though the second wouldn't look bad if the small notes had their *own* semiquaver legs instead of those belonging to the large notes: like a fellow in a borrowed pair of trousers.

All well at Leeds thank you, and they *are* intelligent.

> Yours ever,
> Ed. Elgar

> Birchwood (in peace)
> Thursday [14(?) July 1898]

My dear Mr Jaeger:

First – I don't understand about 'hot wires and noses' – I *trust* nothing serious or very disagreeable and that it's all over successfully.

I was sorry to bother you with so much rot in the last letter but the 'things' accumumulated during my absence.

By all means 'correct-a-cuss' in future.

Why, Why, oh! why did you send me that specimen? at breakfast it came. Speer![1] – the litho: and writing is good – but Speer – you ask 'what's wrong with it?' everything's right with the copy but the music Oh! the music (an awful Exspeerience). I am going out into the woods with my revolver to kill *something*! anything!! *Speers*!!! if I can find any.

I will send all back all the wind (Brass) recd as soon as I get to post. What about the instalment of *strings* recd. two days ago. Am I to retain *them* until the score comes back (for revision).

The copying is festive and the cues seem all right. By the way the 5th and 6th Trumpets need not be complete parts I think, except in Sc. VI: he (the copy-iser) has 'set out' Sc. I for instance where they only have two notes or so – he might have put *'tacent to end of Sc.'*

> Yours ever,
> Ed. Elgar

---

[1] W. H. Speer's *Festival Overture* (Op. 9), Novello, 1898

at Forli [19.7.98 *in pencil, in Jaeger's hand*]
but just leaving for Birchwood
Deo Gratias!

My dear Mr Jäger,
    I am glad you sound better:

Caract: is to take *same as K. Olaf 1hr. 25 mins.* I retd. the *first portion* of
string pts *without* checking them as you will understand the score did
not arrive till Saty.

I think I recd. your secd. telegram *first* – I can't make any sense of it.
I *hold* the score tight now.

By all means lithograph, it's very *nice* – I did *not* go so far as to say it was "nasty".

The portion of strg pts retd. today *are* checked: 'cos why? cos I got the sc: to check 'em by.

Yours ever,
Ed: Elgar

I killed nothing: only put up a notice at the bottom of the wood warning off Speers & overtures and this

nice passage, scored for four muted Jaegers.

Yours ever again,
Ed. E.

It was at this time that Coleridge-Taylor proposed to marry Jessie Walmisley and was rebuffed by her family, particularly her brother-in-law who had lived in the East and had strong views on 'mixed marriages'. Despite this, however, they were married on 30 December.

Birchwood Lodge,
August 21: 1898

My dear Mr Jaeger:

Thanks: I go to Leeds on Saty. next and should like the pages altered *first* if possible.

I forget if I sent in p. 199 with *Lento & a tempo*: *this* is the very last: the score is done and going to you on Tuesday.

Private: Mr Bennett (D.T.[1]) will not be at Leeds as at present arranged – he will be in the *East* he told me; *why shouldn't you* represent the M.T.? don't say I suggested it. No: your natl history is at fault, badgers don't attack wopses – *I* do: I say I wish you were here! I've been cutting a long path thro' the dense jungle like primitive man only with more clothes. But you will see our 'woodlands' someday. I made old Caractacus stop as if broken down on p. 168 & choke & say 'woodlands' again because I am so madly devoted to my woods. I've got the place for years now & another summer – ja! Thanks for the Book plate suggestion – I have a friend[2] *at* one now and we will see later: only he will stick in music which you and others say I don't know anything about, and I want beasts and animals in it. I liked Dodd[3]: he *was* overcome by our sitiwation. Foxhunting yesterday. No proof-correcting done.

Yours ever,
Ed. E.

I'm awfully sorry to hear of C[oleridge]-T[aylor]. I suppose its matrimonial and no possible consolation: oh these boys, if they only knew that a woman's not worth a damn who won't put up with everything except ineptitude and crime.

Elgar arrived at Leeds on 26 August, his rehearsal being on the next day. The chief conductor of the Festival was Sir Arthur Sullivan, who had held this office for fifteen years. It was generally noted that he looked very ill. Alan Gray, a Yorkshireman by birth, was present to superintend the first performance of his A Song of Redemption.

Regarding Caractacus *and the circumstances of its composition and first performance (on 5 October) Miss Rosa Burley wrote:*

'Caractacus: Elgar took the little cottage of Birchwood Lodge which was then in a wood. He loved this wood and was interested in all the wild life.

Caractacus made his last stand here by the Malvern Hills and put up

---

[1] *Daily Telegraph*
[2] probably A. Troyte Griffith
[3] a copyist for Novello's: he lived in Brighton.

a splendid fight. The British fortifications can be traced still and Elgar walked over all the ground. He tramped over the hills and went along the Druid path from end to end, along the top of the hills.

The performance at the Leeds Festival was very successful. Sullivan conducted for the last time, for he was then ill and had to sit down to conduct as he was unable to stand for any length of time. The Lord Mayor (Mr. C. F. Tetley) entertained a very distinguished party at luncheon and Elgar and his wife were placed close to Sullivan.

The Leeds Chorus was considered to be the finest in England and [sic]: this was, of course, before Beecham had hammered it into a new shape, making it flexible, delicate, in fact just the chorus for [sic] which Elgar had in mind when he wrote but which did not then exist. The chorus revelled in the straightforward Handelian choruses & were inclined to resent Elgar's music which they found finicking and fidgety. They could not let themselves go, full blast, as they had always done.

A. J. Balfour was at this luncheon and it would be a very interesting group that was assembled there. The solo artists[1] were invited to luncheon. The Elgars were very shy and rather frightened by the hearty Yorkshire people.'

Forli, Malvern.
Augt 29: 1898

My dear Mr Jaeger:

I only arrd. from Leeds last night (Sunday). You will have had my wire: I will alter no more of C. short of burning the whole thing. I had a good rehearsal at Leeds with the chorus but it makes me, an artist, sick to see that fool Gray allowed as long to rehearse his blasted rot as I am who produce with all its many faults an attempt at something like a 'work'.

Selah!

Now: I have returned everything to you (recd. for corrections) except Bassi. Sc. 1, which will go today. Mr Dodd has had up to end (full sc.) of Sc. V from me: when I saw him a fortnight ago he said he wd. be sending proofs but up to the present I have only *checked Sc. 1 woodwind:* you might ask him how he's getting on – I hope he's not behind – we arrgd. (he & I) that the *Brass* shd. come *altogether* when complete: don't tell him I'm fidgetting because I'm not only it ought to be steadily going on.

---

[1] Medora Henson, Edward Lloyd, Andrew Black, John Browning, Charles Knowles

I lent [Herbert] Thompson my secd. copy with notes: I am writing
to him *now* asking when he can return it if it will do for Mr Bennett?
Shall I send it to Mr B. or to you? if to Mr B. tell me where he is – I
presume not in town unless he's getting his trousseau ready for the
East.

I think that's all the Biz:

I said – Try the E. brand of Badger.

But there aren't any Badgers now – they've gone and deserted the
'earth' near us – never mind I'll track 'em further away. I *should* like
to send one in a sack to Berners St. Sir A. *does* look ill but I've seen
him once before in 1884 so I am no judge.

I am passing thro' town on Friday or Saty. and shall endeavour to
look at you but my movements

> do. mind
> do. music
> are erratic

Ever yrs.
Edward Elgar.

Brewer is very lucky – or rich – to get into the M.T. before he's done
anything, S.T. deserves it and I rejoice thereat (I really must pick up
some shares) (oh!)

P.S. Failing Thompson's copy of Carac: I can, in a few days, send the
proof sheets (which went to Windsor Castle[1]) they were returned at
my request and are binding so Mr B. will get a copy anyhow.

Don't forget to tell me his present address.

It doesn't matter about Sullivan I think.

Forli, Malvern.
Shall be at Hasfield Court[2], Gloucester
[Sept. 1898]

My dear Jaeger,
(The Mister-y is soluted)

Very many thanks for your letter which soothed me immensely – a
3-choir festival always upsets me – the twaddle of it and mutual
admiration. It was a real refreshment to me to see C.T. and know him.
I don't think the *opening* of the Ballade too fast when the 'chaps' are
familiar with it, but, as I told him, the cantabile sections would gain
infinitely by being taken slower (and rubato?) – the fiddles could then
draw "three souls out of one weaver" in many expressive places – I

---

[1] *Caractacus* was dedicated to Queen Victoria.
[2] the home of William Meath Baker, with whom Elgar stayed during the
Three Choirs Festival.

liked it all and loved some and adored a bit: I am always afraid to
criticise orkestration because one never knows what is really wanted
by the composer (how I *hate* that word) so I say nuffin and you know
what I said to C.T. after.

Gratifying to me that you like my expressive flatulations.

Now Biz:

I recd. score & sketch strgs. Sc. VI this a.m. – never send parcels to
me by *G.W.R.* – they are awful and wd. keep it six months before
delivery – I had to send down this a.m. and found the pcl. reposing
peacefully on a shelf – thrown away in fact – they are *awful* here.
Dodd sends me some wind, (a fair quantity) which I am working at.
He shall have the score (sc. VI) on Monday (D.V.) – so all goes on – we
shall be all right if we go steadily on – only avoid the Rly.Co! I find
one error in 8vo. score – the pause (p. 58 2nd bar) tenor solo part shd.
be on the *C* ta-lõns – of course not on the 'ta'! I found this with
Lloyd & forgot it – knock it out of the plate – it need not really go in at
all.

I return chor. pts. S. & A.

I *say:* if you had sent me the m.s. sketch of Alto all the two-line
parts might have been cut out – one never considers Male Altos nowa-
days in a general way as pt. of a chorus – but I *had* to put the note
about 'singing with tenor' in the 8vo score for Leeds where they have
a special set of about 20 men – altos – however its all right only rather
unnec[essar]y.

I'm afraid I gave you a bad impression of my temper the other day –
I am not really bitter and my heart warms to anything like naturalness
and geniality (C.T. e.g.) but I detest humbug and sham and can't talk
it (well). Q's Hall seemed reeking with it those two *daze.*

Yrs.

Ed. Elgar

at Hasfield Court
Gloucester
[September 1898?]

My dear Jaeger:

The enclosed came here: will you – if you can – arrange about the
Analysis with Manns?[1] I have sent him a line saying he will hear from
you or the firm, whoever is the Johnny.

I'm fishing & have ruminated over your letter: so very sorry you're
not well.

---

[1] August Manns was to conduct *King Olaf* at the Sheffield Festival, on 11
October 1899 (see p. 63).

I'm really giving up *all music* & am refusing everything – I cannot afford to waste my precious few years of remaining out door life – so I fish, etc. much better than your damned old blasted music.

Do what you can for Dear old Manns

Yrs ever
Ed Elgar.

I'm going to answer your letter soon.

Forli, Malvern
Sept. 21 [1898]

My dear Jaeger:

I thought it best to sit tight here: I think only a portion of *2nd vio* will be the part I shan't revise & the m.s. sketch pt. shd. be correct enough for your genii to go by. You see the Brass, a considerable portion of which I haven't seen yet, *must* be revised – I am *hoping* to get the remainder of it tomorrow.

I sent *you* the balance of Fl. Ob. Cl. & Fag. (at Dodd's request) completing those parts. I suppose that reached you all right?

I shd. have liked to have seen the *whole* four *voc:* parts again – is there any hurry for 'em and if so, why and where?

Now peg away and be good and remember 'it's not my fault' oh! no!

I am past swearing and am sitting in my shirt with my feet in a bucket of water (it's hot) drivelling.

Oh! my profettic sole.

Yours

Junior Conservative Club,
43 & 44 Albemarle Street,
Piccadilly W.
Thursday [29 September[1] 1898]

My dear Jaeger:

I felt so *guilty* after you had left asking you to be bothered with that

---

[1] Elgar was staying in London for the rehearsals of *Caractacus* at St. James's Hall on 27 and 29 September. On 30 September he went to Leeds, where *Caractacus* was given on 5 October.

copy & should never forgive myself – it was really kind of you to take it – I had so much to carry. If you want me I shall be at the

> Queen's Hotel
> Leeds
> > till Saturday.

Will you jog Rivers' memory as to the *pts & score* for C.P.
Selah!

I am going to congratulate you on your charming Miss D. My wife is also charmed with her – you are a lucky fellow & she – well I think she is worthy of one of the best fellows that ever lived.

Forgive your miserable Frankenstein for [always *deleted*] all his faults & Believe in

Your v penitent
E. Elgar.

The following letter contains a reference to a symphonic project which Elgar had in mind. The 'Gordon' symphony[1], of course, never came to fruition, but the 'heroic' idea none the less went into the character of the two symphonies that did eventually appear. At the end of this year and the beginning of the next, however, Jaeger was sanguine that 'Gordon' would be produced sooner rather than later, so in March he put this note (unsigned) in The Musical Times (p. 161):

'Mr. Edward Elgar has several interesting compositions "on the stocks". Chief among them is the new symphony for the Worcester Festival, which is to bear the title "Gordon". As in the case of Beethoven's No. 3, Mr. Elgar has selected a great hero for his theme, though of a very different type from that of the "Eroica". The extraordinary career of General Gordon – his military achievements, his unbounded energy, his self-sacrifice, his resolution, his deep religious fervour – offers to a composer of Mr. Elgar's temperament a magnificent subject, and affords full scope for the exercise of his genius; moreover, it is a subject that appeals to the sympathies of all true-hearted Englishmen . . .'

In the definitive part of this statement, as on other occasions, it can be accepted that the words are in fact Elgar's.

Malvern
Oct. 20 1898

My dear Jaeger,

Ja! I'm here, tho' I only arrd. last night & found your note – letter rather. No – I'm not happy at all in fact never was more miserable in my life: I don't see that I've done any good at all: if I write a tune you all say it's commonplace – if I don't, you all say it's rot – well, I've

[1] also see *Elgar O.M.*, p. 336

written Caractacus, earning thro' it *15/– a week* while doing it, and
that's all – *now* if I will write any *easy*, small choral-society work for
Birmingham, using the fest. as an advt. – your firm will be "disposed
to consider it" – but my own natural bent I must choke off. No thank
you – no more music for me – at present.

I am glad Hiawatha is going on: but I shall not be in town again for
years I think.

Now Bizz:

Carac: string parts are sent today corrected. (I found on turning
over that this is a half-sheet. Excuse).

I am delighted with the printing & am glad you have some useful
rehearsal numbers at last: one improvement is still required. – the
tempi when a change occurs in the mid. of a scene – the words shd. be
larger & when *divisi* in 2 lines it wd. be better to break the rule & put
Allegro (or whatever it may be) between the staves – the players nearly
always add it in pencil. I want a set for my collection of curiosities.
Now as to *St. George* (By the way compare my rhythm p. 24 with
Cowen's Ode.[1] p. 16 line 2 & later – funny ain't it) By all means let
a soloist sing p. 8. 9. *13* (letter *P*[2]) to S p. 16 & p. 22 &c. only I don't
think *SHE* shd. sing pp. 5 & 6 better for chos. to do this bit.

K. Olaf. I don't really mind the ending of the Thor Chorus – only
how about the *chorus* parts (sep) & the scores & wind &c. &c. &c???
It would be a big job. Let me know. Benson (Lionel)[3] I have just
heard from a friend of his about the proposed pt. sg – why the D.
doesn't he do 'My love dwelt' – *why* does everybody want something
new.

"Gordon" sym.

I like the idea but my *dear* man *why* should I try?? I can't see – I
have to earn money somehow & its *no good* trying this sort of thing
even for a "living wage"! and your firm wouldn't give £5 for it – I
tell you I am sick of it all! Why can't I be encouraged to do decent
stuff & not hounded into triviality.

Write again sometime. I hope your househunting is satisfactory –
don't go too far out.

Yours ever,
E.E.

*Having been in London for a week Elgar returned home to find a letter
from Randegger inviting him to contribute a work to the Norwich Festival of*

---

[1] *Ode to the Passions* (Collins), performed at Leeds Festival
[2] three times underlined
[3] a wealthy amateur who formed the Magpie Madrigal Society in 1897: see
Percy Scholes, *The Mirror of Music*, I, p. 52.

1899. The work was to be Sea Pictures, *but this was the point at which he inaugurated the* 'Enigma' Variations, *as the following letter shows. The composer's intention was clearly rather different from what is sometimes represented.*

Malvern
Oct. 24 [18]98

My dear Jaeger,

Here is the "Grecian ghost which unburied remains inglorious on the plain" or on the hills.

I hope the house-hunting is over satisfactorily and that you have peaceful prospects. Let me know.

Our woods look lovely but decidedly damp and rheumaticky – unromantic just now.

Since I've been back I have sketched a set of Variations (orkestra) on an original theme: the Variations have amused me because I've labelled 'em with the nicknames of my particular friends – *you* are Nimrod. That is to say I've written the variations each one to repre-sent the mood of the 'party' – I've liked to imagine the 'party' writing the var: him (or her) self and have written what I think they wd. have written – if they were asses enough to compose – its a quaint idea & the result is amusing to those behind the scenes & won't affect the hearer who 'nose nuffin'. What think you?

Much love & sunshine to you.
Ed. Elgar.

Early in November Jaeger sent Elgar a copy of Coleridge-Taylor's Hiawatha's Wedding Feast, *to receive its first performance at the Royal College of Music on 11 November. The second part of the trilogy,* The Death of Minnehaha, *was commissioned for the North Staffordshire Festival of 1899.*

Birchwood Lodge,
near Malvern
Saturday, date & month & year unknown 'cos it's Birchwood
[November 1898?]

My dear Jaeger:

Thanx for K. Olaf Indeks &c. &c.

I shd. advise 1st a resetting as marked of the *contents* page – it can be followed much better from the other side.

2nd I think a short rule between the divisions of the Synopsis necy.

It is really *very* well done except "to my poor mind" the first sentence of the Conversion: If you can & think it worth while ask the Johnny to alter it you need not say I suggested it.

Would the note signed E.E. be better at the top of the Contents?

More rain
more gout
more thunder
more dyspepsia
more liver
more music
less money

But King Olaf *is* a mighty work. Wot ye this?

In haste
Yrs ever
Him wot rote it.

All the synopsis will of course go in the book of the words. I *wish* you wd. do an *analysis* of the thing.

[*W.P.S. paper*]

Birchwood Lodge
(Deo gratias!)
Nov 11 [1898]

My very dear Jaeger,

I was sorrowing for a line from you & now comes a nice, *human* letter to me here where you know I find the only really happy times now: thank you a thousand times.

We came up here two days ago & are in fog & the leaves are falling too rapidly but its jolly nevertheless, away from all feuds, intrigues & cranks! I go thro your letter in order except your house business which must come first: *we* are so sorry you have any worry over plans – having lived in Norwood *and* W. Kens: (our *first* house was in Avonmore Rd.) I can only say that I should vote in favour of W. Kensington where we hope you and your wife will be most happy. Well and so the day is fixed. I am so very very happy thinking of your new life, because I've seen Miss. D. and can, thank God, congratulate you and believe you *will* be happy – one can very seldom say this to men who show you the 'modern young women' they are going into partnership with: Lord pity 'em. More of this some day: all good to you both for the present.

Now for worldly matters.

Met[ronome]: marks K. Olaf all retd. yesterday. thanks for them.

Lux. Xti. prelude. I don't think *I* could arrange the Prelude easily

for p.f. but that not saying it couldn't be done. I *could* make a trans-
scription à la Tausig which wd. be pretty useless and I don't want to
do it either.

I am going to send a suggested arrangement to K. Olaf for Military
Band – I spoke to Mr. Littleton long ago about it – thats the best advt.
for anything & its easy to pick out a few tunes.

The Variations go on slowly but I shall finish 'em some day.
Private[1]. I have agreed to do the PRINCIPAL novelty for Birmingham –
Randegger asks me about Norwich wanting, of course, something
new – I suggested Black Knight among other old things but have not
heard anything since the first committee meeting. Then, *un*officially,
poor old Worcester wants a symphony! You see none of this will
pay me a cent! (So I am doing hack work – orchestrating a comic
opera for another chap! for which I shall be paid. Such is life.*)

Now as to Gordon: the thing possesses me, but I can't write it down
yet: I *may* make it the Worcester work if that engagement holds. So
don't please, pass on the idea to anybody else just yet. I would really
ask Edwards to announce it but I must first get to know if the Dean and
Chapter wd. object to the subject in an English Cathedral!

Thanks for playing that Serenade; – it's no good on the piano – the
1st movement is best and is *really stringy* in effect: all the same its kind
of you.

Today I think is the Hiawatha at the Coll. good luck to it and the
young man: I saw in a local paper that the committee N. Staffs:
propose asking him to do something for them.

Now I must stop. I changed on to this paper 'cos the last sheet did
not suit my new toy – a fountain pen – but this is not much better and
I hoped the writing wd. be so good that an apology would not be
necessary – alas! another failure.

Yours ever,
Ed. Elgar.

* [*marginal note*] distinctly private – Beware! the knout is at work!!!

[*W.P.S. paper*]

Malvern
Dec. 7: [1898]

My dear Jaeger,

Very many thanks: please send the Cueen's Qopy *here* – (that
doesn't look quite right): enclosed is my miserable screed value 30/– &
with it Zachoklapper's bill – or Zahnbrecher, whatever his name is –
anyhow he *has* pulled my teeth over it.

[1] twice underlined

I'm not coming to London
    I. Because I hate it
    II. Because I have to play golf just now
    III. Because I ain't wanted
    IV. Because, being miserable, I hate to see anyone happy &
        A.J.J. is just 'slopping over' now (good man)
    V. – ganz genug!

Please: may I send the enclosed letter re St. George to you? perhaps you will deal with it – that is answer it – I have *acknowledged it only* – you see I wrote the work for the firm & *I* don't like to tell this fellow what to cut out – he writes in a twaddley way (I don't know him) & if I tell him what he may do – I don't want to – he may advertise my remarks: – of course he could cut from page 43 to last p. (*orch*) without asking anybody but *I* don't want to tell him he can, unless the firm wishes me to do so – see?

I think that's all. Oh no. A genial soul (whom I don't know either) thinks & writes that, owing to the phenomenal success of my works, I might *pay seventy pounds to publish some of HIS* which he can't afford to do & no publisher will take. I *must* send him to your chiefs.

Much love
Liverly yours
E.E.

[*W.P.S. paper*]

Malvern
Dec. 11: [1898]

My dear Jaeger:
    On looking through your spider-legged notes I find one or two 'loose ends' which I gather up.

As to *J.* Walford Davies[1] (I thought it was & is *H.*[2]W.D.) I fear I *can* do nothing – but I may = you see I am too *near* Worcester to be in it – I'm a Steward & subscribe = I'll see, & you may rely upon me to do my best to introduce sterling stuff – you are wrong in thinking I don't

---

[1] Walford Davies, for whom Jaeger sought Elgar's help in respect of the forthcoming Three Choirs Festival, was represented in the Worcestershire Philharmonic Society Concert of 17 January 1901, by his *Hymn Before Action* (words by Rudyard Kipling). In his programme note Elgar drew attention to the growing merit of Walford Davies, and added: "It had been hoped to include a more important composition than the *Hymn before Action* in the present programme; the bold outline and martial swing of the melody – vigorously complementing Kipling's poem – may serve as DR. WALFORD DAVIES' introduction and lead to the hope that the performance of a more elaborate work may follow." The "more elaborate work" – *The Temple* – appeared, in fact, at the Worcester Festival of 1902.

[2] twice underlined

like some 'forms' of music – anything 'genuine' & natural pleases me –
the stuff I hate and which I know is ruining any chance for good
music in England is stuff like Stanford's[1] which is neither fish, flesh,
fowl, nor good red-herring!

Never heard of Lady Curtis[2] in these parts so cannot appreciate her
graceful remarks to Miss D.

What I said about reorchg [Imperial] March was simply a proposal
to make the Organ pt (at prest. obbligato) *ad lib*: I don't want to in the
least – it wd take time & I should get nothing for it: so we won't
trouble – but after all it wd be better, for occasional use, that it were
done.

I think *we* may be up in town on Tuesday – if so prepare to be
bombarded with questions galore.

I reserve a lot in case this happens.

Yours ever,
E.E.

With both Gerontius (*a project possible, thought Elgar, for the Birmingham
Festival*) *and the* Variations *in mind and with neither appearing to meet with
the approval of Littleton of Novello's Elgar felt frustrated. During the coming
year he was about to transfer his music to Messrs. Boosey. But this was
averted by a reconciliatory conference with Littleton on 8 September 1899.*

Forli, Malvern.
Dec. 17 [1898]

My dear Jaeger:

Here are two letters: this one to wish you every good thing now
and always; you are too sensitive about the invitation. We have been
trying for weeks to find some little thing for you and now the thing
fixed upon won't be ready* – an inkstand of Worcester *Faience* (not
china) – however our intentions were, and are, good & the trifle
must find you on your return – from Düsseldorf or where you go.

If I *can* get to town I will gladly and gaily turn up at St. Mary's but
I fear I may not be able to get away.

Now our best and most heartfelt wishes for you both.

Ever yours affecty,
Edward Elgar.

* It's being 'baked' now specially

[1] On 11 November Stanford had written somewhat discouragingly about the
possibility of introducing one of Elgar's works to the Bach Choir, of which he
was then the conductor. In due course, however, Elgar was to perform some
Stanford, the cantata *Last Post* partnering Walford Davies's *Hymn Before Action*
in the patriotic concert of 17 January 1901.

[2] wife of Sir Arthur Colin Curtis (1858–1898)?

Forli,
Malvern.

private

Dec. 17 [1898]

My dear Jaeger,

I put this on another sheet & I shd. not have bothered you with it – only you ask: for the last six weeks (about) I have been very sick at heart over music – the whole future seems so hopeless. I wrote to Mr. L. because I had talked to him of it previously – about the Bir. Fest. work & he does not reply: also I have asked how my egregious debt to the firm (K.O. &c) stands and they tell me nothing. Now I have worked steadily and honestly till I am offered all the festivals & then the firm seem to have had enough of me. I can quite understand that my big works don't pay – i.e. show any good return but I shd. have hoped that on artistic grounds the very small remuneration I ask shd. be forthcoming for things which at least interest the better portion of the musical public. No! the only suggestion made is that the Henry VIII dances are the thing – now I can't write that sort of thing & my own heartfelt ideas are not wanted: why K. Olaf should be worthless when its done often is a mystery to me when things by, say, MacKenzie, which are never touched, shd. be good properties. You see I want so little: £300 a year I must make, & thats all. Last year I subsisted on £200. It seems strange that a man who might do good work shd. be absolutely stopped – thats what it means.

Now you see how things are. do *not* tell anyone all this or any of it. I did not intend to write as it may seem disloyal to the firm but apparently this is the end of all things, so it doesn't matter.

Ever yrs.
E.E.

The letter from Jaeger referred to is not now in existence.

Forli [*deleted*]
Malvern.

Dec. 21 [1898] 7 p.m.

My very dear Jaeger:

I am just in & find your good letter: I will not say a word now. This is only coming because I cannot get away alas! – to wish you again *everything* & may you be as happy together as I & my dear one have been and are.

Ever yours,
Ed: Elgar.

The bout of pessimism expressed in Elgar's "private" letter of 17 December
was answered by Jaeger as follows:

'December 31: . . . "Glück auf zum Siegen!" England expects every
man to do his duty and no musician in your great and glorious country
has a greater duty to fulfill than you. So don't dare to talk about your
new work being squashed. Nonsense! A day's attack of the blues,
due to a touch of indigestion or a blast of east wind will not drive away
your desire, your necessity which is to exercise those creative faculties
which a kind providence has given you. Your time of universal
recognition will come. You have virtually achieved more towards
that in one year than others of the English composers in a decade.'

Malvern
Dec. 31: 1898

My dear Jaeger,

One line to greet you on your return home. I was much touched
by your letter – written in your busiest time & should have sent a line
to Düsseldorf, only, with wisdom, you gave no clue to your address.

I don't know *when* you return but I am D.V. coming to town next
week (8th) & shall look for you.

I *could* not get away for the wedding or nothing wd. have pleased
me more than to have assisted.

All good wishes be yours in the New Year.

Yours ever,
Edward Elgar.

On 7 January Elgar conducted a concert of the Worcestershire Philharmonic
Society, the programme including works by Mozart, Goetz, Wagner,
Dvořák (Slavonic Dances 2 and 8), as well as Elgar's arrangement (lost) of
'The Holly and the Ivy'. Two days later he went to London where, on
14 January, he interviewed Alberto Randegger, conductor of the Norwich
Festival, and Clara Butt, for whom Sea Pictures were written. On the
following day he attended the Sunday Concert Society's performance at
Queen's Hall where Rimsky-Korsakov's Fantasia on Serbian Themes
(Op. 6) was played. The 'Russian craze' encouraged by Henry Wood and
George Riseley, conductors of the Sunday Concert Society, was not to the
taste of the more conventional critics.

During this month Elgar was revising his Three Characteristic Pieces
(Op. 10) and the song 'Love alone will stay' – the 'Lute Song' (Op. 37 no. 2).
Work on the former was completed on 24 January, on the latter on the day
following.

While in London Elgar visited the Jaegers on 15 January.

III

1899

Forli
Malvern.
Jan 5 1899

My dear Jaeger:

Welcome home! I won't say much on this particular piece of paper 'cos I'm coming to town on Monday next for a space & shall see you, and if I'm good, perhaps I may be allowed to see Mrs. Jaeger too.

I'm so sorry I shall miss your A[t] H[ome?] on Saturday – I'm conducting a sort of a kind of a concert.

No! we did not design the Inkstand – I will tell you about the ware one day.

Ha! ha! here's a nice well-behaved letter, not one expletivious word: don't I know that Mrs. J. is looking over your shoulder????? dear me! I was young once myself & now I'm only your old

Ed: Elgar

I say – those variations I *like* 'em. My wife joins me in all messages.

Malvern
Jan 20: [18]99

My dear Jaeger:

I am not well: ever since I got my head wet last Thursday – 'along of you' – now it's sort of neuralgia & will go merrily on.

Business.

Ja! it is somewhat of a contradiction but I thought it wd. do – it shows the conductor that he may hurry up a little more – I don't really think it's worth while to put *piu mosso* for this scrap but as you please.

The dinner[1] is digested, also the speeches, also–hm!

[1] 'E. to banquet to Cowen Maccabean Club', Lady Elgar, Diary Entry for 15 January

Analysis [King Olaf] is proceeding & I hope to send it tomorrow with my notes to you. It's an *awful* job.

All right – omit *everything* in the March.[1] *I've wrote about it already.* My wife is really laid up in bed & mimsy.

In great haste

Yrs sincly

Ed. E.

We were glad to get a small peep at your home & the pretty picture dwells with me.

Malvern

Jan. 22, 1899.

Creature!

Cease reviling mine instruments: there are only three bangs on the GONG in the whole of Caractacus & I'll wager a pound a bang you can't tell where they are – so artfully are they dispersed. Yah! Let's call it, as in 8vo score–

The Roman Triumph (March) eh?

it's handy for programmes; see?

March . . . "The Roman Triumph" . . . (Caractacus) Jaeger.

Chorus Sc III

words want altering a little before arranging.

Verily: I know Sinclair & wd be delighted to see him arranging my 'stuff' – or preferably the stuff after its arranged: but I don't know if he *does* arrange.

I *really* hope to send the Analysis tomorrow . . .

Now GRIN: – we, that is the Phil. desire some *English Music*[2]

– English I know well;

– Music I know well;

but *English-music* generally

*   *   *   *   *   *   *

very urgent this! Now will you, in your might, get one of your myrmidons(!) to send all, or any, of the enclosed list for me to select from. I want to see that of *W. Davies* & shd like to do it: I am sorry his oratorio was not accepted for Worcester: but all the *lumps* in programme were cut & dried before I appeared on the scene: – then I offered to retire in favour of young England (bless it!) but the Committee jeered – at my retiring, I mean – and you think it's a d—— lie; (your very words) but it isn't. I have reduced the Analysis to Marks &

---

[1] from *Caractacus*, see pp. 39, 40, 51, 58

[2] four times underlined

pfennige & corrected it with Bradshaw & am tearing my hair – it's a trial to your usually very sane

Ed. Elgar.

My wife is somewhat better but has a vile cough. I am better altogether and extremely venomous just now.

In fulfilment of his wish to produce an English work at a concert of the Worcestershire Philharmonic Society Mackenzie's Dream of Jubal *(Op. 42) was chosen, and performed on 4 May.*

Malvern
Jan. 22 Sunday. [1899]

My dear Jaeger:

Froissart.

Here's the skore. *p. 48.* two first bars require alteration. Parts affected

    Tromba 2a

    3 Trombones &

    Strings.

It was an awfully stupid bar & the 'stuff' may, nay probably will be played again this year: it will do for an old work, not bad, but I could not stand that one bar.

Yrs ever
Ed. Elgar

Put the Op: no in anywhere you can when occasion arises.

Monday.

I did not post this last night: & now here's the Analysis: I have tried to make the end clean – it was all omitted in the original. I have used some of J. B[ennett]'s remarks in *his subsequent criticisms*. I think if you send me *two* copies of proof I wd. send one to him as I promised & I always keep my word!

Hurry up.

Yr
Ed. E.

pcl post regd brings the two things together.

Malvern
Jan 27 [1899?]

My dear Jäger:

All the pages seem correct except p 40 with your lovely 'ancor etc which shd. be in the next bar. I've marked it.

As to Sinclair, I think you had better ask him.

As to Jabberwock[1] the English never take to anything of that sort –

---

[1] Jaeger suggested a cantata on a text from Lewis Carroll.

treated mock-heroically – the whole book of 'Alice' is now on the stage done by children – go & see it & weep – I know my twaddly grown up countrymen & women & am sick of 'em

Always (but in haste this time)

thy

E.E.

At the beginning of February Elgar went to London and was present at the inaugural meeting of the Folk Song Society.[1] He had visited Leipzig in 1883 (see Elgar O.M., p. 49) and the enclosed excerpt from The Daily Telegraph *of 4 February[2] recalled that visit.*

The Mandeville Hotel, W
Saturday a.m.
[4 February 1899]

My dear Jaeger:

I'm sorry I shall not see you again: I have to return home to-day.

The enclosed cutting amused me because I saw two dancers once in Leipzig who came down the stage in antique dress dancing a gavotte: when they reached the footlights they suddenly turned round & appeared to be two very young & modern people & danced a gay & lively measure: they had come down the stage *backwards* & danced away with their (modern) faces towards us – when they reached the back of the stage they suddenly turned round & the old, decrepit couple danced gingerly to the old tune.

I tell you all this because it gave me the idea of the III° movement

[1] This took place on 2 February at Mrs. Beer's house at 7 Chesterfield Gardens. Mackenzie was in the Chair. Parry gave an inaugural address, and Edgar F. Jacques read one paper ('Modal survivals in folk-song') and Mrs. Kate Lee (hon. sec.) another ('Some experiences of a folk-song collector').

[2]
AMERICAN SOCIETY
THE REVERSIBLE DANCE
FROM OUR OWN CORRESPONDENT

NEW YORK, Friday.

Mrs Stuyvesant Fish says that her coming 'reversible dance' is to be called the Bellamy party, because her guests will seem to be looking backward.

She got her idea from a frolic in a country house on Long Island during the Christmas holidays, when no end of fun was created by the ridiculous appearance of dancers who seemed to have their heads and clothes turned the wrong way round, while they pirouetted as usual. This is accomplished by the use of masks on the backs of the heads, and wigs or caps over the face, the women wearing dominoes and the men reversed dress-clothes. In the case of a stout person the effect is often more laughable than elegant.

of the three things[1] I sent to the firm – tell Mr Littleton any of this if you think it worth while.

In haste,
kind regards
Yrs
Ed. E.

Give your boys my blessing to-night.

Feb: 13 [18]99 Malvern

My dear Jaeger:

I was glad to see your scrawl again. No: there's no sunshine going just now anywhere. As to things you name: you won't believe it but I haven't a copy of Caractacus in the house! I forget how the Lament intertwines with the Chorus. I could of course remember it but before I attempt that feat you might order a copy or two to be sent from the shop dept. say 2 paper
1 board &
1 cloth.

I *suppose* I ought to possess my own works!

We are all well: I've caught a cold on the common (golf I mean) & have a headache in consequence & am mouldy.

I say: I ordered some score (20 stave) paper – I mention this because we talked it over, & they've gone & sent me ½ quire (*all* they have) but it's not the same – the staves are smaller & doesn't suit me – I'm keeping it because it will just finish my present 'job', but I hope you are bringing out that graduated series on superfine paper at a subfine price.

Ever yours
Ed. Elgar.

I will write about the ptsong[2] (out of Carac: I mean).

At this time the Elgars were negotiating for a new house at Malvern and by 24 February (see Diary) they had settled on that to be named anagrammatically 'Craeg Lea'. Elgar had been in touch with Nathaniel Vert, Richter's manager, and a score of the 'Enigma' Variations was sent to him on 21 February. During this year the idea of a 'Gordon' symphony was being pursued, not only by Elgar, but also by Jaeger.

Sunday [19(?) February 1899]

My dear J.

Sorry! I thought you understood about Gordon – I imagined I told

[1] *Three Characteristic Pieces*
[2] 'Britons alert'

you that I had annexed the idea – I only wanted to see my way to ease
& affluence to write it – that has not arrived but anyhow I'm making a
shot at it – you needn't be afraid of gongs – I'm not the man to make a
noise (??) We've gotten us an house!

You will see my letter to the firm about the Variations I expect;
only for mercy's sake don't tell *anyone* I pray you about Richter becos'
he may refuse. Vert is keen about it & it wd. be just too lovely for
anything if R. did an English piece by a man who hasn't appeared yet:
& now your arguments about Q's Hall wd. receive a clencher – but I
fear R. has been 'got at'.

I have begged for a very early reply from Vienna.

I note the rest of your letter.

I wish sometime you wd. let me know how many copies of K. Olaf
you have – or rather could a new edn be ready for Sheffield. I much
want to rewrite a few declamatory passages but it won't do until you
have sold out – perhaps the plate cd. be altered now?

yrs
E.E.

[*W.P.S. paper*]

Malvern
Feb 21 [1899]

My dear Jaeger:

I feel out of it! having been busy, really busy – we are leaving Forli &
getting us another cot.

hence the abstraction.

I did not write to Mathews for the score but you can send it to me
(Vol. II) any time you can spare it.

It does seem an awful shame that you shd. go to the expense of
copying the score – it should be *printed*! I am going to conduct at
Leeds next season (Oct)[1] & its probably to be done at L'pool,[2] & a
monumental (!) score wd be a credit to your department.

Perpend!

We hope you & your wife are flourishing. I'm just off to the Beagles
& shall be away all day – no music like the baying of hounds after all!

[1] 8 November, see pp. 64, 67, 68

[2] The 'Triumphal March' from *Caractacus* was played in Liverpool on 16 July
1899; also included in the programme were the *Imperial March*, the *Serenade*, and
the *Variations*.

Thanks for the things sent. I should like a set of strings of Caracta: for my collection when issued.

In much haste & tribulation,

Yours ever

Ed. Elgar

Write someday.

Forli

Malvern

Feb. 25 [1899]

I wrote this on Saturday

My dear Jaeger:

Here comes the score of Caract: I have been thro' the March & have *red-inked* some passages in the wind which will make it clear: I have scarcely touched the *strings* but some small notes must go in in one place – I think they can easily be put in the existing plates. I have made

Arpa,

Organ,

B. Clar. & Trombi III & IV

C. Fag:

    ad lib. – there:

isn't that virtuous.

I think it is the best scoring I ever saw! & the worst written. How are you? I hope well.

I expect your silence is connected, as usual, with the M.T. nicht wahr? You must forgive me much just now for we are changing house or rather preparing for it & all is anyhow.

You will see my letter to the firm which I hope is clear. I suppose there wd be no difficulty in getting out the parts.

I trust Mrs Jaeger is well & that you are flourishing generally. I could not think where that pig Betts[1] got his yarn from on Friday & his wicked joke.

Yours ever

Ed Elgar

[*W.P.S. paper*]

Malvern.

Feb 28 1899.

My dear Nimrod,

Capel-Cure[2] sends me the enclosed – but he has forgotten where he took the *Tenor solo* section from – or rather he has forgotten what

---

[1] *Note by Jaeger:* 'Betts critic of Daily News'

[2] The Rev. Edward Capel-Cure, a Malvern clergyman who prepared the libretto of *Lux Christi*

the words are – I don't know either as I have sent all back to you.

Chor pt is Amos V. 8.

The ps used in the T. solo cd easily be found by looking in the Concordance – if any trouble send the sheets back to me. Don't think the parson has forgotten *his Bible* but poor chap! he ain't seen or heard of the thing for about 18 months.

Yours ever in haste

Ed: Elgar

The Club,

Malvern.

Friday [10 March 1899]

My dear Jaeger:

I hope you are not ill but I've managed to get my letter writing – owing to scrambling about moving – in an awful muddle & seem to have missed a letter from you.

The new house will be called

Craeg Lea

Wells Rd.

name not on yet.

– I am awfully worried with this moving & do anything to escape – I *fled* out yesterday straight across country to think out my thoughts & to avoid every one – will you believe it? I had walked 9 miles & was on the road and a man rode silently (on a bicycle) behind me & said 'Oh! Mr. Elgar! can you tell me if *Novello's have any performing right in &c. &c*"

I was speechless.

In haste

Ever yours

Edward Elgar

Shall I send the P.F. arrgt of the variations now complete – for inspection or wait for the return of the full score?

Forli,

Malvern.

March 13 [1899]

My dear Jaeger:

I am sending the pF Variations to-day.

I daresay it, or rather, they will come under your eagle eye: I have tried to make the arrgt as simple as possible: the 'pretty' one X shd do very well as a separate venture, if only the piano solo is easy enough: *do* tell me if you think it could be fined down more: the score is easy & for a few insts

the demisemiquaver groups are thus throughout

do *you* think I have made the passage easy

or would this be better

I have kept to ⊕ which sounds all right but which wd. Mary Ann of the ladies' schools prefer? Nimrod does not do for piano so well as orch:

Mrs J. will recognise your portrait quicker than you will: I have omitted your outside manner & have only seen the good, lovable honest SOUL in the middle of you! and the music's not good enough: nevertheless it was an attempt of your

E.E.

Craeg Lea,
Wells Road,
Malvern.
March 20 1899.

My dear Jaeger:

I send 'Sursum Corda'[1] to *you:* how wd it do for Newman[2]? It has only been done (in town) at Blair's Church[3]. I forget which ch. it is but you were there. It makes as you know a good effect but it's *obvious* music: tell Newman it would make a gorjus effect with the organ.

One other thing there's the String Serenade: now (Breitkopf) that's never been done in London: failing anything else he might do the *slow movement* only from that – or he might do it as *well as* anything else: it made a sensation at Antwerp & elsewhere: it wd. be fine to do it with double strings & is quite easy, not much rehearsing required.

As to Sursum Corda if he cares about the idea I'll come up on Friday & talk with him, you & the firm: but the slow movement from the string thing wd be a good novelty.

Yrs in haste
Ed Elgar

If he has a Chorus why oh! why not the Te Deum? or Blk Knight.

The Serenade (Op. 20) was first performed in Antwerp on 23 July 1896. It was repeated, by the Orchestre de la Société Royale de Zoologie under the direction of Edward Keurvels, the Flemish composer and conductor, on 30 November 1898. On both occasions the work was included in a programme of Scandinavian music – a fact which would have appealed to Elgar on account of his claim to be of Scandinavian descent. The Serenade was given yet again in Antwerp on 21 February 1900, this time in a programme of British music presented by Granville Bantock.

Although the previous letter is as from Craeg Lea the Elgars did not move, according to the Diary, until 21 March, on which day Edward was rehearsing Caractacus *at the Albert Hall in preparation for the performance of 20 April.*

Craeg Lea
Thursday [23 March 1899]

My dear J:

I arrd. home (*new home*) all right & found my dear one flourishing although tired.

---

[1] Op. 11, composed in 1894 and published by Schott in 1901(?)
[2] Robert Newman, manager of Queen's Hall
[3] Holy Trinity, Marylebone (also see p. 66)

Here is the sheet of corrections – can you make it out?

If not let me know they are *all* for the *score* – the p.f. is right.

– Do send a wire & say if the score has arrived – I am getting in a *fit* lest it shd. miscarry. This *is* a jolly nice house but of course all in confusion just now. However it will be ready for *your* inspection any time. My study is a dream! & the view.

I want a photo of you as Nimrod (my view of you)

Much love,

Yours

Ed Elgar

Craeg Lea,

Malvern.

March 24 [1899]

My dear Jaeger,

Here come the proofs of the three little pieces.

I want to know if you could get the *title* done *very soon* as Lady Mary [Lygon][1] is going away & I should like her to see it first–

I propose

    Three Characteristic pieces (as [head *deleted*] chief title)

       I. Mazurka

      II. Serenade (Mauresque)

     III. Gavotte.

Then above I want

To

Lady Mary Lygon,

Madresfield.

———

Just so.

———

If its against the rules to do the title first – squash it. If issued separately the dedication should go on each one. She is a most angelic person & I should like to please her – there are few who deserve pleasing – I've tried to please you & know I can't!

Yours ever,

E.E.

[1] Sister of Lord Beauchamp, of Madresfield, near Malvern; she was shortly to accompany him to New South Wales where he was appointed Governor. Lady Lygon is memorialized in the thirteenth of the '*Enigma*' *Variations*.

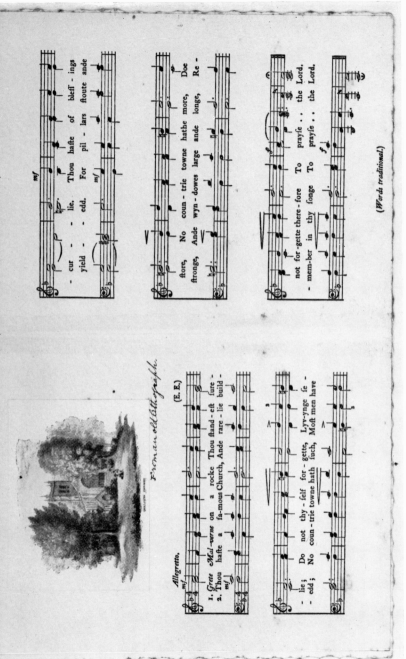

From an old lithograph.

Allegretto.

(E. E.)

1. Grete Mal-vurne on a rocke Thou ftand-eft fure -
2. Thou hafte a fa-mous Church, Ande rare - lie build -

- lie ; Do not thy-felf for-gette, Lyv-ynge fe -
- edd ; No coun-trie towne hath fuch, Moft men have

- cur - - lie. Thou hafte of bleff - ings
yield - - edd. For pil - lars ftoute ande

ftore, No coun - trie towne hathe more, Doe
ftronge, Ande wyn-dowes large ande longe, Re-

not for-gette there-fore To prayfe . . the Lord,
- mem-ber in thy fonge To prayfe . . the Lord.

(Words traditional.)

Christmas card, 1897

Whitsunday, 1900
(See page 88)

WACHT AUF!

WORCESTERSHIRE PHILHARMONIC SOCIETY

[*W.P.S. paper*]

Malvern,

Ap 5 [18]99

My dear Jaeger:

All your words of wizdum sink deep & will be acted upon. I am sick of gavottes too – & Mazurki (thats a good plural). If you want a sub. (or Haupt) title for the Mazurka put

"In Kaprun".

The gavottes are more puzzzlin.

1) 1700–1900
2) Dignity & impudence
3) Skirts v. Tights! (good)
4) Then and Now
5) Ranelagh & the 'pav':
6) Old & New
7) Hims & hers Ancient & Modern
8) De mal en pis
9) Sedan chair & motor-car
10) Q. Anne & Q. Victoria
11) Farthingales & petticoats

Oh lor! won't some of these do?

I think you had better send the Analysis to J.B. *only* tell me when you send & I will send a note to him synchronisticallifyicationally (I made that word)

I *may* come up on Saturday but will let you ken if I do. I *must* come up on Monday[1] and back on Tuesday a.m.

In haste

Yours ever

E. Elgar

Craeg Lea

Malvern.

Sunday, Ap 9 [1899]

My dear J:

Deo gratias!

I wonder where IT has been:

I'm coming up tomorrow arriving at 12.15 and shall come down – Berners St. – to you as soon as I'm *thawed*[.] it's bitter cold here today. If you have preserved my list of corrections (& I'll scalp you if you haven't) I will make 'em myself in two minutes only I *should* like to see an example of your scoring.

[1] to rehearse *Caractacus* on April 10

Some of 'em (vars:) are so short that I don't think dear Brause[1] *can* begin each one on a fresh page, so perhaps it wd. be well to remind him that X will probably be wanted for separate use.

I don't think there is any restriction at the Albert Hall: *do* come if you like but I don't know that it will interest you to hear my struggles. Look here if you have any proofs or revise for me on Monday do send them to

　　3 Tedworth Square
　　　Chelsea[2]

I have to leave by 1st train on *Tuesday* and could 'do' them in the train and save time and it wd be something to do. Dr. McNaught is in Malvern for competition and comes to us this p.m. – I sh. like you to have seen the view first!

Yrs. ever
E.E.

Craeg Lea,
Malvern.
April 12 [1899]

My dear Jaeger:

I *am*[3] glad you did not come to the Albert Hall! I won't say a word but – I've rote to Vert asking to be in a Joon programme if humanly possible but we will sail on as hard as we can with the printing. I had no reply from the firm about H[erbert]. T[hompson].'s Analysis (Caract.) Also I sent a *small* tune for the fiddle[4] – its not much but don't lose it! Because I can sell it only I might know your views soon.

I will let you know my movements later.

In the meantime
Yrs ever
E. Elgar:

P.S. If you (M.T.) give Richter's list the following are spelt wrongly:
　　R-Korsakow shd. be Snegour*och*[5]ka
　　Tschaikowsky – Air*s* de Ballet "Voyévod*a*"
　　S. Wagner – Bärenhäuter (fancy A.J.J. being told that!!)
C.A.B. sent me a corrected copy.

---

[1] Brause, Novello's chief engraver, and sometimes foreman
[2] the house of Basil Nevinson (B.G.N. of No. 12 of the *'Enigma' Variations*)
[3] three times underlined
[4] *Chanson de matin* (Op. 15 no. 1, pub. 1899)
[5] italicized letters much underlined to end of postscript

Craeg Lea,
Malvern.
Ap 27 [1899]

My dear Jaeger:

I feel like a criminal at all I have to answer.

I. I forgot all about the wind of Caract. March. I *think* the score is
marked and Mr. Rivers[1] cd. insert my notes – I *think* I wrote to the firm
about making organ B.Clar. & c. Fag *ad lib*[2]. but it may be that I
only put some such direction in the f. score. Let me know what Mr.
Rivers makes of it.

II. I thought I explained about the Royalty – it is as you say Mr.
Augustus [Littleton] thought they might do it. I pointed out that I had
been promised a royalty by Mr. Alfred [Littleton] long ago on *something* – the next thing they took – they wanted an easy violin piece and
I furnished it – but they said it wd. not *bear a* royalty. I am furnishing
3 small pieces on which I suggested a Royalty – no notice taken – so I
suggested this sword song – that's all! of course they will do as they
please.

Oh! I am so anxious to have done with the whole art – it's only my
wife who begs me to go on, but I hate & loathe the whole business.

III. Yes, in the page of Vars: put the chords small – I did not think it
worth altering. I return the Meditation [*Lux Christi*] and the Sword
Song [*Caractacus*]. Ought not the work (in each case) from which the
things are taken to be stated? Surely.

In much haste,
Yrs. ever,
E.E.

Forli
Malvern.
Ap 28 [1899]

My dear J:

Sorry about your rheumatism and hope you are better. If you *really*
think it wd. be better pray do add Finale to the title – I of course should
prefer simply

Variations
Op. 36
Edward Elgar.

[1] Chief of Novello's Hire Department. He spent fifty-three years in the service
of the firm and retired in 1935. For many years he was a familiar figure at the
Three Choirs Festival, where he acted as librarian for the orchestral and vocal
material.

[2] twice underlined

That's modest & becoming but if necy. I will sacrifice my own bruised feelings on the altar of Mammon (high priest – Nimrod) I think its too bad to put the price as high as 3/6 – Nobody will buy the damn things.

Yea! kite-flying is a fine art but I don't do it now but I am going to start again soon.

Yrs. ever,
E.E.

Craeg Lea
May 2 [1899]

My dear Jaeger:

Many thanks for looking after my proofs: I have to thank West[1] for many [suggestions] – I think I have adopted 'em all. Barry writes this a.m. that he has discovered a lot also and is returning his sheets to you: if he has discovered anything else let me know: he talks also of consecutive 5ths and suchlike luxuries about which I don't care a tinker's damn! Anyhow let me know. Thanks for rushing that partsong[2] thro:

Now, Var 13. – I have altered the phrase to

The pretty Lady is on the sea & far away & I meant this (originally) as a little quotation from Mendelssohn's Meeresstille u. Glückliche Fahrt – but I did not acknowledge it as the critics – if one mentions anything of the kind – talk of nothing else – so I have now cut out the reference – I think you can alter the score in two places – it's only clart.!

Tell me what else reminds the critics of something else I might alter it.

As to Contrasts! I think the name will do – I only sent you my list for nonsense. I have made the tempi clearer now.

[1] John E. West, musical editor of Novello's, 1884–1929
[2] probably 'To her beneath whose steadfast star', prepared at Windsor Castle on 24 May

I am in a fit & cannot eat or drink until I hear what else sounds cabbagey.

In woful haste & woful want,

Yrs.

Ed. E.

Between 8 and 17 May an ambitious 'London Musical Festival' took place at Queen's Hall. There were two orchestras employed, those of Henry Wood and Charles Lamoureux, of Paris, under their respective conductors, and also the Queen's Hall Choral Society. Elgar was represented by the 'Meditation' from Lux Christi, which received its first performance in London, although it had been played at the Gloucester Festival of 1898.

On 11 May Elgar was present at an 'At home' at Frank Schuster's (see Letters of Edward Elgar, p. 350). This would appear to be the first time he met Schuster, who was to become a close friend.

Malvern

May 3 [1899]

My dear Jaeger:

I'm acoming up on Saturday a.m. (may be Friday p.m.) So hold anything you have for me & I will call on Saturday morning & see wot's wot. (I may not be able to be at Berners St. till 1.0)

Barry's ideas are futile but I have put in some of his axidentles – most of wh: I omitted purposely as being superfluous: you will see what he says – that wooden idea of cutting out the consecutive fifths is enough to turn one gray.

I shd. think 'Contrasts' might do – I do hope you did not shew the "firm" *my* list!

Meditation is to be rehearsed on Saturday at *2.30* – I'm going

I can when in town alter the skore & cut out Meeresstille – I'm in a fit & take no food thinking of your horrid words about another reminiscence.

I'm d—d if ever I try to write any more music.

In haste

Yours ever

Ed: Elgar

xqqq this paper

[*W.P.S. paper*]

Malvern

May 17 [1899]

My dear Nimrod:

Yes, I think these kleine noten will do. I am so sorry about that Olaf analysis – it went last night to you.

Look here – in the Variations *pianoforte* look at p. 30 (first bar of Var. XIII) in L.H. I want

If too late never mind but you may not have started printing yet.

I hear all our skemes for Whitsuntide are smashed – our little girl is home from school with a suspicious throat. I don't think it's anything but it plays the bear with our private junketings.

Yrs ever in haste,
Ed. Elgar.

Forli [*deleted*]
Malvern
May 19 [1899]

Dear J:

Tharnks:

entered was J.B's words so I dare not alter it–

put the Ex thus for choice

I think J[oseph]. B[ennett]. meant *ended* so we'll put that & it won't mess the plate too much.

§ "but in the minor" it *is* minor, but so it was before (more orders)–

Now I'm v*ery* much laid up with an awful cold: if you know tomorrow (Saturday) a.m. what I shall receive on Sunday a.m. in the way of score & proofs from you will you *wire* & tell me – 'cos I cd. engage my man (the human 5th.-trap) for the Sabbath – if you're not sure of sending me anything, never mind; but if all the wind or all the strings *with all* the score are coming without fail do drop me a wire.

It is *so* cold & comfortless here outside[1] I really prefer London I fear this neuralgia

Good luck!

Yours ever

Ed E

Craeg Lea, Wells Rd.

Sunday May 28 [1899]

My dear J.

Many thanks for yours:

all right, the *name* will do for the Caraktus March and it shd. do well for Military band. If your organ *arrgers* had a ghost of the average Frenchman's arranging ability a fine (effective I mean) organ piece cd. be made of it too.

Another 'Enigma' – the Black Knight you say is unsuccessful commercially – and its the only thing I ever recd. any royalty on yet – I see how it is. I think it is too artistic for the ordinary conductor of Choral Societies – I find they are an inordinately ignorant lot of cheesemongering idiots. the chorus & orchestra *go* for my things but the *conductors* always, or nearly always, find them too difficult – to conduct. Vocal parts would help of course *and*[2] a printed score. Imagine a poor devil of an organist put up to read one of my m.s. scores & pity him & me & you & Messrs. N. and the audience.

As to the "Batterie" in the Cactus march – I should print it in score as copied in.

[*end of letter wanting*]

[*W.P.S. paper*]

Malvern.

Friday [2 June 1899]

My dear Jaeger:

Wood is rehearsing the Vars. at *10.30* tomorrow (Saturday) I am just starting to town & shall return at 1.30 tomorrow.

I hope all is well at your house & that the new arrival likes this world better than some of us old stagers. Thanks for the Bonn programme; I should like to go very much.

I want you to get a further opinion about your nasal business: I have asked a doctor friend in town who recommends Greville

---

[1] added in pencil

[2] twice underlined

MacDonald.[1] I will remind you of this when I'm up again next week &
we'll talk it over.

Much love

Yrs. ever

Ed: Elgar

Craeg Lea,

Malvern.

June 8 [1899]

My dear J.

Only an urried line. thanks for seeing to the Imp. March.

I shan't trouble about the *chorus* in Lux – I was only going to alter
two notes to make the *time* easier – but they can grind at it.

The solos I remind you I *am* going to overhaul.

I say do get those 3 pieces Autogravured or we shall never get 'em
played. Every pier band is going to do that old boyish thing Tuckwood
has done[2] now the skoughre is printed! Geideling[3] is good enough
for those. No! you did not shew me any Kölnische Zeitungen at all
or anything nice except your own old phiz.

Yrs.

E.E.

P.S. our Baby has whooping cough after all so the whole house is
upset and so am I. I say will those 3 pieces be ready by the first week
in July becos I've got to make out a *final* programme for Bantock[4].
I *shall want the Vars:*

*The Elgars went to London on 16 June and Edward immediately visited
Richter to go through the score of the* 'Enigma' *Variations with him. This
had already been rehearsed on 3 June, Elgar having been present, was rehearsed
again on 17 June and on the morning of 19 June. On the evening of that day
it was given its first performance at St. James's Hall. As later letters show, the
Finale was subsequently enlarged.*

'To write a really original set of variations is no easy matter, but this
Mr. Elgar has done. The theme displays dignity and at the same time
simplicity, while of the variations we may say there is not one that
could be termed feeble; they are remarkable for charm, variety,

---

[1] Greville MacDonald, M.D. (b. 1856), E.N.T. specialist at King's College
Hospital

[2] *Sevillana* (Op. 7)

[3] Herr Geidel, head of the music-engraving firm in Leipzig

[4] for a concert at New Brighton on 18 July. This was one of a series devoted to
modern music. Composers other than Elgar prominently represented were
Tchaikovsky, Cowen, Dvořák, and Rubinstein. Bantock was conductor-in-
chief, but Rodewald and Chevillard also assisted.

character, rather than for the skill both of structure and orchestration, by which, however, these qualities are enhanced. We regret that the composer has dedicated his work "To my friends pictured within". There was no harm in his working, like Beethoven, to pictures in his mind, but it would have been better not to call attention to the fact. The variations stand in no need of a programme; as abstract music they fully satisfy. If the friends recognise their portraits it will, no doubt, please them; but this is altogether a personal matter. The performance, under the direction of Dr. Richter, was perfect, and at the close the composer was called to the platform and loudly applauded. It was no mere *succès d'estime;* the variations will, we feel sure, be often heard, and as often admired.'

– *from* The Athenaeum, *24 June 1899*

'Effortless originality – the only true originality – combined with thorough *savoir faire,* and, most important of all, beauty of theme, warmth, and feeling are his credentials, and they should open to him the hearts of all who have faith in the future of our English art and appreciate beautiful music wherever it is met.'

– *from* The Musical Times *review of the first performance of the* Variations, *July 1899, pp. 464–5*

[*W.P.S. paper*]

Malvern
June 27 [1899]

My dear Jaeger,

I waited until I had thought it out and now decide that the end is good enough for me: as to the points in the score I am puzzled – I always said those celli were – bar one or two – the worst in the world – and a whole heap of passages they have did not come out – including that passage (unheard) on p. 26 (I had forgotten that they actually have it with the bassoon and we never heard it). Again on p. 27 the Celli got *no* tone out of those 7ths – I will assist 'em. You won't frighten me into writing a logically developed movement where I don't want one by quoting other people!

Selah!

Do let one of your men alter the score of Lux (*Damn the composer*) and also the 'cues' in orch. parts if necy.

I have had a nice rapturous letter from C.H.H.P[arry]. most kind of him.

As to the parts of the 3 new pieces – I had no idea you wanted to engrave the wind in time for New Brighton. I send back the M.S.

parts as soon as possible. As to engraving the score of the Vars. hadn't
it better wait until after New B[righton]. – that is on the 18th. I think
that's all – I've a frightful headache today – sunheat.

Yrs ever

Ed.E.

How wd. this do – use the skoughre & parts just as they are (Variations)
at Bantock's concert – I would touch up the thing *after* & let you have
it say on the 20th of July? Commonsense ain't it?
N.B. Do get those corrections in Lux score made at once dear man. I
spoke to Mr. Alfred about the Tenor song as a separate thing, and,
if Mr. Bantock can get the vocalist, we are going to try it: if you could
get me a set of the revised 8vo. sheets of the song I wd. send it to
Brophy if he can come.

Malvern.

June 30 [1899]

My dear Jaeger:

As to that finale its most good of you to be interested & I like to
have your opinion – I have my doubts as to some of the rest 'cos its
generally *suggested* to them.

Now look here, the movement was designed to be concise – here's
the difficulty of lengthening it – I *could* go on with those themes for ½
a day but the *key* G is exhausted – the [1st theme *deleted*] principal
motive (Enigma) comes in grandioso on *p. 35* in the tonic and it *won't
do* to bring it in again: had I intended to make an extended movement
this wd. have been in some related key reserving the tonic for the final
smash. In deference to you I made a sketch yesterday – but the thing
sounds Schubertian in its sticking to one key. I should really like to
know *how* you heard that Richter was disappointed – he criticised
some of it but not the end – the actual final flourish was spoilt in performance by the insts. going wild. You see there's far too much of
this sort of thing said: somebody wants to find fault & in course of
conversation says "the end did not please so & so – I find it very poor –
don't you?" the other chap hadn't thought of it at all but says "Yes it's
very abrupt" & so it goes on.

This sort of thing is of no value to me – what *you* say is your own
opinion and wd. be given on anybody's work. All the other fellows
wd. never have made a remark if the work had been written by any
great man. If I find, after New B[righton]. that the end does not satisfy
me, I may recast the whole of the last movement but it's not possible
to *lengthen* it with any satisfaction I fear. If I *can* find time to make a

readable copy of my "end" I'll send it to you and then you'll see how good

E. Elgar
is at heart.

Mrs. Elgar to Jaeger:
July 4
'. . . what intense pleasure the notice of the "Variations" in the M. Times gave me, it seemed exactly to realize my idea of what I wanted said regarding the music . . .'

Craeg Lea,
Malvern.
July 7 1899.

My dear Jaeger:
   Many thanks for your letter re 'Lux Xti': I don't think – short of burning the whole thing – that there's anything further to be done. The principals[1] will want copies and when they are ready I will send a special line to Lloyd drawing his attention to the amendments: he has sung it before from the old copy – the others have not : I see they have cast Marie Brema (!) for the little easygoing contralto part – I expect she will 'chuck it' – a festival committee is funny.
   I wish you were going to be at New Brighton but it is extremely doubtful even at this late date whether the quaint performances of your secretary will not prevent the concert taking place. I can't think the letters are written by one of the firm.
   I will write again when anything turns up: things is dull. *Your* opinion is not a 'Nebensache' – some people's are: I am hoping to send you a sketch of a proposed extended finale: there's one phrase wh: I can use again.

Yours ever
E. Elgar.

Birchwood Lodge,
nr. Malvern. Deo Gratias
[July 1899]

My dear Jaerodnimger:
   Aha! I'm here & *at* work in my woodlands. Now: hither comes pp. 1– to 144 incl. of the Score and *all* the wind &c. revised to 76 at this point the Jaerodnimgeresque coda cometh on – I am scoring this prestissimo.
   Look here – shall I put in *organ* ad lib: just at the end? If so (perpend)

[1] for the Three Choirs Festival at Worcester in September

it shd. be named on the 1st page of printed score: I suppose the *1st page* will give the names of *all* the insts. as usual & then less staves will be used (only those necy) afterwards: anyhow tell me at once about the organ *ad lib.*

In haste
Yrs. ever
Ed Elgar.

Otter hunting three days this week.

A Fox

P.S. [*in pencil*] If you think *not* organ, cross it *out* on p. 1 of score.

Malvern.
July 12 [1899]

My dear J:

You're a trump! I'm heartily glad you like the TAIL. *I do* now it's done: I haven't time for a word, only here's the M.S. I think dear Mr. Brause can make it out, but, as usual, I've used up (pasted it on) my sketch where not illegible. just look it through again there's a good chap.

Now. I am going to New Brighton tomorrow – back on Tuesday; *then* I will revise the points in the sc: which he discussed before & score this new end (coda) – Can you rush the piano copy thro' – I send it now on the chance – if it *must* be delayed, let me have the M.S. back to score on Tuesday from, 'cos, (as I said before) my sketch is cut up to gum on – see? So I shall be waiting. If anything is ready on Saturday, it might come on to me c/o G. Bantock Esqr.,

Holly Mount
Liscard
Cheshire.
Yrs ever
E.E.

While staying with Bantock Elgar went to Sheffield on 17 July for a

rehearsal of King Olaf (*to be performed on 11 October*). *Mrs. Elgar noted in the Diary:* '*Glorious* reception and rehearsal'.

> Malvern.
> July 20 [1899]
> prestissimo.

My very dear J.

Owing to some oversight your letter never came on to me & we arrd. home late last night!

Here's the final revision of the Coda: thanks to West and you for suggestions: I see it will do to include the rhythmic bars and have done so – I can't put in *more* runs: they really *begin* at first bar of p. 39 and are (orchestrally) the feature. I couldn't put 'em in for pf. they simply 'culminate' where introduced in the P.F. arrgt. Now. I've no copy but am *revising* the score (on the points we mentioned before) & will score this (new) *coda* directly I receive the engraved copy from you – *send two copies* of proof. I will keep one.

I think I can send you the score [for engraving] by the 26th but alas! we've lost a few days by the infernal postal arrgts. Anyhow leave full directions as to the score going to Germany. We had a glorious time. Bantock *is* a brick and *really* understands things. Then I went to Sheffield & heard that chorus and was lifted into the seventh paradise: never you complain of my choral effects again – they're grand and mighty when properly sung and by Heaven I've never, never heard *anything* like that chorus – you *must* hear Olaf at the festl. Coward must be a genius to get the dramatic force & perception; it is simply marvellous and colossal.

> E.E.

The first of Jaeger's letters for this year to have survived is dated 24 July, and deals with the engraving of the string parts of the 'Enigma' *Variations and the wind parts of the* 'Triumphal March' *from* Caractacus *and the* 'Mazurka' *and* 'Gavotte' *from the* Three Characteristic Pieces. *Jaeger continues:* 'The Serenade M[auresque] is at Cardiff being used as a test piece in orchestral playing (adjudicator Sir J. F. Bridge!!! I[1] recommended it to him!!!) I enclose 2 *un*read proofs of *the* Koda [of the *Variations*] & have just seen Geidel's agent. Now look here, cut up that Full score of the Variations in slices & send us a portion *at once*[1], that I may hand it over to Geidel's agent who promises to have the score ready in time for the *Worcester Festival if only you read the proofs quickly*! So buck up! Don't wait till the Koda is scored. Send a bit at once; every day is precious.'

[1] twice underlined

Just off to Birchwood
[c. 25 July 1899]

My dear Jaeger:

I seize this packing paper[1]!

All right: I *do* look 'ere. By this post comes pf. proofs – p. 40 last bar: it's too quick for any one to grab the chord I think & as it stands it makes the next p. sound fuller (1st chord p. 41 I mean). As to p. 41 do you like the *look* of those *3*'s all down the page? wd. *one* do & then *one* 4 (as it is now) – p. 42 – there are 3 bars L.H. of *E*'s – they shd. have been *small* – anything to save time so don't alter 'em unless you think fit. Now as to the score & wind. I'm going to plunge into 'em tomorrow & you shall have the score (*except Finale*) sent tomorrow. I can score the new end quickly: tell that nice woolly-lamb young man from Geidel's that the score must be taken care of – I don't mind the 'laying-out' figures if necy but I bar greasy thumbs.

Now as to the percussion of Caractacus march: if you print the *combined* part only – leave room for a *note* which I'll invent when I see the proof "When possible three performers shd. be employed in which case etc. etc." Something like that eh?

In haste

yours ever

Ed Elgar

[end of July 1899]

Dear Nimrod,

Xqqqq this scrap: I forgot to send back proofs of vars title. You'll see the suggested type which I think wd. look nice & friendly & not *too* far removed from the austerity of the title.

On 21 August Elgar went to London, interviewed A. H. Littleton, of Novello's, and as a result 'broke with Messrs. Novello for a time' (*Mrs.*

[1] on which to write

Elgar, Diary). The late Harold Brooke observed on the contretemps as follows: 'I think A.H.L., who was a very obstinate man, was peeved at the objection to a charge of 30/– (presumably for the hire of the material) & made a silly remark from which he refused to retreat. The small sum involved at least indicates the difficulties with which English publishers of orchestral music were faced in those days. On the other hand, if A.H.L. had had a fraction of the prescience of A.J.J[aeger] he would have financed the whole thing, & E.E. as well!'

The dissension was, however, of brief duration, for on 8 September Elgar saw Littleton again and their differences were resolved.

Birchwood Lodge
nr. Malvern.
Sep. 1 [18]99

My dear Jaeger:

All thanks to you for your note: sorry you are so busy & short-handed.

As to analysis of Lux my wife sent J.B. a copy of the Queen's Hall affair but I said I would like him to do it off his own bat: no harm done however.

Now: I don't think I ought to worry you with my business & purposely refrained from saying anything about the songs to you. Don't think I depend on singer's promises – I have my *small* piecrust.

I have had to write to the firm on one or two matters & have gone on just as of old & they reply: I think we have only one 'thing' between us & that is A.H.L's objection to my expression of disgust – this is very real & I can't withdraw it – Vert has lost heaps over the old gang's orchl. attempts & did the work as a favour – an *extra rehearsal* cost him £40 – the letter to the firm containing this information was *not before* A.H.L. – my note to Vert was in reference to the fact that he had *paid* £40 as well as taken the risk of producing an English piece & the publishers 'try it on' to get 30/– more out of him – this certainly aroused my disgust. I would have withdrawn the expression &, if need be, apologised as far as A.H.L. was concerned, *but, – this annoyed me more than anything* – he said V. ought to have got the extra rehearsal out of his men for *nothing*!! I was shocked at the sheer brutality of the idea but he repeated it: I confess the prospect of a rich man seriously considering the fleecing of those poor underpaid, overworked devils in the orchestra *quite* prevented me from feeling Xtian. If that is "business" – well damn your business – I loathe it. Now, my dear man, do not worry about me in the least: I have told you over & over again that the state of music in England is simply farcical & depressing & I

am well out of the vortex of jealousy, chicanery, fraud & falsehood, I
have to thank music for your friendship & for this I am grateful.

Yrs ever

Ed E

Craeg Lea,

Malvern,

Sep 9 1899

My dear Jaeger:

Don't you think I ought to send a note to Miss Bache[1] about those
libretti, 'cos I 'mind weel' how that you introduced me to her:-
she knows I had 'em? eh? If she *don't* know of course I needn't write
but I like (SOMETIMES) to be decently civil now don't I?

Drop your eye on the enclosed newspaper[2] – the British composer
will look up now.

Also *do* read the letter[2] & preserve it. & shew it any one you think
will appreciate it* – I have roared for days – "leaving legs behind"
etc. etc.

Misprint (slight) bar before 3 1st Vio Carac: March.

a shd. be crotchet & triplet after!

Is it my fault?

Goodbye

Yrs

E.E.

* [*marginal note*] I've declined – would Pitt like to take it on????????

At the Three Choirs Festival at Worcester Coleridge-Taylor's Solemn
Prelude, 'the only actual novelty', *was, according to* The Annals of the
Three Choirs (Continuation, *Gloucester 1931, p. 24*), 'heard with much
interest and attention'. *Regarding the concert in the Public Hall,* 'Mr.
Elgar received an enthusiastic welcome on appearance at the conductor's desk to direct his *Variations on an original theme*, which had lately
been produced in London at a Richter concert. The prophecy of an
eminent critic that "this music will soon travel round the earth" has
been realised.'

[*W.P.S. paper*]

Craeg Lea

Thursday (14/9/[18]99)

My dear J.

Only time for a line.

Taylor's prelude went *well* except a trifle of unsteadiness in the scale
passages and one other place – at least that is all I (a borrel man) could

[1] probably Constance Bache (1846–1903)
[2] not preserved

discover: I revelled in the opening and the close but I could not 'sequentiate' (!) the middle: he is a dear chap & its all so *human* & yearning.

The performance of the variations was really good especially *you* – slow & fine it sounded. Finale sounded gorgeous but the room is small.

Yrs ever
Ed. Elgar

Craeg Lea,
Malvern.
Sep 17 1899

My dear Jaeger:

Why not address as above and not *Forli* which we left 6 months agone? Perpend:—three times have ye done this thing.

Now: biz – I really do not mind about the score – it is better to reduce the weight – paper, price – in every way: the *first* page should shew everything employed: after that only the insts. actually in use need be shewn: the names (curtailed) shd. be placed at the beginning of each new device: it looks very well if not cut too fine in the way of elimination – (B[reitkopf]. & H[ärtel]. are good style when they *do* abbreviate) but of course Litolff is not 'classy' in appearance and I think they are discarding their old scores which were so much cut about. I think if each *var:* had its own 'system' that wd. be best – but then it may be difficult to make 'em fit ends of pp.

Sinclair is playing (organ) some (all possible) of the variations at Tenbury Commem[1]: I think you published an arrgt. *by* him of something. How is it done – practicable, saleable? And wd. it do to ask him to perpetrate an arrgt. of (some of) them for organ? I'm glad the Meditation is going on: anybody with any *real* feeling (emotion) was quite stricken and overcome by 'Lux Xti" – Albani was quite tearful over the expression of it, so was I. It is naive but there is nothing else like it – most of the critics think that a good thing but the audience don't – they love it!

Yours ever,
Ed. E.

[*W.P.S. paper*]

Malvern,
Sept 21 [18]99

My dear Jaeger:

I've been so very busy with all sorts & conditions of rot that I could

[1] Annual Michaelmas Commemoration of Foundation of St. Michael's College. Sinclair always played an organ recital at this occasion (see *History of St. Michael's College*, 1943, p. 55).

not spare a minute. No, I don't think I can just now *do* with S. Eliza [St. Elizabeth, Liszt?] I shall be in town very shortly & shall hope to see you – I should like to see 'it' but it will belike have left you before that. I am sending oh! such a pretty note to Miss Bache.

I heard from C. Taylor in response to a friendly note I sent him – I wish the critics had a little more imagination when British music is concerned: if it's cut and dried they sneer at it, and if we do show a bit of real feeling and emotion they laugh at it – I'm sick and so are you of me.

Yrs ever

Ed: E.

Sea Pictures were performed on 5 October, at Norwich. Meanwhile requests were coming in for further performances of the Variations. *That projected in Glasgow does not seem to have taken place, at any rate not in the winter series of 'Classical Concerts'.* St. George *was given at Tunbridge Wells in the Great Hall on 4 December; at a 'Conversazione of the Vocal Association', and conducted by W. W. Starmer (see* Letters of Edward Elgar, *p. 351).*

Bank House,
Norwich.

Oct 6 [18]99

My dear Jaeger,

I've been ill! bad cold but owing to good nursing I'm improved but still a weakly beast. Dear man: much as I shd like to see you Saturday p.m., I fear I can't get out.

The cycle went marvellously well & 'we' were recalled four times – I think – after that I got disgusted & lost count – She sang *really well*.

The letters, for wh: thanks – are about the Vars: at Glasgow & 'St. George' at Tunbridge – I've never heard the last named & wonder what it's like.

Much love

Yrs

Ed. E.

Jaeger to Elgar:

1, Berners Street,
London, W.

Oct. 10, 1899.

My dear Elgar,

I send you today a bit of full score of "Contrasts". The remainder will follow quickly. On Thursday or Friday you will receive the whole of the proofs of the Variations. Must I send them to Sheffield? Or

where?? Return them quickly won't you? We are trying to publish
before the 23rd., but fear it will be impossible because of the d——
American copyright. Still I hope Richter will have a proof copy corrected, to conduct from and the work shall be ready shortly afterwards.
I suppose Richter couldn't postpone the performance?[1] We mustn't
worry him lest he or Vert get sick of us. Geidel has been very quick
over the work.

Tell me, were there any corrections necessary in the string parts of
the three pieces (Opus 10). I see only one in the parts that were played
from at New Brighton. May I print for stock? Directly the Festivals
are over (thank Heaven) and the full score of these pieces out, we shall
'push' them, and there were no further mistakes in the Variations
strings, were there? I can't see any. I want to print them also for stock
at once. Any other business? I don't think so. How is your cold?
Better, I hope. I wish I were at Sheffield to hear K. Olaf done properly
for once. Don't bring down the roof with the challenge and the wraith
and the dragons. Good luck to you and good health. I had to go home
disappointed last Saturday, couldn't get in.

Ever yrs. sincerely,
A. J. Jaeger.

The Sheffield Festival of 1899, conducted by Manns, gave King Olaf *on
11 October. The* Imperial March *also had a place in the programme. The
programme notes for the former were written for this occasion by C. F. A.
Schöllhammer (see p. 288).*

By now the Imperial March *was a national symbol. After its first performance at the Crystal Palace, on 19 April 1897 (by five Guards' Bands
and the Crystal Palace Orchestra, under Manns), it was played at the Jubilee
State Concert and at the State Garden Party at Buckingham Palace, and
now, in 1899, it was used for the Royal Birthday celebrations in St. Paul's
Cathedral, Westminster Abbey, and St. George's Chapel, Windsor.*

Wharncliffe Hotel,
Sheffield.
Oct 11: 1899.

My dear Jaeger:

Thanks for your letter:

Now: I'll be ready for the proofs on Thursday or Friday (as you
say) and will *do all I can,* (& that is a good deal!) in the way of haste.

Perpend! We leave here tomorrow for Ashfield Hotel, *Settle,*
Yorks. where we shall remain until Monday: on Monday evening I

---

[1] The performance of the *Variations* at the Richter Concert on 23 October
duly took place.

have a rehearsal of 'Caractacus' at Leeds – Tuesday I travel to London & shall be at Chelsea. Richter's rehearsal is on the *Saturday* a.m. (21st ain't it?) so that everything will be wanted for then. I don't *think* it will do to suggest postponement at all.

I don't think there are *any* corrections in the strg pts of the three pieces (Op. 10) – they were carefully played at N. Brighton but as you know the men often play correctly what isn't there – but I think you can print. I think also (I *wish* I was *sure* of something!) that there are no errors in the string pts of the Vars: – wouldn't you like to cut out the whole of the Nimrod movement by way of improvement????????????? Olaf will go well. Chorus superlative. orch. – v. middling [Edward] Lloyd very good. [Charles] Knowles – frightened, [Alice] Esty – worse! There! – I wish you were here with your very nice friend *Ibbetson*[1].

Yrs ever & ever,
Ed Elgar

Have seen Edwards[2] etc. he's here (in the house I mean)

[*in pencil*]

Ashfield Hotel
Settle
Yorks.
13/X/[18]99

In bed!

My dear Jaeger,

Here's the cszquōrrr & very nice it looks – I've got a chill & am supposed to be badly – anyhow I'm smoking a pipe & breathing pure air off the moors – for all of which D.V. after Sheffield smoke & a d—d bad orchestra.

Tell Mr. Brause his pretty score assists me to feel better.

One word of sense, we arranged to omit *all* cues 'cos any conductor wd. find that they were in the parts – But pp. 15 & 16 – there's a *solo* passage for Ob. II – Here the cues *should* go in the score because if the small orch. arrgt. is played, the conductor will know where to look for the solo pt – in all other places its doubled & don't matter.

"Am I subtle? Am I Machiavel?"

Where's that from? Yah! I wish you had heard the chorus at Sheffield. I am hoping to write to you.

Yours
Ed. E.

---

[1] Ibberson? see p. 214

[2] F. G. Edwards (1853–1909), Editor of *The Musical Times* from 1897 to 1899

P.S. I Hope the *dedication* may go on the scores & I hope some copies of the 3 together may be stitched up.

From a letter of Jaeger to Elgar, dated 14 October: 'Your Olaf seems to have knocked them in the old Sheffield place. I wish I'd heard that chorus. Did you see last night's "Pall Mall"? . . . I thought I had a high opinion of E.E. the composer & often written so, but Blackburn caps it all. . . . I should have liked to see Stanford's face as he read it . . . I hope Mrs. Elgar is well and happy over your great success everywhere. I'm sure she will be delighted. *I* am!!!'

After staying at Settle (where his old friend Dr. C. W. Buck rejoiced to see him again) Elgar went on to Windsor Castle for a royal concert and thence to London for the Richter Concert on 23 October. On the previous day he went to Jaeger's house where 'he had promised to play part I of Gerontius from Ms.' *(Jaeger)*

[*W.P.S. paper*]

Craeg Lea,
Malvern
Thursday [19 October 1899]

My dear Jaeger:

This is in answer to yours just recd. in case I don't get to Berners St this week. I *thought* I'd come round on Sunday – if Wood is doing anything on Sunday afternoon we might go to that: s'pose I, *or we*, came about 5 – and skipped about 6.30.

I think that wd. be best.

I only want to play you a few frazes

Yrs ever
E.E.

Sorry – very sorry – about the M. T. you were the only critic.

[*postcard*]

[*postmarked* 20 Oct. 99,   7.30 p.m.]
at Chelsea.
Friday p m

Oh!
Really!!
Prodigious!!!
But I'll come as soon after four as I can on Sunday, E.

Gadzooks! P.S. My wife's out but if not engaged she will be delighted to come.

Worcestershire Golf Club,
Malvern.

Wedy 25th Oct [1899]

My dear Jaeger:

We arrived home last night all safe but I hadn't time to get to Berners St as Mr. Hedley[1] wanted another sitting.

I thought it went well on Monday night but I wanted the finale quicker – the martial pt. anyhow. I hope you liked it all. I fear the 'party' are very sick at its being done again.

It's lovely here in the sun & I shall feel better soon in the bright air. It's a jape about the Miniature score![2] I hope you saw my letter to the firm you see there must be a demand for scores if people will pay to be allowed to print 'em!

No more now but much love & kindest regards to Mrs. Nimrod.

Yrs ever

Ed: Elgar.

On 1 November Jaeger wrote saying that he had sent a score of Coleridge-Taylor's Death of Minnehaha, which he had heard at Hanley and which, despite a bad orchestra and no choral and orchestral rehearsal, had made a deep impression. The letter was accompanied by a set of proofs of the Variations.

Craeg Lea,
Malvern.

Nov 2: [18]99

My dear Jaeger:

Bless you – I didn't want the beastly *music* – I wanted to hear of *you* – don't you know I (almost) like you. - you are a brute to me nevertheless and then you write and say I must not think you're 'not at work because you don't write' – damn the proofs and bust the Variations. I hope you are better and your nose is not *really* a trouble. My wife is very unwell and does not mend as yet. I will write about the proofs and send a lot back very shortly. The Scottish Orch has put down the Vars: for Decr 26.[3]

Yrs ever

Ed Elgar.

P.S. Blair is doing at Marylebone Church on Sunday Nov 12 (four o'c) an old piece of mine 'Sursum corda' – I wrote it & it was played many times as an intro: to the orchl. services in Worcester Cathedral – if

[1] see p. 75
[2] a suggestion for inclusion in *Payne's Miniature Scores*?
[3] see p. 72

you *cd.* hear it & tell me what it's like & if worth publishing I shd. esteem it a favour?

Craeg Lea,
Malvern.
Nov 5 [1899]

My dear Jaeger,

My wife *has* been worse but is now better & I hope mending – chill.

I am sorry to hear about your own worry – do see a Specialist if you haven't already done so.

I am hoping to finish the Mazurka score at Leeds whither I journey tomorrow (Hotel Metropole, Leeds) until Thursday a.m.

Look 'ere. I'm working at the Vars: I have finished all you've sent – but I think I ought to compare the remainder which is – or are

    Contrafagotto [*added in pencil by Jaeger*]

    Bass Trom

    Tuba

    Tim

    Side Dr. [*deleted by Jaeger*]

    Gr.C.

    Organ [*deleted by Jaeger*]

with the score – my people here will post to you all I can send tomorrow morning. If anything is ready to come to me send it to Leeds.

Don't, dear man, *trouble* about the *Sursum Corda*, but if you are within easy reach I should be glad if you heard it and reported to me.

It's no good trying any patriotic caper on in England: we applaud the 'sentiment' in other nations but repress it sternly in ourselves: anything like 'show' is repugnant to the *real* English – whom you don't know or understand yet nor ever will.★

Kerl! with your caricatures.

Yours ever,
Ed. E.

★ My wife says this is rude and untrue so for fear you shd. believe it I say its rot!

Jaeger had enclosed some German caricatures, apparently of some nationalistic significance, with his letter of 1 November. He himself had received them from a friend in Krupps. 'Don't think', he wrote, 'I sympathise with them . . .' On 7 November Jaeger asked again about the symphonic project. 'How is that Gordon Symphony getting on!! Why dontcher answer???'. He also expressed himself as mystified by the golf score-card which Elgar enclosed with the following letter.

Hotel Metropole,
Leeds.[1]
Nov 8 [1899]

My dear Jaeger:

Thanks for all – enclosed I return the pages I select as being best –
I've only "?" the spacing but I expect it's all right – these fancy types
are awkward I know sometimes.

Ja! there *is* a Contra-fagotto part – I hope Mr. Brause, bless him!
has not fagotton it! (ahem!)

You refused 'Sursum Corda' cos' I wouldn't let it go forth to the
world scored for two *Cornets* and one *Trombone*! I made it playable
therewith but I insisted that my artistic full brass shd. be issued ad lib.
A German firm offered good terms for it but I was patriotic and waited
and now I've forgotten the piece.

Hope you're all right now and flourishing at home.

Yours ever
Ed. Elgar

The golf score is nought! only it looks gomplicated. All composition
is a dead secret but I say I have written a *theme*, alas! orchestral and it's
no good on the piano.

[*W.P.S. paper*]

Malvern, Nov 15 [1899]

My dear Jaeger:

Biz:

By this post I send M.S. scores of Mazurka & Serenade Mauresque
which I retained for further corrections: I also return Tr. Basso (or III
I prefer to call it) of Vars: corrected. I'm awfully glad you went to hear
'Sursum Corda' – the 'linking' passage *should* sound all right if they
arrived at any balance between org: & strings. Blair has the score – I'll
send it on to you *perhaps*. I must see if it would knock into an organ
(solus) piece – curtailed of course. You are an angel to have went & I
send a very dutiful, especial little bundle of thanks to Mrs. Jaeger for
letting you go.

Get out! I'm not going to send you any themes yet. Some day I
will – I think you deserve a refreshing one after the Underground Rly.
on Sunday.

Here's Judas! & another scrap.

[1] Performance of *Caractacus* at Leeds on this day

Cheerful ain't it? Tell me how Mr. Alfred is cos I want to see him soon.

Yours ever

E.

I can't write as my finger is very painful – I knocked it about at golf as usual.

It was Elgar's intention to write an oratorio on the theme of the Apostles (see Elgar O.M., pp. 317–319). The 'Judas' motiv now mentioned became, as will be seen, a dominant motiv ('Angel of the Agony') in Gerontius. In an incomplete letter of 16 November Jaeger observes: "That "Judas" or "night" theme from your new work is a *discovery*! It makes me *shiver* when I think of the effect of soft low brass (Five Tubas, Eh! You'll get them at Bayreuth, but where else?) But no doubt you'll get your effect with one tuba and four trombones, though the colour will not be the same, dark copper glow & gloom.'

On 17 November Jaeger wrote: '. . . When I heard the new finale [of the *Variations*], both at the Worcester rehearsals and the Richter [Concert], I was a little disappointed that the sudden burst into E flat at 82 did not come off quite as explosively and surprisingly as I had anticipated. When I look at the score p. 126 I put it down to the fact that the first fiddlers have not the short quaver rest that many of the other instruments have. They seemed at the performances to glide up to the B flat instead of sharply plunging, hammering on it with stroke of Thor's war axe! Would it not give you a stronger E flat chord and a greater surprise if all instruments had the crotchet rest before 82 . . . Think on it and if perchance you mean to alter anything let me have the corrected proof quickly that I may send it to Geidel. Otherwise ignore this long palaver, pray, and excuse my impertinence. By the way, are you not revising a set of strings (finally) with the score? . . .'

[*without address*]
Nov 18 [18]99

My dear Jaeger:

Thanks. Here's p 126 of the Vars. I've altered it to "suit purchasers", only I ought to see this one p. again – cd. Geidel post it direct to me & might I send it to him straight to save time? I've not had the strings again as your letter suggests – so I wired to-day. I will gladly look 'em thro' once more.

As to the bar before 82 I've done it to please you (grrhh!) & must put it right in the wind pts when the revision comes if it ever does.

I'm glad you like my idea of Judas. I'll send you another wildly

expressive bit but it's very hard to try & write *one's self* out & find
that one's soul is not *simple* enough for the British Choral Society.

Yours ever

Ed Elgar

I will answer your letter shortly.

[*letter-card*]

[Malvern] Nov. 22 [18]99.

My dear Jaeger:

Here's the concentrated essence of a cuss! [*drawing of a hand points to
a spot of red ink.*]

Anyhow I've obeyed orders & asked Wendt[1] to luncheon on
Friday: I don't suppose he'll come: too far.

I've had to hire a MAN to look at proofs, I'm too busy.

Yours ever

Gérla-Deradw!

Russian Composer

[*no address*]

Friday (24/XI/[18]99)

Nimrod dear!

'*K'ere!*[2]

Wendt's a-coming now. – it's your fault & he will go away a
miserable youth for daze.

Now: All Carac: parts & score are coming to you – I wish I could
train my scores & things to fly like a homing pigeon – I'm pigeoned,
it costs a weary lot in postage. Look 'ere the score's coming all to
pieces – probably from publishing fragments! It did ought to be
printed to save its life: also as an example of *English* art – not British –
really Jaeger it *is* a damned fine piece of work looking at it as if I
weren't the parent.

Twiggez vous, s'il vous plait gefalligst bitte schon the note on the
percussion part & see if it'll do. I say, they asked me to suggest some-

---

[1] Theophil Wendt, a minor composer of light music and part-songs in the
Novello catalogue (see *Mus. T.*, 1899, pp. 550 and 619). In 1898 he composed an
Ode for the Opening of the Grahamstown South Africa Exhibition. He emigrated
to South Africa – in 1901 he lectured on Scandinavian music in Grahamstown –
and as conductor of the Capetown Orchestra gave first performances of works
by W. H. Bell (see p. 280 f.). In 1929 Wendt published *A Set of Part-Songs based
on South African Native Tunes* (Schirmer).

[2] i.e. 'Look here!'

thing for a patriotic-T. Atkins-fund-Boer-war-fund-Concert. I said perhaps the *Flying Dutchman*! wd. do. jape.

Yours liverally, Antipyrinically, phenacitinally, calomellically podophyllinically-Carter's-small dose small price. Oh!

E.E.

[*W.P.S. paper, in pencil, undated*]

[end of November 1899]

Dear Jaeger:

Awfully busy! Wd. a note like this* do to go on all three pieces. I *did* propose it but thought *ad lib* was very dear to the publishing heart (? gizzard)

It looks *wordy* but then all English is – was & ever shall be.

If you put a *note* (prefatory) I wd. knock out those asterisks(Leonids) which spoil the look of the ssczowough*oh*[1]r I think. perpend.

P.S. on the title pf. arrgt. of Contrasts you have '1700' out of place! I return everything of Vars: I shan't want to see the skorh of that again.

Hope you're well. I've a liver & can't spell çkor nohow nowise & not at all.

Yrs. ever,

Ed. Elgar

* Note to precede all three full scores of Op. 10

Note.

This piece may be effectively performed by an orch. consisting of
[†]1 Fl. 1 ob. 1 Clar. 1 Fag. 2 Horns, 1 Trumpet (Cornet) Timpani & Strings Any other inst. in the Score may be added with corresponding gain and effect.

[†][*marginal note*] ? in English

Bissoons, Drums

Craeg Lea, Malvern.
Sunday night [26 November 1899]
(so it won't reach you for days)

My dear Jaeger:

Don't be cross 'cos I don't mind altering the score at all: nothing can make me miserable regarding my music thank you: never mind the cuss – your nice friend, after being prevented on Friday, came (& Wendt) on Saturday. Lunch & a walk & found us deadly dull I know & pitied himself for having expended two marks on railway fares.

Businesssss.

Leave the Trombone out of all the notes – I don't think there's

[1] three times underlined

anything obligatory in the Mazurka but that you can see & act according in concatenation accordingly. No revises of Var: score from Geidel yet – maybe in the morning.

I can't send you any more themes yet 'cos I'm busy with 'em. You shall see one or two some day.

In great haste

Yrs ever

E.

How like you my new name?[1]

Craeg Lea, Malvern.

Dec. 27 [1899]

My dear Jaeger:

I want to know a heap of things: how and where are you? Better I hope & fit for the fray.

When *will* those Vars: (score) be ready? I think my M.S. must have frightened poor Bruch at Glasgow – so they have put off the performance &, probably, I shall have to thank your firm for another entire loss of performance. Are the *pts* of Caractacus whole work & March out? You did not send a set for my collection.

Don't worry about anything of mine if you ar'n't well. But tell me any news that's going.

We had a really nice artistic concert the other day[2], Berlioz's 'Enfance du Christ' – a work of real 'atmosphere' & charm.

In great haste & worry

Yrs ever

Ed E

Craeg Lea, Malvern.

Dec. 29 1899.

My dear Jaeger,

I *was* and *am* so glad to hear of you again – please go on getting weller. Bless you! it wasn't my corrections (or *yours*[3]!) I was thinking of a certain 'countermanding' in the summer.

All right send copies of anything you can – they will augment my funeral pyre which is coming on shortly.

I can't tell you any news: all is flat, stale & *unprofitable*.

[*end of letter wanting*]

[1] see p. 70
[2] Worcestershire Philharmonic Society, 21 December
[3] three times underlined

1900

On 1 January Mr. G. H. Johnstone, Chairman of the Birmingham Festival, visited Elgar at Malvern to make the final arrangements for the inclusion of The Dream of Gerontius *at the forthcoming Festival. Elgar confirmed his acceptance of the proffered terms by telegram the next day and, according to the Diary, then 'began again at former libretto'. On 12 January he went to the Oratory at Birmingham where his friend Father Bellasis[1] was available for advice on textual matters. In the letters of 1900* Gerontius *is frequently discussed. Five which have already been published in* Letters of Edward Elgar *(pp. 81–8) are not repeated here; their dates are 29 April, 7 May, 19, 20 June and 11 July.*

At the beginning of this year the full score of the 'Enigma' Variations arrived.

[*W.P.S. paper*]

Malvern.
Jan 4: 1900

My dear Jaeger:

I wonder what has become of you?

I recd. *the* score all safely & some odd parts for all of which thanks: how lovely the score looks, I am so delighted with it & only wish it were a harbinger of peace & good will, but–

Do let's hear how you are – I've not had a decent word from you since you sent Wendt[2] here – do you ken that? All goes slowly here: I'm working like a —— fool & get kicked for my pains & – or pleasures – I don't know which they are.

---

[1] either Henry Lewis or Richard Garnet Bellasis, brothers and members of the Oratory at this time, the first described in an obituary notice as 'no mean musician', the other as 'a talented musician'

[2] see p. 70

We hope all is well at your home & with all good wishes for the New Year – wh. by the way I think I sent before – from us all to you both.

Always dear J.

Yours affctly.

E. Elgar

Tell me any news of fellow criminals

Malvern.

Jany 10: 1900.

My dear Jaeger:

I've been so busy that I couldn't find time to write – I received with joy your long letter[;] please thank Mrs. Jaeger for letting you sit up to write it – its dated a *year ago*! Yah!! 1899!!!

Now. Imprimis – I recd. the scores of the 3 innocents – *many thanks*[.] Secundus. "As I laye a smoughkynge" – I hate the idea of the firm losing anything & I only knew of its withdrawal from your letter: now – the song is boyish[1] & the compass is large but if the firm like to issue it I cannot possibly object – I can revise it but I don't see how to make it like unto my new vagaries: please tell Mr. Alfred [Littleton] all this if you like–

Judas is dropped! I may have some news for you concerning my works very shortly – but I am sick of the whole thing and wd. never hear, see, write or think of music in shape, form, substance or wraith again.

I think you are right about C. Taylor – I was cruelly disillusioned by the overture to Hiawatha which I think really only 'rot' & the Worcester prelude[2] did not show *any* signs of cumulative invention or effect: the scoring is altogether uninteresting & *harsh* of both these works: wherever I've been people are sympathetic and kind on acct. of the colour question and he is well advertised & backed but his later work is insincere & cannot do any real good: this is what I feel: I have never worked so hard for any man before – on *your* recommendation – & I took a real pleasure in him.

As to St. Elizabeth [Liszt?] send it on. I shd. like to see it – at owner's risk.

I am glad your criticisms are appreciated all round – I don't see the Musical papers – which you live on in London – & those sent me I rarely open – anything about golf or kites now!

[1] Title not given in extant correspondence

[2] *Solemn Prelude*, Op. 40

Now I must be prepared to stop: I fear I didn't make much of Parker[1]. I think that's the last item in your scrawl.

Now goodbye.

Tell me what you charge *me* for the full score Op. 37 [36?]. I'm afraid I can't afford it but I shd. like to give one away.

Yours ever,

Ed. Elgar

On 18 January Elgar conducted Sea Pictures *in Manchester, Stanford appearing at the same concert as conductor of Glazunov's fifth symphony. Although the performance of* Sea Pictures *was, according to the* Manchester Guardian, *a little less good than that at Norwich because of insufficient time for rehearsal the music made a big impression on critic and public.* 'One of the most striking musical phrases in the cycle', *it was noted,* 'occurs in the first song, at the beginning and, with modifications, again at the end. It is an image of the moving multitudinous sea, and is a superb piece of invention. The lyrical unity and perfect simplicity of the ensuing "In haven" forms a delightful contrast. In the third song given yesterday – fourth of the series – we have again a kind of utterance that is perfectly lyrical. The characterisation in this very beautiful and original song seems, in some mysterious way, to bring back the very taste of the Shakespeare lines:—"Full fathom five . . ." It is the iridescent mystery of the sea-bottom. . . . Miss Clara Butt gave a performance of these songs that was on the whole very fine, though here and there marked by* vibrato. *At the end she shared with the composer, who had conducted the brilliantly orchestrated accompaniments, the enthusiastic greeting of the audience. There was no mistaking the genuine enjoyment that the songs had afforded.' (Manchester Guardian, 19 January 1900)*

Elgar (see also p. 66) was being placed in an illustrious gallery. Percival M.E. Hedley (b. 1870)[2], educated in Vienna and a competitor in the Goethedenkmal Competition held in that city in 1890, had made his name as the painter and sculptor of likenesses of composers and actors, and a slender fortune through his marketing of 'plaquettes' based on these works. A friend of Brahms, whose portrait he did well, he included Richter, Saint-Saëns, Paderewski, and Nikisch among his subjects, as well as Queen Victoria, King Edward VII and King George V.

[1] *Hora novissima* (Worcester 1899) was succeeded by *A Wanderer's Psalm* (Hereford 1900). See ref. to *The Legend of St. Christopher* (1898), p. 9 above.

[2] see *Allgemeines Lexikon der bildenden Künstler*, Leipzig 1923

Craeg Lea,
Wells Road,
Malvern.
Jany 28. 1900

My dear Jaeger:

I must find time to send you a scrawl although I've really nothing to say except, how are you?

I am working away at my thing for Birmingham – you will hear all about it some time soon, I suppose – but I have nothing to do with the publishing this time & must not talk about it even to you.

I saw Stanford at Manchester the other day. I conducted the Songs at the Halle Concert – & we are quite as before — this between ourselves: we smoked & supped together.

Where's that genial sculper, Hedley? Its quite time I saw myself in bust form.

Send a line occasionally to your forlorn soul in arid regions.

I am sick of music and all that's connected with it & long for Birchwood & pigs & cattle.

Yrs. ever,
Edward Elgar

Malvern,
Jan. 31 [1900]

My dear Nimrod,

Thanks for yours: I'll try for the score of Caractacus from Cheltenham but it'll take a long time to go thro' & I can ill afford the time. Also, the idea of a piano arrgt. of Froissart is a wild scheme & it wd. take me weeks to do & it won't *pay*. If one could see a full score of anything in print one might hold up one's head, but piano arrangements only lower one in one's own estimation. When I have met German musicians (for instance) I never talk about having written anything: cos why? Cos they ask to see a score & think nothing of you if you haven't one in print, *and they are quite right too*. Imagine any of the third & fourth raters appearing here with m.s. scores!!

We are out of it all artistically, and I am out of it commercially likewise. Music is a trade and I am no tradesman.

Yours ever,
E.E.

On 4 February Jaeger wrote to Elgar, saying: 'The 1st result of your Stanford-Entente Cordiale is that he is going to do your Variations at the [Royal] College [of Music] . . . I am always bothering Wood about them, but I fear (entre nous) the Q[ueen's] Hall management is

Birchwood, 1900

Llangranog, 1901

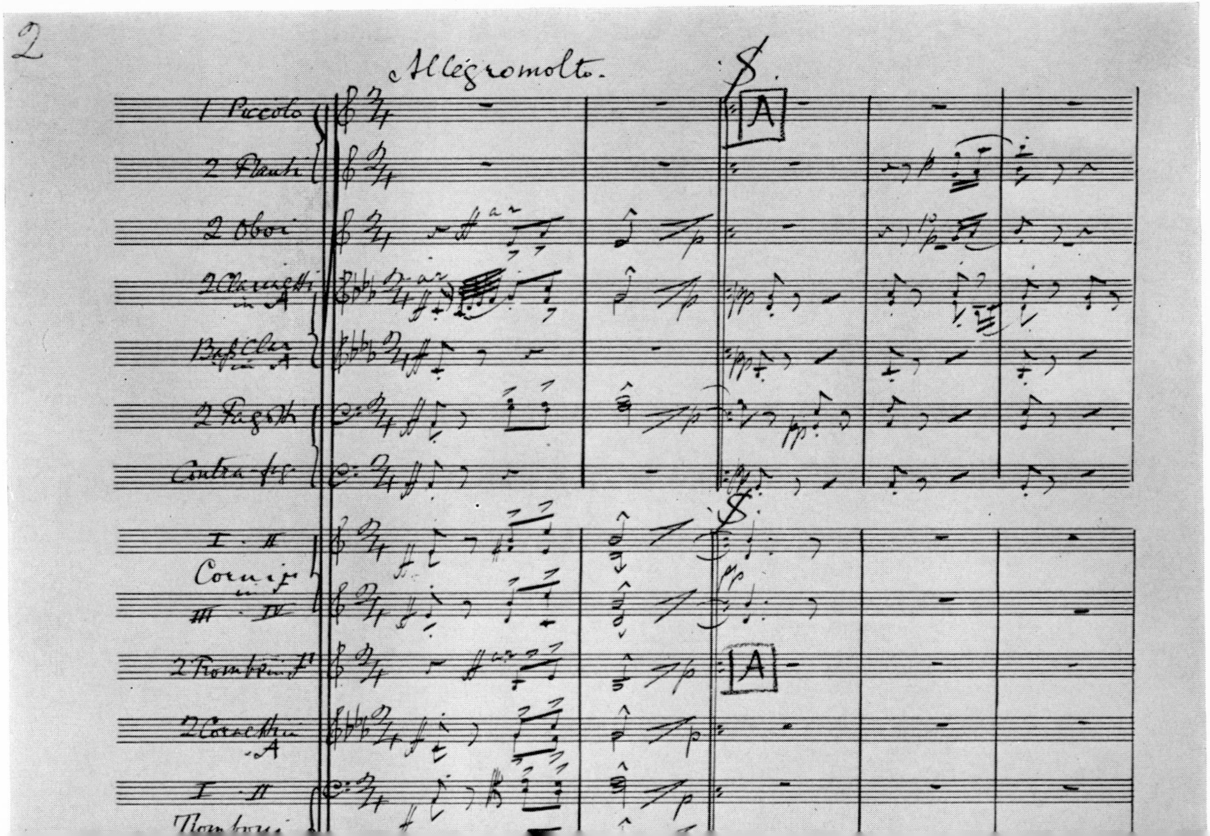

2
Allegro molto.
1 Piccolo
2 Flauti
2 Oboi
2 Clarinetti in A
Bass Clar. in A
2 Fagotti
Contra-fag.
I . II
Corni in F
III . IV
2 Trombe in F
2 Cornetti A
I . II
Tromboni

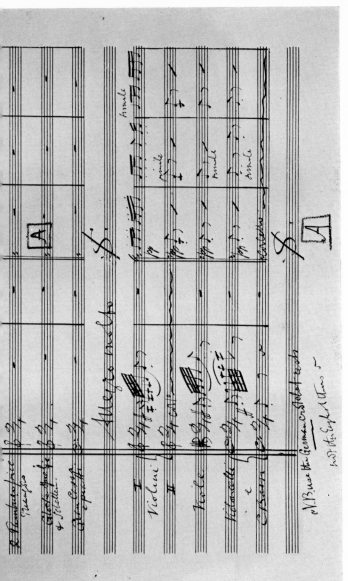

Manuscript of *Pomp and Circumstance March No. 2*
(by courtesy of Messrs Boosey & Hawkes)

Worcester
Cathedral
with demons

summat in a "bad-ish way".' *Jaeger asks why Elgar must not talk about*
the publishing of Gerontius *and if he has sent a score of the* Variations *to*
Richter. 'So you are "sick of music" eh? Papperlapapp! That's what
Wagner said while he was creating his crushing efforts of genius.'

[*W.P.S. paper*]
                                               Craeg Lea, Malvern.
                                                       Feb 5. 1900
My dear Jaeger:
   I was awfully glad to get yours cos I was awfully afraid you were
vexed with me. Well, I can't help it but I hate continually saying 'keep
it dark' – 'a dead secret'. Now – you must not say a word to anyone
please but sometime ago I gave up Birmingham as I really could not
afford to go on writing – so the Committee have relieved me of all
trouble in the matter rather than lose me. I hear from the Chairman &
from nice good Mr. Alfred [Littleton] that they've settled it between
'em & your firm are to publish the work. I am setting Newman's
'Dream of Gerontius' awfully solemn & mystic.
   Mr. Alfred will no doubt tell you about plans someday, but there's
no harm in your knowing, only *don't* tell anybody else.
   I'm *awfully* hard up just now for a space, but I want to give you a
score – can't you take one and put *it down* to me and I'll write your
name in it someday.
   I've *not* sent a score to Richter – but might do so later, only I really
haven't a brass farden to spare.
   Now I must go on to my Devil's chorus – good! I say that Judas
theme will *have* to be used up for death and despair in this work, so
don't peach.
                           Much love from us both to you both,
                               Ever yours,
                                   Edward Elgar.

[*W.P.S. paper*]
                                               Craeg Lea,
                                                 Malvern.
                                               March 2 [1900]
My dear Jaeger:
   Here come 44 pages M.S. – I'm afraid it's not a good copy but I
think it's no worse than usual. To improve it my wife's sal-volatile

bottle bust a-coming home – hence the stains! When I get old & fat I'll be able to furnish you with a really clean M.S. to work at[.] Let me know by wire, if you can afford it, that this has reached you – I'll be in a fit 'till I know

Yours ever
Edward Elgar

Deal tenderly with it it's the *only* copy there is – I can't yet afford a copyist
poor divvil

[*W.P.S. paper*]

Sunday
& a brute of a day
[18 March 1900]

My deary Jägerer,

poor thing: I hope you're better – take a teaspoonful of   and mix it thoroughly with   then add a like quantity of   put the whole into an   and carefully   it until it   ; take four or a lump of   or a small   will do equally well if desired, & it suits the   of some people better; the   can be mixed in without adding the   but most patients consider a dose of safer.

Phew! there's a prescription for you – I fear I left something out after all.

Poor beggar! do get better: I say those people at 1, Berners St. have sent me only *one* proof – I wanted two at least: do send 'em a card or somethink if you aren't there – I don't like to write for fear it wants engineering – is it a krime to have two copies of a proof? By'r lakin a parlous fear.

Its snowing awfully & I'm precious glad you are not here for the sake of your health – you wd. however be about good enough to put in an armchair to smoke with & talk to. Don't let Mrs. J. see this, she'll think it rude – so it is!

I hope you're better & am

Yours dispersedly
Edward Elgar

I'm sending you the balance of the first hundred pages [of *Gerontius*] tomorrow I hope.

Craeg Lea,
Malvern.
Tuesday
[20 March 1900][1]

My dear Corporal Nym:

By this post come pp. 44–99 incl. up to the end of pt I. the final chos. is godly effective &, I think, not quite cheap: if the score required viz 1 solo, 4 semich; *8* full ch, & 2 accpt. 15 staves in all is unmanageable the *semi*chorus might go in short score on *two* staves – but don't say a word unless the printer takes the Button[2] off his foil & shews real fight.

All right let 'em do 'Froissart' – it's old & not quite what I'd write now but it's good, healthy stuff: one thing – you say 'combined bands'.

– I don't suppose for a moment the *two* orchs will *combine* over me, but if they should be mad enough, remember you've only *one* set of wind. I shall be curious to hear the over. again – anyhow it's better than either ——, ——, ——, ——, ——, ——, (names on application) cd. write now.

Thanks for proofs: I *am* glad to get 'em.

Wire me that the new batch arrives safely there's a dear, 'cos I get angkschzsuszcs over it sometimes. Hirschen sie auf! (Buck up!) translation, with the remainder, 'cos if the Bir: people want something to go on with they can have pt I as soon as you've done it. As soon as this 'Dream' (nightmare) is done – I'll write such a lot of things for Ysaiah – & all the profits – I *should* dearly love to get out some of my chamber music! No time.

Yrs ever
E Elgar

[*W.P.S. paper*]

Malvern
March 26, 1900.

My dear N.

Thanks for your telegram: 'tis not well that the Skore shd not have arrived yet & 'by'r lakin, a parlous fear' possesses me.

Rot! go & be *took* & send me a copy at once . .

I enclose the p. of Cello & bass: – I think I shd simply label it '*B.Clar.*'

---

[1] *Diary Entry by Alice Elgar:* (March 20) 'Sent 2nd set of M.S. Gerontius to Messrs Novello'.
[2] H. E. Button of Novello's staff

then *on the score* (I suppose there will be a separate copy of the March[1])
write solemnly
"*In the absence of B. Clar: C.Fag: etc the small notes should be played*"
or some such legend.

I *shan't* be able to write music in this room – it's too distractingly
lovely.

I say why shouldn't you & Mrs. J. come on Saty before *Whit*sunday
& stay till Whit-Chewsday – there's an idea.

Yours ever
Ed. Elgar

Send the (2) revises of those piano trifles[2] *prestissimo*. I want to finish
the score.

Jaeger to Elgar, 25 March:
　. . . 'As to those invocations or whatever they are called to all the
Saints and prophets we think you should choose those lines dealing
with the best known incidents in the Bible, e.g. select Moses & his
doings in preference to Abraham & his guilt of heathenness. That is
rather too suggestive of a Roman Catholic priest's reference to us
Protestants as heathen isn't it? The poem is wonderful & must appeal
to you most forcibly. But by Jove! what a task for you. Yet I feel sure
you will be equal to it, for like most first-class composers, you seem to
grow with your task, & the greater the difficulty the more surely you
will rise to it. So I don't think you will disappoint us over your present
great task.' . . .

[*letter-card*]

Monday
[*postmark* Malvern, 26 March 1900]

My dear Jaeger: (Nym.)

That's just what I wanted to know about those sporting prophets[3]:
how will

Noe,
Job,　　　　　　　　　　　　　　★
Moses,
Daniel do?

Please put 'em in. I will write about Wrochester to-morrow – why

---

[1] 'Triumphal March', from *Caractacus*, Sc. VI

[2] *Chanson de Matin* and *Chanson de Nuit*?

[3] cf. Elgar's text in *Gerontius* with the fuller original of Newman and also
pp. 84 and 91–2

not come here next Sunday: do – I'm sure you could, only you're
PIG-HEADED.

Much love

yrs E.E.

Don't let old [J.E.] West keep my proofs long.
* [*marginal note*] Thanks about Queen's Hall news.

[*W.P.S. paper*]

Craeg Lea,

Malvern.

March 27 [1900]

Dear Jaeger:

Thanks for yours: I forgot to say that if you shd. require to reprint
either K. Olaf or Caractacus, certainly the latter, don't do so before
letting me hear:

Ben Davies has accepted Caractacus for Bradford on the understanding that I make the part more suitable: this I think very advisable
as Lloyd is retiring – I haven't had time to look thro' the work, but I
don't think much need be done: the question as to the alternative
notes being added to the vocal score I will of course refer to the firm
when the time comes.

Yours ever

Edward Elgar.

You might however ask Mr. Alfred about it or if not worth troubling
him tell me what has been done in similar cases – If any such have
arisen.

P.S. Why shouldn't you come down this week over Sunday? you
could if you tried & wouldn't sulk in state: do try – it might do you
good. I've pills – draughts – lotions – whiskey – tobacco – golf – all
waiting for you.

*The Rochester, Strood, and Chatham Choral Society, with the Orchestra
of the Royal Engineers, planned to perform* Caractacus (*and the* Bavarian
Dances) *at the last concert of the 1900 season. The Bradford performance is
noted on p. 128.*

Craeg Lea, Malvern.

March 30 [1900]

My dear Jaeger:

I have been thinking over Rochester & have finally decided that I
cannot go: it takes too long from this countryside & I hate & detest
rehearsing choruses etc etc. So get me out of it as nicely as you can.

Tell 'em I'll come next year & conduct Caractacus if they'll do it but
I really cannot afford the time just now. Of course one *has* to do this
sort of thing sometimes but I always feel that's lowering to art & to
oneself – imagine a painter having to travel about with his own
picture to exhibit it! It's all very well for boys & such vermin & vanity
stricken asses but I'm none of 'em or rather have grown out of it I
suppose.

Yours ever
Ed. E.

[*letter-card*]

Monday a.m. early
[*postmark* Malvern, 2 April 1900]

My dear J.

I'm so very sorry to hear Mrs J. is not well[1] & that her buoy is also
coldified – *do* get better soon – Very soon.

Look here – I have sent back a batch of revises & boldly put atop –
another proof! If you want the type only send me the *necy* pages again.
I quite forgot to put Pt I or anything of the kind at the beginning!

Yours ever
E.E.

[*W.P.S. paper*]

Craeg Lea,
Malvern.
Sunday [8 April 1900]

My dear Jaeger:

I think the weather may be better now: how about arranging to
come for a mournful frolic next Friday to Tuesday – or inside those
days if anything should prevent the whole time: ask Mrs. J. prettily
& she'll let you come.

Hey! – I felt so angry ever since I was at your house that I did not
carry my pitiful M.S. to you: I have tried to find time to write out the
Angel's song, all my own scrawl, for your own Angel to sing as a
peace offering to HER – not you – you old – Nimrod.

Write & say about coming

Yours ever
Edward Elgar

[1] Mrs. Jaeger was pregnant and a daughter was born on 26 April, to which
event Elgar makes a touching reference in his letter of 29 April (see *Letters of
Edward Elgar*, p. 82).

[*W.P.S. paper*]

Malvern

April 12 [1900]

My dear Jaeger:

We are very anxious to know how Mrs. Jäger & yourself are: you needn't send – unless you like – a long letter, but a p.c. or scrap wd. do. Here we're *all* down with more or less of colds – I have been really *ill* with mine – but enough.

We hope you are all right but must hear.

Yours ever

E.E.

On 13 April Jaeger wrote that his wife had written to thank Elgar for the copy of the 'Angel's Song' (Gerontius) which he had sent to her as a gift some days before. Jaeger describes this song as 'uncanny'. 'I say "uncanny" because it has a character unlike anything else in music as far as I know. Simple as it is, its very simplicity is its wonder, for it is a kind of simplicity I have never met with before, so aloof from things mundane, so haunting and strangely fascinating. . . . I spent this morning and afternoon a few hours with the proof of Part I of your work and have been tremendously stirred by it. There is some gorgeous stuff in it, better than either King Olaf or Caractacus, though one should not compare. Since Parsifal nothing of this mystic, religious kind of music has appeared to my knowledge that displays the same power and beauty as yours. Like Wagner you seem to grow with your greater, more difficult subject and I am now most curious and anxious to know how you will deal with that part of the poem where the soul goes within the Presence of the Almighty. There is a subject for you! Whatever else you may do, don't be theatrical. But it is insulting to you to even hint at such a possibility. If I did not fear that you might jump down my throat, I would like to make a few very trifling suggestions. But I won't spoil your Easter.'

Craeg Lea,

Malvern.

Easter Tuesday [17 April 1900]

My dear Jaeger:

I was delighted to get your letter for several reasons: 1st because I wanted to know how you where [*sic*] & 2nd. I've been really ill with awful chill – throat everything in fact & *all* has perforce been at a standstill for a fortnight, alas!

Thank you for all you say about the 'Dream': I shall however be glad to hear your emendations before too late to alter anything: I altered – in the 'Litany' – Daniel to *David* to avoid for literary reasons, the *rhyme*. I meant to tell you but was too ill. I could send you another batch but strictly entre *nous* am waiting to hear definitely who is to sing who. confound it my pen's gone gammy.

Please remember that none of the 'action' takes place in the *presence* of God: I would not have tried *that* neither did Newman The Soul says 'I go before my God" but *we* don't we stand outside – I've thrown over all the 'machinery' for celestial music, harps etc.

But you will see anyway tell me what's wrong &, if not too violent, I'll do my best

So meek am I!

Yrs always

E.E.

Craeg Lea, Malvern.

Sunday

[? April 1900]

My deary Jaeger:

I hope you found your dear wife better. It was a real pleasure old Mosshead to see you again & I thought you looked well.

We shall be delighted to see you in Worcester on Saturday – I say only this much because I hope my wife is coming to town with me for the rehearsal and we shall all meet and will fix times etc.

Do make Alfred L. pay you for coming or something or offer t' boom somebody in the M[usical]. T[imes]. if they'll fork! We (Alice & I) shall probably stay with friends if she accompanies me.

Much love,

Yours ever,

Ed. E.

I hope Walford Davies is pleased with the Worcester business[1] – I'm so deadly afraid of him that we never talk – I have a feeling that he *hates* me and I choke. I suppose I deserve to be hated but I don't like it much. Yah!

[Percy] Pitt's pt. song is good I'm going to write to him about it – good old 'antique' Pitt. I say what an *awful* photo of Parker.

Craeg Lea, Malvern.

Wedny. May 16 1900.

My dear Jaeger,

I send some pages of Part I with a few alterations – some of 'em are already done I *think* but am not sure – don't swear!

---

[1] see *Letters of Edward Elgar*, p. 88

Hope you are well and your wife and the Angelical.

Yours ever,
Ed. E.

[*W.P.S. paper*]

Craeg Lea, Malvern.
May 18 [1900]

To A. J. Jaeger esq:

Musical tinker: Amender of immoral piano arrgts: Improver of oratoriacal recits: Prof. of the English Church style: intendant of Novello's musical conscience: Greeting!

Puppy[1]!! Enclosed are – no they're not – I've kept 'em – well anyhow I have seen your work & approve – only, my dear, the flute 'sighs' as you call 'em reappear on pp. 23. 24 – I don't know if you want 'em in again – perpend! Bargiel[2] don't matter. He's dead & the bar is only a recit: out of time.

I think the little notes look well in the p.f. Dorabella – if a *good* pianist played this movement on the piano it wd. sell like steam – only no pianist – amateur – ever buys anything until they've heard it.

Thank you for all you say about my Baby. Much love from us all to you all.

Furiously yours,
Ed. E.

The wife sends her translation for your inspection,

condemnation,
vituperation,
concatenationally together.

[*W.P.S. paper*]

Craeg Lea, Malvern.
Sunday May 20 [1900]

My dear Jaeger:

No I'm not touched over Bargiel – 'cos why – 'cos I've never heard a —— ed note of his to my knowledge – & shdn't mind if I did.

Camel! the passage in the Intermezzo[3] comes again on pp 23 & 24 – you've sent me proofs of pp. 20, 21, 22. what's the unheavenly good of adding what isn't there to what shdn't be there or anywhere and why shd. passages playable on pp. 23 & 24 put themselves in this agreeable

---

[1] twice underlined

[2] Woldemar Bargiel (1828–97), stepbrother of Clara Schumann, a disciple of Robert Schumann, and a well-known Berlin composer

[3] 'Dorabella'

proximitious confusion on pp. 20, 21 & 22. Why shd. A.J.J. send to
me and ask me to
there that's enough! In other words. I've got no copy and its the same
jape all over again. I must look at the chorus parts carefully & *can't*
send them back today.

I'm sending some more M.S. tomorrow with a note as I'm not
sending the chorus (continuing) complete but I think you might go
on with *Dummy* paging and so save a little time:

I'm glad you're enjoying the hawful spirits of us – I was in Hereford
yesterday and the folks were really mad I think.

Bless you my Angel. Send your long letter about nothing.

Lovely day: sun – zephyr – view – window open – liver – pills –
proofs – bills – weed-killer – yah!

　　　　　　　　　　　　　　　　　E.

I wish you were here.

[*W.P.S. paper*]

　　　　　　　　　　　　　　　　Craeg Lea,
　　　　　　　　　　　　　　　　Malvern
　　　　　　　　　　　　　　Monday [21 (?) May 1900]

My dear J.

I send m.s. down to big chorus – this said chorus I want to '*dwell on*'
for a space – but I think you cd. go on with the soli parts (also enclosed)
putting dummy paging etc.

Please ask Button about the key of the *Angel of the Agony*.

It's in D♭ – but the enharmonic changes are so ghastful that I've
written it phonetically – if anything plainer can be devised I don't
mind.

Thanks for sending to the child & for the h'kerchief just come

　　　　　　　　　　　　　　　Tout a vous
　　　　　　　　　　　　　　　　　E
　　　　　　　　　　　　　　　　　E

Jaeger to Elgar:

　　　　　　　　　　　　16, Margravine Gds., W.
　　　　　　　　　　　　22nd. May 1900.

My dear Elgar,

I have just spent an hour over your last batch of proofs, pp. 103/111
& pp. d – f) and, Oh! I am half undone, and I tremble after the tremendous exaltation I have gone through. I don't pretend to know everything that has been written since Wagner breathed his last in Venice
17 years ago, but I have not seen or heard anything since 'Parsifal'
that has stirred me, and spoken to me with the trumpet tongue of

genius as has this part of your latest, and by far greatest work. I except, perhaps, the Pathetic Symphony, although that is but worldly, pessimistic, depressing, whereas your wonderful music is inexpressibly and most wonderfully elevating, "aloof", mystic, and heart-moving, as by the force of a great compassion. I cannot describe it!

But that solo of the "Angel of the Agony"[1] is overpowering and I feel as if I wanted to kiss the hand that penned these marvellous pages. Those poignant melodies, those heart-piercing, beautiful harmonies! I recognise the chief theme as having belonged to 'Judas'. Nobody could dream that it was not originally inspired by these very words of Newman's.

You must not, cannot expect this work of yours to be appreciated by the ordinary amateur (or critic) after once hearing. You will have to rest content, as other great men had to before you, if a few friends and enthusiasts hail it as a work of genius, and become devoted to its creator. As for myself, I almost fear I shall not be able to tackle the work in that "analysis". I am such a wretched amateur. I must think the matter over while there is time.

That long letter re some little points in Part I and the early portion of Part II I must reserve. I'm not in the mood tonight. Also my letter to Mrs. Elgar re her poem.

Goodnight, my friend, and go on with your magnum opus to the joy and benefit of us poor ordinary mortals and ad majorem dei gloriam! Much love.

Ever yrs.
A.J.J.

[*letter-card*]

Malvern
Thursday
[*postmark* 31 May 1900]

My dear J.

By this post comes the great Blaze; as soon as I return the proofs already here everything will be straight. There's still some more M.S. to come but not much.

I can't tell you how much good your letter has done me: I *do* dearly like to be *understood*.

No time for more,
Yrs. ever,
E.E.

Don't you think of shirking that Analysis. I'm not sure about the B'ham book of words yet. Please wire receipt of M.S. I'm angshuss.

---

[1] vocal score, p. 151 *et seq.*

In respect of the performance of Sea Pictures *at the fourth concert of the Philharmonic Society's season the* Musical Times (*June, p. 393*) *stated:* 'In these poetically attuned lyrics Mr. Elgar gives further proof of his artistic intuitiveness and his mastery of dainty orchestration. It is no wonder that the subtle charm of "In Haven" secured for it an encore.'

[*W.P.S. paper*]

Craeg Lea,
Malvern.
June 1 [1900]

My dear Jaegerer,

Thanks for the proofs etc. etc. I'm not returning the stereo set 'cos they're *all right*. In the set which goes with this scrawl you'll see a note about '*Angelicals*' which please see to as nicely and amicably as you can. I hope to *bring* the rest of the M.S. and will stay in town to correct proofs etc. & hear some music D.V. and see you and jawwww like blazes.

Love to your Angelicals at home.
Yours E.E.

P.S. M.T. just come. Good! but no time to read just now. I can't help (it'll only cost the firm 1d. stamp to return the packet) sending you the enclosed whole *bag of tricks* re St. George – it has amused us vastly. Also the flag – tickets – bills & general mild excitement.

[*W.P.S. paper*]

Whitsunday.
[3 June 1900]

My dear Jaeger

I'm bitterly sorry to trouble you. But it has struck me that Mr. Brause may be devoting some of his well deserved holidays to drawing out the chorus parts – I want the voices re-arranged on the enclosed 3 pp. Do like an angel just complete the address for me and swear as much as you like at Yours truly.

This letter together with the snapshot affixed by Elgar in place of a signature is reproduced as the plate facing p. 45.

WACH' AUF!

WORCESTERSHIRE PHILHARMONIC SOCIETY

CRAEG LEA,

WELLS ROAD,

TELEGRAMS:.
UPPER WYCHE.

MALVERN.

Thue 7 1900

God bless you, Nimrod.

Here's the end

Edward Elgar

On 6 June Mrs. Elgar had written in the Diary: 'E. finished the Dream of Gerontius. Deo gratias. Rather poorly.'

The Elgars travelled to London before 9 June, seeing a performance of The Rivals that night and attending the Philharmonic Concert on 10 June.

Jaeger to Elgar:

1, Berners Street, W.
June 8 1900

My dear Elgar,

Delighted to hear you are in town once more! I wired you this morning & wonder what the telegraphist may have made of my latin. I say, I have invited two fellows, Allen Gill and Henry Beaumont (tenor) to my home on Sunday at 4 p.m. to enthuse them over 'Gerontius'. Gill wants to do it and H.B. wants to sing it. Can't you come to give them the proper impression? My enthusiasm is unbounded but my pianism and singism is but small. The more I study the work the more I marvel. It is wonderful. Come & discuss some little points with me. I have today sent to Malvern the original m.s. pf. score of Caractacus – and the first part of 'Gerontius' which I thought Mrs. Elgar might like to have.

No time for more–
Ever yours,
A. J. Jaeger

[*W.P.S. paper*]

Craeg Lea, Malvern
June 14 1900

My dear Jaeger,

I'm sorry that the libretto shd. be a worry and you are an *ass* to muddle it all up: on second thoughts you're not – I am.

Look here: I obtained permission before I began to work and told Mr. A. what I'd done. The revd. owner is anxious, (in deference to the memory of his dear friend the Cardinal) to know how the work goes on and wanted a check (or knowledge) as to how many copies were sold. I really do not think he wants to make any *money* out of it. I wanted to do the best I could, and as Fr. Nevile refused a sum down and, knowing that the firm made a charge for printing libretti, (to concert givers) I suggested the form of the permission which I now enclose. When I told Mr. Alfred this he informed me that the firm were *not* going to make a charge, in future, for printing libretti of short works: I then pathetically observed that when I *did* try to do something to please the firm it turned out wrong. Selah! Now I think – I intended it so – that the enclosed letter leaves the 8vo. edn. and any other *free:* will you shew this to Mr. Littleton and then tell me what is required to be altered and of course I'll do all I can to make things as he wishes.

Fr. Nevile tells me he consulted Longman's and they approved of his letter so they may know all about it.

Yours ever,

Ed. Elgar.

Of course if this permission is all thats wanted the B'ham people will have to pay for their programme.

[*W.P.S. paper*]

Craeg Lea, Malvern.

June 14 [1900]

Dear Jägerissimus:

I have sent off a librettistical letter which you will consider & write about again. Now: I went to the Coll: and conducted the Variations! & arrd. home late. As to your letter I'm glad the Angel's song is to be made legible. Thanks for sending Skour to Pitt – but the Bill's wrong ain't it? it was to be ½ price to me. I enclose it although its not your business.

Plunket Greene leaves middle of July & wd. like to squint at his part previous. Will the rough 8vo. copies be ready by the end of this month think you? If not, I daresay he cd. have proofs of his few pages – but I shd. think the whole thing will be done by then.

My wife is delirious over her copy of Caractacus.

In frantic haste,

Yr. ever,

Ed. Elgar

The ideological (or theological) impediments to Gerontius are illustrated by Jaeger's letter of 14 June: '. . . There is a lot of Joseph and Mary about the work: very proper for a Roman Catholic lying at death's door to sing about, but likely to frighten some d—d fools of Protestants. I had a long talk to the Secretary of one of the big Glasgow Societies yesterday and showed him proofs and so generally enthused over the work that I hope he will strongly recommend Gerontius to his Society. But he at once, on reading the words, spoke of the Roman Catholic element being so prominent. Tommy rot you say: ditto says I, who am rather an Agnostic than anything else. But alas one must deal with people as one finds them, and if, without bowdlerising a superb poem one can remove Mary and Joseph to a more distant background, it may not be a bad thing.'

Craeg Lea, Malvern.
June 15 [19]00

My dear Jaeger:

p. 35[1]

"Rescue him, O Lord, in this his evil hour, As of old so many –
(such as) Noe, Job, Moses, David – so to show thy power" etc. seems
to me to be sense, but if it isn't put the asterisks on p. 35 in the places
you suggest – it then reads

"Rescue him, O Lord, in this his evil hour – Noe etc." But as you
sensibly please.

I'm tired.

As to the Catholic side, of course it will frighten the low Church
party but the poem must on no account be touched! Sacrilege and not
to be thought of: them as don't like it can be damned in their own way
– not ours. Its awfully curious the attitude (towards sacred things) of
the narrow English mind: it puts me in memory of the man who
said, when he saw another crossing himself 'Oh, this *devilish crossing*'.
There's a nice confused idea for you. End of all received: I like★ it!

Yours ever,
Ed. E.

★ [*red ink blot*]
  xqqq blot

[*W.P.S. paper*]

Craeg Lea,
Malvern.
Wedy [20(?) June 1900]

My dear Jaeger:

The P.F. Dorabella is *alright* – I don't return the proofs 'cos I'm
short of envops. & you say you don't want 'em.

I'm awfully glad you are going to 'do' Gerontius in the M.T. & I
hope you'll spread yourself.

I've been waiting for the letter about *suthing*[?] but it hasn't come

In haste
Yrs ever
Ed E

P.S. I've 'done up' the proofs for post. *please*

p. 91 [*sic*] 56

small t for *thy*[2]

there's a good man it'll save me undoing the parcel

[1] Vocal score, *Gerontius*, cf. Newman's original text
[2] twice underlined

Craeg Lea, Malvern.
June 24 [1900]
Johannes Tag.

My dear Jaeger,

Here are one or two things: first, your last letter came through all right with the ½d. stamp and no surcharge – which, ensmiled me: your beastly 1d. is therefore adhesived above.

Now I've had a proof of the finale for *ten* days and no *read* proof or M.S. yet! Where the divvle is it – aren't we wasting time sadly? Do send it on if possible. Thanks for sending Plunket Greene his 'songs'. Now he'll be happy.

I hope to send about 60 pages full score tomorrow or Tuesday and the remainder as usual a bit at a time.

Don't forget about the *full sc.* fair copy – that is to say, if it is to be made at all, why not now? I'm awfully busy – letters to write. All good things to you all.

Yours ever,
Ed. E.

In a series of long letters Jaeger made critical observations on Gerontius *intermingled with expressions of enthusiasm. Thus:*

June 15: '. . . There is one page, (159), I can make nothing of, i.e. nothing adequate to Newman's words or the situation, though I have played and sung it over and over again and imagine all sorts of orchestral dodges to make it good to this critical ass! But all the rest is most beautiful, exquisite, ethereal. That lovely contrapuntal movement beginning at 126 has gone straight to my heart and burned itself into my brain. I fancy I have not seen any such lovely writing of a quiet soothing character since Die Meistersinger . . . . One thing: can you not make the solo part at top of p. 167 a little more melodic and really attractive. The words are lovely, and the effect of the whole no doubt A 1 but the "Angel" is badly off for "tune", ain't it?'

June 16: 'I have spent by far the greater part of this lovely day over your work instead of going to Richmond or somewhere to get some fresh air: the wonderfully beautiful and impressive finale especially held me captive and entranced, and the more I study the work the more I say to myself – remembering full well all Brahms', Tschaikowsky's, Richard Strauss', Verdi's, and Bruneau's doings: this "Gerontius" is the most beautiful and elevating work since "Parsifal". Your music is in turn as original as Bruneau, as wild and strong as Strauss, as impassioned as "Tshai", as ecstatic as Verdi (the latest Verdi) and as sane and noble and dignified as Brahms knew how to be. [*See Elgar's letter of 20 June,* Letters of Edward Elgar, *pp. 85–6*]

June 27: '. . . Now for your last long letter [20 June] . . . Don't
think you have convinced me, and don't imagine that I have delayed
because I want to ask other people's opinions. Nothing of the kind. I
have opinions of my own (& prefer them often) to other people's . . . .
Now I have read the poem well, and appreciated situation at the end
(Soul after seeing God) well. But, surely, the first sensations the Soul
would experience would be an awful overwhelming agitation; a
whirlwind of sensations of the acutest kind coursing through it; a
bewilderment of fear, excitation, crushing, overmastering hopeless-
ness etc. etc. "Take me away"!! Your treatment shirks all that and if
you will allow me to become for a moment downright vulgar and
blasphemous, your view, as expressed in the music, suggests to me
nothing so much as an "Oh lor, is that all. What a poor show, take
me away, it gives me the miserables". Yes, a whine I called it. You
may take it for gospel that Wagner would have made this the climax
of expression in the work, especially in the orchestra which here
should shine as a medium for portraying emotions. . . . I don't want
your "Soul" to sing a dramatic song – Heavens! But what is your
gorgeous orchestra for? and why should you be dull and sentimental
at such a supremest moment? Don't tell me you can't do it in 50 years!
Here is your greatest chance of proving yourself poet, seer, and do-er
of impossible things, and you shirk it. Bah! I see your point of view
quite. It's alright for the despised Brixton Baker and Bayswater
Butcher, not for an inspired poet-musician like E.E. . . . Did I not hold
your splendid powers in such reverence and admiration, and were the
rest of the work less superb, I should hold my peace and be content
with mere English cantata.' . . . [See also Elgar's letter of 11 July, Letters
of Edward Elgar, pp. 87–8]

Craeg Lea, Malvern.
June 27 [1900]

My dear Jaeger:
Gerontius
    see p. 130 *last* proofs, 1st tenor fourth bar – < > ♪ I don't know
how these marks got in.
    Lee Williams suggests the enclosed correction – which will make a
better *vocal* sound than "His" [.] may it be altered? On p. 11 (the first
entry of Chorus) it ought to be, according to libretto Chorus
(*Assistants*[1]) – can the omitted word go in? I don't think the succeeding choruses need have "assistants" again.
    [1] three times underlined

All right – I'll send score direct to Mr. Dodd. Tell him to put in plenty of *vocal cues* in all parts (especially in pt. one 1st tenor solo).

I've put largamente instead of *comodo*, but I don't know why – only to please you, & after all comodo has only *one* M. Ja! Jae! Jaeg! Jaege! Jaeger!!

I've kept p. 159 back for consideration, but all the time know I'm right & that you're wrong. However I'll see – one thing does annoy me. You say I've 'shirked it' – now I've shirked nothing – I've only set the thing as I feel & see it, which is not shirking at all, at all.

I can't stay to refer to the rest of your sermon, which is very Nimrodisch as pictured &c.

Yrs. ever,
Ed: Elgar

Birchwood Lodge, near Malvern.
Sunday [1 July 1900]

My dear Jaeger:
Very well: here's what I thought of at *first* – I've copied it out & sent it – of course it's biggity-big. *Now:* perpend – the following alterations will have to be made: viz: the *souls* chorus will *follow* the 'Take me away' That is to say: I enclose* p 157 – the top of it is all right & I've attached the Judgment theme, (I can't get in the rushing string passages!) at end of second p. (of my M.S. enclosed) the Solo 'Take me away' comes in, as it stands in type.

Now enclosed I send the *end* of the solo which *must join* on to the *Souls* Chorus, it is in type. And again the Souls' Chorus joins on to the end (last) movement – this 'join' I also enclose.

Now: *important*, immediately you get this tell me if the printers can understand it, if they cannot, send me a wire at once here & I'll come up at once. *Don't delay* 'cos we're going to Birchwood on Tuesday & it's very difficult to get away to trains. It'll relieve my mind (what *you have* left of it) to get a wire anyhow.

I hope you'll like the emendation.

But wire-wire-wire or I shall be gone into the woods.

Yours ever

Ed. E.

* [*marginal note*] The rehearsal figs: will want correction later. Hurry this up, all of it. I'm quite tired of seeing it.

Birchwood Lodge, near Malvern.

July 5 [1900]

My dear Jaeger:

Many thanks for the pens safely recd. I wouldn't have troubled you only it's miles to a p.o. to get an order & stamps are a trouble also to procure. I'll pay you, bless you!

Well: here we are! There are a lot of young hawks flying about – plovers also – 150 rabbits under the window & the blackbirds eating cherries like mad. E.E. is cheerful & is now learning 'potato' culture, – what names – 'Beauties of Abram', (they mean Hebron!) Adirondacks etc. etc.

Many thanks for the proofs, all returned. I don't really know if *p. 12 Chorus* is worth altering, as the folk don't sing from the copies. I pointed out once before that it shd be *chorus* & not *tutti* for uniformity's sake, but I suppose the sheet got lost somehow. I am very anxious to get all the Chorus copies out now, & a voc: sc. as *soon* as possible, 'cos I must consult the Birmingham people early about semi-ch. etc.

Can you tell me if *Dodd* is solely employed by your firm, or may I ask him to copy the score for me – if he has time etc etc – let me know this as time is short enough. I sent him about 40 pp on Monday & a p.c. to acknowledge same but have heard nothing & am in a fit!

Much love, yours ever

Ed. Elgar – write soon.

P.S. I return *only* the pp 12 & 34 all the others are right. *tell me if you want 'em back*. Hope your house is all well, & the angelical (minor).

[*W.P.S. paper*]

Saturday a.m.

[14 July 1900]

My dear J.

Do beg & pray from me that the Chorus parts *bars* may be ruled thro'. If you look at p. 9-12 etc of Alto part you will see it looks *quite* well for the bar line to break off. Breitkopfs' do it &, as a matter of principle it's just as good for the barline to *dodge* the words, as (in many cases) for the words to dodge the barline, nicht wahr?

It will be *hopeless* to get a Chorus to follow as it stands while the additional barlines (see p. 12) make it quite clear.

Birchwood Lodge, near Malvern.
July 17 [1900]

My dear Jaeger:

Thanks: I am glad about those barlines. I've no time to write really; I *won't* alter p 159 & be darned to you. I'll explain the idea sometime – at 120 for *one semi-quaver* value fffffffzzzz is the one glimpse into the Unexpressible – then it (the Music) dies down into the sort of blissful Heaven theme which of course fades away into nothing. I think the long notes for Tenor are better in anyone else's hands or voice – other than E. Lloyd –

Do send me a complete copy – *3* very soon – I'm going to Birmingham on Thursday to consult as I told you.

Ever

E.E.

Don't envy me. All your *london* asses – because I choose to give up everything & lead a simple life on farm labourer's wages – about half what *you yourself* live on – think I have an easy time. I believe it's blasted laziness.

On 11 July (see Letters of Edward Elgar, *p. 87) Elgar had promised to try to arrange details concerning the* Analysis of Gerontius *while in Birmingham. This caused Jaeger much concern during the following weeks. He was, in fact, overworked, sitting up late to write notices for* The Musical Times, *concocting an* Analysis *for* Hiawatha's Departure, *preparing works by Coleridge-Taylor, Parker, and Parry for the forthcoming Hereford Festival, as well as seeing* Gerontius *through its various stages. In his letter of 12 July Jaeger took another swipe at the Parry cult, instigated by the new* Te Deum *(Thanksgiving) of that composer.* 'Parry!', *he wrote,* 'Oh, Parry!! very much Parry!!! Toujours Parry!!!! Fiddles sawing all the time!!!!! Dear old Parry!!!!!! Now if you could compose a skoughre like that!!'*

[*W.P.S. paper*]

B'wood July 20 [1900]

My dear Jay:

Please send 2 cop[ie]s to Mad. Brema at the incomprehensible address I've written to her to prepare her.

Enclosed I return the libretto marked as you wish.

I think we'll treat it as a *libretto* & bracket the two bits that run together.

Thanks amany for tackling Wood & Co but I fear they are quaint.

Now we hope that you & your Angelicals will have a nice resting time & fine weather: let me know your address & all that happens re Johnstone & B'ham. I must work, I've nearly done.

Yours ever
Ed. E.

Birchwood Lodge, near Malvern.
Monday Jly 23 [1900]

My dear Jaeger:

I think our letters have – or rather will cross. 'Cos why? 'Cos I've not heard from you yet, & if you posted on *Sunday* it won't reach here until Tuesday. Now (Monday) the copies have arrived & by Jove how well it looks! I wrote to Lloyd asking *where* cops. shd be sent but he has not replied so please send 2 cops to

Hassendean

Hove

Sussex

to be forwarded.

Greene you know all about.

Madame Brema

17 Sussex Villas

Kensington W.

But I'll write to her & ask if she's there so let her wait until I hear & let you know.

I don't say a word about the Analysis because I may hear your remarks to-morrow – see?

I'm happy Mr Dodd supplied & shall (D.V.) have finished in a fortnight.

How about the Libretto in printing for the 8vo edition, don't you think the *omissions* had best be marked by dots . . . . & *not* asterisks which are heavy.

Also I've heard nothing from you for an age concerning the *permission* which you hold – does the firm want it altered or not?

P. 92 At 56 2nd note in Bass shd be Fx *not* Gx (we all missed this).

P. 159 at 120 there shd be a *p* thus *fffzp*.

P. 106 – rule shd join.

Yours ever
Ed. E.

On 26 July Jaeger wrote to confirm that the necessary permission for the use of Newman's text of Gerontius *had been obtained, and that he was trying to organize performances of* Gerontius *in Edinburgh and possibly Glasgow. 'Walford Davies last Saturday played through portions of the work at my house & got most excited – enthused. He thinks it "great" & "most beautiful" & he asked me to tell you that he loves you, though he knows you not. He is the most severe critic I know, but he recognises your qualities like few others . . ,'*

Birchwood Lodge,
near Malvern.
Wedy [August 1900]

My dear Jaeger:

Good:

I hope you're better the heat has been really awful & upsetting everyone – I don't like to say a word about these woods for fear you shd. feel envious but it is godlike in the shade with the snakes & other cool creatures walking about as I write my miserable music. Is it music? I fear not.

Biz: I enclose Mr. [G. H.] Johnstone's[1] letter (20th) on the strength of which I wrote to you – now today I've written again mentioning 10/10/ & the copyright & have given him your address & asked him to communicate with you. Let me have his letter again or take care of it.

about the Libretto: – I'll write to Father *Bellasis* about it, but I really don't see why the poem shd. be *given away* by the proprietor at all, at all. But I'll do what I can.

Directly you have 'closed' with Mr. J. I'll send you some books or something about the poem. You ought to come

HERE

I learn all about it at the shrine in the wood. Think on it.

Glad to hear of W. Davies.

I know I'm in a state of *callow assdom*★ all alone in the cold here & don't know nuffin but I like to hear of things, people & (occasionally) of A.J.J.

in haste

Yours ever

Edward Elgar

★ don't waste this please! I made it!! it's better than Gerontius. Write as soon as you can.

P.S. By all means use the copy for printing from. do you think at the End the 3 things wh. are worked together [?]

shd. be bracketed
[*in the Contents*]

$\left\{\begin{array}{l}\text{Softly \& gently} \\ \text{Lord Thou} \\ \text{Praise to the}\end{array}\right.$

[1] see p. 73

Birchwood Lodge,
near Malvern.
Tuesday [August 1900]

My dear Jaeger:

One line to catch post: I was out all day yesterday with a sawmill, sawing timber into joists, planks, posts, rafters, boarding yea! boarding with feather edge: how little ye townsmen know of real life. anyhow I got a chill over my exertions I have a liver today. I used to say 'come & see' & shall now say 'come & saw!' only Mrs. J. wdn't let you – it's dangerous.

Now to come down to the *damned*[1] music.

I am delighted with your analysis so far as it goes & if its all like that I shall expire in one roseate [*red ink mark*] blush. Really, my dear man, it's just right, only I don't call that one motif '*Sleep*' You will have had my note today (yours has only just come!) & we can foregather all day on Sunday & mend everything.

I suppose after all 'Sleep' will be right – I meant 'to be lying down weary & distressed' with your poor head buzzing & weak & – have you ever been really ill? Sleep will do but it's the ghastly troubled sleep of a sick man.

Look here: I imagined Gerontius to be a man like us not a priest or a saint, but a *sinner*, a repentant one of course but still no end of a *worldly man* in his life, & now brought to book. Therefore I've not filled *his* part with Church tunes & rubbish but a good, healthy full-blooded romantic, remembered worldliness so to speak. It is, I imagine, much more difficult to tear one's self away from a well to do world than from a cloister.

Your 6 might be Anguish but Despair will do.

'Kere, can't you drop the *Mr.* all the way thru & say Edward Elgar – & the composer after – I hate *Mr.*

p. 8 "Strange to say" etc. I didn't give this 'prayer' theme to Gerontius too plainly – solidly – cos he *wanders:* rather

If he'd been a priest he wd. have sung or said it as a climax but as he represents ME when ill he doesn't – he remembers his little[?] Churchy prayey music in little snatches – see?

He's of the world – or was & is going thro' a bad time, even if quite repentant etc.

Now, go on, there's a dear, & don't be frightened: my wife fears you may be inclined to lay too great stress on the *leitmotiven* plan because I really do it without thought – intuitively, I mean. For

[1] three times underlined

instance, I did not perceive till long after it was in print that – (p. 34) "In Thine *own agony*[1]" & the appalling chords

I last bar p 150

II 3rd line, bar 2, p 154 introducing & dismissing the *Angel of the Agony* were akin but they are, aren't they.

Yours ever & ever
Ed Elgar

[*W.P.S. paper*]

Birchwood.
Augt 9 [1900]

Dear sea-serpent:

For all your remarks many thanks. I've sent some to Novello's & some to *W.P.B.*

I meant that theme

line 2 p. 92[2]

„ 1 „ 149

„ 1 „ 155, to mean an indefinable feeling that there's more around you than you know: Have you ever been in a pitch dark room & have *felt* the presence of people when you have no proof or knowledge that anyone is there. I *have* & it feels like that.

Yah! don't bother me about music. I ride a Bicycle.

Much love, yours ever
E.E.

I've heard about the libretto & your firm is to arrange as they wish & can with Longman, so I hope that is settled. I do hope you are having better weather now – it is truly deplorable here – gales & rain.

Birchwood Lodge,
Malvern.
Augt 14 [1900]

My dear Jaeger:

I'm truly glad you are to do the Analysis, only you *must* get more for it.

I said to Mr. J[ohnstone]. *ten* and if that were too much wd. he make a proposal to you? I am woefully disappointed that he shd. have written to you about five [guineas] and you must stick out for more. I will gladly help all I can but I am sick of the whole thing and your firm is enough to make one disgusted with one's fellow creatures

---

[1] *own agony* twice underlined
[2] see vocal score, *Gerontius*

forever. I will not say what I think, but all other publishers are so
different and nice and pleasant to do with even if things are not smooth,
and all others are reasonable and obliging and considerate – I say no
more.

Boosey wd. fly rather than ask *me* to arrange about the libretto in
order to save himself a possible small fee, but your firm is incomp-
rehensibly —— I don't think the Big Chorus need worry you, its
quite simple. Send me your copy and I'll do all I can with it.

Glad to hear Pitt's music[1] is good and shall look forward to hearing
it much.

I hope you are all better for the change only you must have had some
awful weather.

Yrs. in haste & ever,
Edward Elgar.

Birchwood Lodge, Malvern.
August 15: 1900.

My dear Jäger:

Sorry you are back for your sake but precious glad for my own.

I *must* have the score to read the parts by or with & Richter wants it –
he said – first week in September. I am to go through it with him then.

I think you had best proceed as rapidly as you can with the engraving
of the parts & I'll correct 'em in a lump – more or less – when I can get
a sight of the score to work with – by – or from. Proofs of cover &
A.M.D.G. page retd. if the latter *can* 'face the music' please do let it,
but don't waste paper over it.

If Dodd had already done 56 pp when you wrote that is more than
1/6th of the whole so he ought to soon finish.

I'll keep the 9 pp string pts recd until I get more anyhow.

Yours ever
Edwd Elgar

On the title page which I saw long ago it only said Price – nothing
about boards or cloth.

Birchwood Lodge, Malvern.
Aug. 19: [19]00

All Hail, great Faun!

Here's your Contents – I've added a bit & scrawled it over. Ja!
gewiss Duet is fatal. Dialogue is correct tho' unpleasing: why not
Recit!! or palaver!!! or gossip!!!!

---

[1] presumably the part-song 'Shepherds all and Maidens fair' (P.S.B. 844),
published in 1900

No. dialogue will do very well. You are right about the slurs: they are misleading, irritating & useless; but I gave up as I thought they were immutable – following your directions, I return a *marked* copy which I pray you send to me 'cos I pine for it – make the best of it. 'K'ere; a quaver rest has dropped out at $\boxed{25}$ pt II. I don't care a d–mn. I say the *scoring* of this work is A.1. now I look back at it – you hold your stummick.

Yours ever with much consideration & a bad tooth & a shaky hand from Bike riding (falling off I mean) & refreshments

E.E.

Ja!

Birchwood Lodge,
near Malvern.
Sunday Augt 25 or 6 [1900]

My dear Jaeger:

I expect you are buried in the M.T. & speechless: so mote it be. – I've now recd. & checked & *returned all* strings of Part I.

I retain score (also recd.) of pt I for wind etc. I sent all Longman's letters to your firm but, as they've got what they asked for, they are not yet polite enough to acknowledge the receipt.

Now: I am D.V. coming to town on Saturday next[1] & may find time to look at your lovely phiz: for five minutes before I leave on the following Friday: I'm not at the Hereford rehearsal.

Now, please address Craeglea after *Tuesday* next: we climb down to the valley on Wedy a.m. & I cuss every step away from these woods.

Grrrhh!

Much love

Yrs ever

Edward Elgar

[1] for rehearsal of Hereford Festival music. Elgar was represented by *Caractacus* (Act III). A new work of interest to the citizens of Gloucester was Stanford's *Last Post*, since the text was by W. E. Henley, a native of the city. Edward Lloyd appeared this year at a Three Choirs Festival for the last time.

[*letter-card*]   Sunday [*postmark* Malvern, 9 September 1900]

My dear Jay:
   I hope you settled down after the jaw & japes at Pagani's – I can't
mark a par: to fit[.] Send on your 'stuff' when ready – I like to insult
your work by calling it 'stuff', a sort of return for your years of scorn
                              Yah!
                              E.E.

                              at Herefordshire Club,
                              Hereford
                              Thursday
                                   [13 September 1900]

My dear Jaeger:
   I sent a wire this a.m. on my return from Birmingham[.] I return
home *per Bijck* on Saturday a.m. so please direct to Craeg Lea on
Friday so that I shan't have to carry my own rubbish about the county
                         All well
                              Yours ever
                              Ed. Elgar

                              Craeg Lea,
                              Malvern.
                              Saturday a.m.
                                   [15 September 1900]

My dear Jaeger:
   These pages reached me now 8 o'c. – I don't know where to send
em so I send to your home address with a stamped envelope to save
you trouble.
   We go over for *today* only – & back on Tuesday evening. I hate
going.
                         Yrs ever
                              E.E.

*Jaeger, temperamentally akin to Elgar in so many ways and liable at all
times to work himself beyond the point of endurance, was nervously exhausted
by his work on the Analysis and by his general anxiety for the welfare of*
Gerontius. *He had, he said, done his Analysis after his daily routine in the
office and by giving up all his recent Sundays to the task. He was incensed by
rumours. So in one (undated) letter he wrote*: . . . That ass Betts has been
at it again in the D. News talking about a *massive* 8 part chorus as a

Finale to Gerontius & last Friday he talked of Gerontius being done at
the Albert Hall. I think it's a lie. I hope it is for Gerontius at the
Kensington Katacomb will be awful. Queen's Hall is the place & I
hope Wood may do it . . .'

In another letter, also without date, he spoke of a row with his employers:
'. . . It seems to me they are jealous or disgruntled because so many
people, i.e. musicians write to *me* & come to speak to me. They seem
to want to tie my unworthiness down to mere "clerking". Well if
they do, I shall leave. I hope I'm a little better than a clerk . . .'

*But the Analysis was eventually ready in proof and Jaeger retrieved his
spirits when he heard appreciation of* Gerontius *from a respected source.*

Jaeger to Elgar:

1 Berners St., W.,
13–9–1900

'Your movements worry me. You say "off to B'ham" did you not
mean to Hereford? I sent several parcels of proofs & letters & a copy of
Gerontius there. Did you get them all? Tell me. I spoke to Lloyd re
Gerontius at the London rehearsals. He said "very fine music but
wants getting at & understanding". Just so, I said, I hope so. Brains
generally want understanding. You shall get a proof of *the* Analysis
today or tomorrow. Please *knock it about as you like*, as long as you
don't deprive me of the right to have an opinion sometimes! I could
say nought of Orchestration of Pt. II. If you can add that, very well. I
had no score to refer to.'

On the following day Jaeger wrote again, to say that 'Professor Sanford
[*of Yale University, to whom Elgar was to dedicate the* Introduction and
Allegro *for Strings*] & Mr. Knight have just been & told me the greatest
treat of the Festival (sic!) was their first acquaintance with bits of
Gerontius, as sung by Lloyd. They *raved*, & I smiled & said unto them
"There, what did I tell you".'

at 44, Bridge St.,
Hereford.
[16 September 1900?]

My dear Jaeger:
Gar on:
I told you I was to be out of town on Thursday and home on
Friday. I am going all I can with the parts but where are the rest and
where are the M.S. things. I'm anxious to correct 'em.

My wife, in my absence, replied to the telegram in error I fear and added to the general confusion.

I biked over from Malvern.

Yours ever, E.

On 18 September Jaeger wrote to Mrs. Elgar: '. . . I sent the other day a score of E's Variations to Professor Buths of Düsseldorf, one of the ultra-moderns of Germany, great propagandist for Richard Strauss and I enclose his remarks which I won't attempt to put into English. The Firm at my suggestion have invited him to B'ham to hear some English music. He is conductor of the Lower Rhenish Musical Festivals. Do you guess something? But mum's the word. I think his critique of the Variations (after one day's perusal of the score) is the best I have seen. German is the language for criticism.'

The enclosure ran as follows:

'Heute haben Sie mir etwas Feines geschickt; die Variationen von Elgar haben ein musik-aristokratisches Gepräge. Wenn der Himmel diesen feinen Geist einmal mit einem poetischen Vorwurf beschenken wird, der ihn ganz innerlich packt, dann erhoffe ich ein Bedeutendes von Elgar. Das Variationenwerk ist feinfühlig, sinnig, empfindungsvoll; es ist ja noch bis zu einem gewissen Grade nur "tonspielerisch" um mich kurz auszudrücken, aber es ist nicht nur ein äusserlicher, französischer "Esprit", wie die Aufgabe der verschiedenen Charakterdarstellungen aus gleichen Notenmaterial behandelt wird, sondern es ist Empfindungsgehalt vorhanden. Ich habe so den Eindruck, als ob die Saite "Elgar" noch eine grössere Spannung verträgt, und dass ihr Grundklang noch nicht herausgeholt ist. So viel im Allgemeinem für heute; vor allen Dingen aber: "Hut ab" vor solcher Künstlerschaft.'

['You have today sent me something fine; Elgar's *Variations* have, musically speaking, an aristocratic character. If Heaven will endow this fine intelligence with the stuff of poetry, which inspires him, I shall look forward to something of significance from him. The Variations are sensitive, thoughtful, and full of feeling. To be short, to a certain degree they are only "effect for effect's sake", but the way in which the different character sketches are treated in corresponding musical terms is, unlike a merely detached, French *esprit*, extremely expressive. I have the impression that the Elgarian string could bear a greater tension, and that the foundation tone is not yet extended. So much, in general, for today. But above all: "Hats off" to such artistry.']

Craeg Lea, Malvern.
[19 September 1900]

My dear Jaeger:

The Analysis is splendid but I must keep it until the a.m.

I am coming up tomorrow to the Langham Hotel[1], arriving about 4.30. I shall receive here everything till second delivery.

Tell Dodd *not* to send anything more *here* but to *you* and you can let me have it at Langham. I return by this post *all* remainder of string parts, proofs and revises. I've now at last got the *score*. It must be stitched somehow on Friday belike.

Much love,
Yours ever,
Ed. Elgar

Craeg Lea, Malvern.
Sep 27 1900

My very dear Jaeger:

We arrived all right this afternoon & found our peaceful little home very bright, clean and *quiet* after London and the greasy pandemonium yclept Pagani's. Somehow, after thinking of the rehearsal, I feel very much ashamed of myself as author of "Gerontius" – a sort of criminal – and wonder if I shall ever get up sufficient courage to go to Birmingham at all. I suppose I must however, if only to conduct for the siren whom Manns writes of – privately – as "Cara Clara" [Butt].

'K'ere – you Annalist – I read your 'stuff' in the train and its clever beyond words I think and thank you for it. Save and except your adjectives over some of which I 'splutter and growl'. Also 'K'ere – as usual, when a work is out of hand I tear up my sketch books. I'm an ass – "Jaeger's pet ass" – well I don't mind – and I looked at these two *very first* sketches and I wondered whether you'd like 'em – if you don't want 'em throw 'em in w.p.b. I am not getting conceited (don't fear) and think my scrawl worth having – ciel! but somehow I couldn't tear up these two bits and I'm an ass.

Yrs. ever,
Edward Elgar.

P.S. A damned ass.
P.P.S. Certainly.
P.P.P.S. Forsooth.

The first performance of Gerontius *took place at Birmingham Town Hall on the morning of 3 October. It was an indifferent performance, the chorus especially being at fault (see* Elgar O.M., *pp. 89–90), and the critics were*

[1] for rehearsals of *Gerontius* at Queen's Hall.

Sketches for a
'Welsh' overture (1)

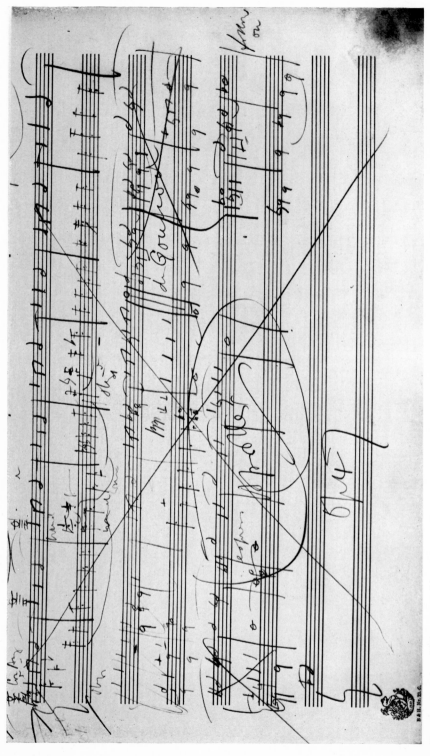

Sketches for a 'Welsh' overture (?)

generally little more than lukewarm in commendation. The Manchester
Guardian *notice of 4 October, to which Elgar refers in his letter of 12
October, was, however, less reserved:* '. . . Here a comparison with
Berlioz is simply inevitable – for Edward Elgar's dramatic power
admits of comparison with the great masters. His demons are much
more terrible than those of Berlioz, who was a materialist in the
profound sense – not, then, in virtue of more or less shifting beliefs,
but of unalterable temperament. Infinitely remote from that of Berlioz
is the temperament revealed in Edward Elgar's music, which, like
parts of the poem, fairly merits the epithet "Dantesque".

'In the performance this morning the part of Gerontius was most
conscientiously given by Mr. Lloyd. The utterances of the officiating
priest, more unimpeachably written for the voice than most of Elgar's
vocal parts, were delivered with admirable and perfectly appropriate
eloquence by Mr. Plunket Greene, and the grand style of Miss Brema
was very finely exhibited in the sweetly and beautifully conceived
part of the Angel. The orchestral rendering, under Dr. Richter, was
in every way admirable, and the only serious defect was the occasional
flat singing of the chorus. At the end there was a scene of very genuine
though restrained enthusiasm, the composer appearing only after
much persuasion. I am more than usually troubled by the sense of
utter inadequacy in these notes, and can only hope that I may have
some opportunity of doing better justice to a deeply impressive work.'

[*W.P.S. paper*]

                                              Malvern
                                          Oct. 9 [1900]

My dear Jaeger,

I recd. the St. Francis this a.m. but no word with it: we hope you
and yours are well and that you are recovering from the effects of last
week: I was very well and not worried by the infernal music: we had
however news of severe financial loss – (since partially amended to our
great relief) and that made me very worried.

I hope *you* are all right: I have not seen the papers yet except one or
two bits which exuberant friends insisted on my reading and I don't
know or care what they say or do. As far as I'm concerned music in
England is dead – I shall always write what I have in me of course.

I have worked hard for forty years & at the last, Providence denies
me a decent hearing of my work: so I submit – I always said God was
against art and I still believe it. anything obscene or trivial is blessed in

this world and has a reward – I ask for no reward – only to live & to hear my work. I still hear it in my heart and in my head so I must be content. Still it is curious to be treated by the old fashioned people as a criminal because my thoughts and ways are beyond them.

I am very well and what is called 'fit'! I had my golf in good style yesterday & am not ill or pessimistic – don't think it, but I have allowed my heart to open once – it is now shut against every religious feeling and every soft, gentle impulse *for ever*.

Write soon,

Yrs. ever,

E.E.

[*W.P.S. paper*]

Malvern.

Friday

[12 October 1900]

My dear Nimrod:

Of course you're all on the wrong tack. I was not grumbling about the performance much – not so much as you made out – I only say the usual curse came upon my doings: what I was really upset about was my wife's throat – I think I told you a slight operation was performed in B. & our financial troubles. The result of it all is that we can't go away for a change. I'm rather pleased with my work – privately – but it is annoying – whatever *you* may think, to know that it's *no good* commercially, and that with *one*[1] exception (your own good self) all my best friends including the highest thinkers only made one remark during my 'exaltation' "now you must write a few popular songs" instead of a word of appreciation, in its best sense, fifty times, by the men even who had promised to finance my work, during the week, nay on the very moment of performance did they drum it into my poor ears "now a popular song or two will make up for this" – my wife ill, and our money gone.

Damn Gerontius: I'd really forgotten it when I wrote to you last.

You are a dear old mosshead, but I can't really trust you – 'cos you don't work on the '*really* popular song' idea. If I'm X this is the sort of thing which has done it: as to the papers I've not seen one yet and shan't see 'em for a long time – Stay, I lie – I saw – under compulsion – the Manchester Guardian. Thats all. Write soon. I send the score and a letter to the firm. *Edwards* wants to see the *writing* in the score so let

<hr>

[1] twice underlined

him see it and draw his attention to the orchestral figs. [?] at the end.
Yrs. ever, with love to the 'ouse

E.E.

*If Elgar did not take the advice to write popular songs he did move out of
the* Gerontius *ambit and early in November (the letter is not extant) announced a new intention to Jaeger, who wrote to Mrs. Elgar on 7 November.*
'. . . I am glad to get E.E's. cheerful letter of the other day with news
of the "Cockayne" overture. Ye gods! what a capital title! I can
smell the Steak and the Stout already. I'm glad that E has done something *jolly* after the serious and awesome Gerontius. Let him finish it
with a *"Bang"* though, & give us a really *rousing* piece. We can all do
with it.

'Professor Buths tells me he *means* to do "Gerontius" in Düsseldorf!
He is battling with that Translation I sent him & will submit some
specimen pages soon . . .'

*With Elgar cheerfulness had a habit of breaking in, but this was a de-
pressing period, and* Cockaigne *was sketched against a background of
dejection, financial embarrassment, and concern about the business arrangements of* Gerontius. *The note at the end of the manuscript of* Cockaigne,
quoted from Piers Plowman, *was a fairly accurate summary of the situation –*
'Meteless and moneless on Malverne Hills'. *There was, however, one
encouraging gesture: the conferment of the honorary degree of Mus. D. by
the University of Cambridge (at Stanford's suggestion) on 22 November.*

*Regarding this Miss Burley left the following note, which requires modi-
fication. Elgar was offered the degree by letter on 17 October and notified his
acceptance the next day. The robes, subscribed for by friends, arrived eventually on 3 December 1901.*

'One morning in November, 1900, I had an urgent message from
Alice Elgar, asking me to come to Craeg Lea as soon as possible for
something important. I hurried along and Alice met me in the dining
room looking very anxious. "What is it?" I said. "They have offered
him the degree of Doc. at Cambridge University and he says he will
not accept it. Do go up and talk to him." (His study was upstairs – he
never liked to work on the ground floor.) I went up cautiously and
found him sitting at his table with his head in his hands.

He said gloomily, "They've offered me a Doctor's Degree at
Cambridge University, but I shan't accept it. I'm just writing a
refusal."

Miss B. "Won't accept it, but why not?"
Elgar, "It's too late."
Miss B. "Too late, for what?"
Elgar, "For everything."

Miss B. "I don't understand it. Why, it's the greatest honour they can offer you. This is a recognition of *Gerontius*. You can't snub Cambridge University."

Elgar, "But I can't afford to buy the robes."

Miss B. "You need not buy them. You can hire them. You are not the first impecunious Doctor of Music. Why! I could almost lend you enough for the hiring."

Then I laughed & said, "I'll go round & sing & collect money in a shell!"

Then the mood passed and he looked more cheerful.

Then I said, "Now, just write a nice polite letter thanking them for the honour which you appreciate most keenly." I went away at once & reassured Alice, telling her it was all right and it would be better not to say any more about it.

A few days afterwards he asked me which day would be the most propitious of three that they offered, and I chose, at once, Nov. 22, as it was St. Cecilia's day. His friends subscribed the money for the Doctor's robes and he much enjoyed the reception at Cambridge.'

at Hasfield Court
Gloucester
Oct 26 [1900]

My dear Jaeger:

Thanks for your congratulations – it is too true about the Doctor. I enjoyed your long letter & it is good of you to write but you can't get me to work. Aha!

Seriously, my dear friend, look at the position: e.g. I'm asked to write something for the Phil:–well I've practically got a Concert overture ready: the P. won't pay *anything*.

Now look at this.

To copying parts	12.0.0.
Rehearsal ex.	3.0.0.
Do. & Concert	6.0.0.
	————
net loss	[£]21.0.0.

Now what's the good of it? Nobody else will perform the thing – if I take it to your firm they might print the strings but the result wd. be the same.

No thank you: I really cannot afford it and am at the end of my financial tether. Don't go and tell anyone but I *must* earn money somehow – I *will not* go back to teaching & I think I must try some

trade – coal agency or horses [houses?] – I really wish I were dead over &
over again but I dare not, for the sake of my relatives, do the job myself.
Well we shall see – I've not read the papers yet re Gerontius & never
shall now. I'm sorry you've been bothered over it – just like my
influence on everything & everybody – always evil!

All thanks for sending the Variations to Lessmann. it's no good
however. I'm sorry I forgot to answer your question about chamber
music for Miss Prout – but I can't do it: – the 'stuff' wd. want looking
through & perhaps clean copies made & it's not worth the trouble – I
would not do it even for Joachim so we'll drop it.

We are very well & jolly – having a little change which my wife
needed very much – she's really well again after the throat business &
I'm riotously well thank goodness.

The degree is not conferred until Nov. 22 – I should of course have
told you about it (only knew a week ago) but it was not to be mentioned – I only saw it in print two days ago:

Edwards ought to give a list of the people on whom it has been
conferred – not officials but the composers – it wd. be only fair to
Cowen & myself – the general public don't know the difference
between 'it' & the stupid Canterbury commercial transaction.

Much love to you & you all.

Yours ever

Ed: Elgar

[*W.P.S. paper*]

Sunday Nov 4 [1900]

Dear Nimrod:

What a jolly fine tune your Variation is: I'd forgotten it & have
been playing it thro' – it's just like you – you solemn, wholesome,
hearty old dear.

I *could* give another side of your character but won't (musically)
just yet.

All right – I note what you say & won't write to you anymore – that
is if you bully me.

Don't say anything about the prospective overture yet – I call it
'Cockayne' & it's cheerful and Londony – 'stout and steaky'.

I'm not proceeding with the coal business but am going to try
taters – sacks not 1d. worths so I can't supply you. I hope to be in
town *en route* for Cambridge about the 20th. & will make the pts. &
score of Gerontius agree then – I mean the corrections made in the
parts. Also if I can bear to look at it again I'll trim the orch. version of

the finale & tack it on to the prelude. Selah! I want you to see how Henzen[1] has done the Sea Pictures into your wonderful language – it (the translation) goes *well* with the music, but I don't know enough to say if it's good poetically. I do want to see you or somebody as knows suffin – I am bored to death with commonplace ass-music down here – the bucolics are all right when they don't attempt more than eat, drink & sleep but beyond those things they fail. Can't you come down here for a weekend?

Much love from us to you III.

Yours ever

E.E.

Craeg Lea, Malvern.

Nov. 14 [1900]

My dear Jaeger:

Many thanks for Gerontius in french: my wife has taken it off for solemn perusal & I will have a good look at it soon. It is probably good as the *editeur* or whatever a French beast is – traducteur I suppose – has not attempted rhyme.

Sorry you are not well but I suppose it's a small temporary LIVER – & not real worry which Heaven forbid.

I hope to be in town on *Tuesday* – this Cambridge jamboree (!) is on Thursday 22nd. after which the deluge. I feel Gibbonsy, Croftish, Byrdlich & foolish all over.

Music progresses slowly. I've written some tunes which will 'make a methody swear' – the whole quotation is too good for you – (Devon Hunting Song, ancient, adapted) (I believe its Somerset after all)

    "Oh! Elgar's work's a d—able work,
    the warmest work o'the year,
    A work to tweak a teetotaller's beak
    And make a methody swear."

(This is Cokayne!)

Sweet, ain't it?

Now get better and have a tonic and tell us how your house is and give our love to it, them, and kiss the Angelical for me.

Yours gownily,

E.E.

---

[1] probably Karl Georg Wilhelm Henzen (1850–1910), Director of the Leipzig Stadttheater and also of the Association of German Dramatists and Composers from 1890. He wrote important books in connection with drama.

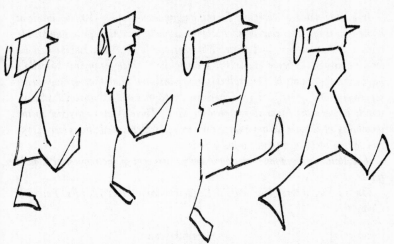

Philharmonic ladies going to Cambridge for the event – (great excitement Pitt has sent me his score: it's jolly good – *fine* & the wretch has written the Harp part correctly I believe – it is *too* bad of him (I forgot to tell him so,) because *I* shall have to try to be correct now. PIG. tell him this & don't, in this connection, omit the *pig*[1].

[*W.P.S. paper*]

Craeg Lea, Malvern.

Nov. 29 [1900]

My dear Jaeger,

I'm home:

They did the Variations very well indeed at L'pool[2] and my procession of friends dear to me was nice to see – I mean hear – but the sounds I have connected with them are very vivid (to me) and I feel the corporeal presence of each one as the music goes by: you sounded, you old preacher, gorjus.

'K'ere: add *Op. 19* to all the parts and score in fact whatever is printed or to be printed of Froissart.

I'll send ye the rest of Op. 18[3] (pt. songs) whereof you've only *one*, some day. I hope you are well and flurrrrishshshing. It's raining piteously here and all is dull except the heart of E.E. which beats time to most marvellous music – unwritten alas! and ever to be so.

Yours E.E.

[1] three times underlined
[2] 24 November
[3] 'O happy eyes' (Op. 18, no. 1) was published in 1896. 'Love' (Op. 18, no. 2) did not appear until 1907. Both had been written in 1890 together, presumably, with other part-songs originally intended to form part of Op. 18.

In a letter dated 2 December Jaeger, having been playing chamber music at home, put it to Elgar that he should write a violin and pianoforte sonata. He reports the enthusiasm of Charles Macpherson, J. E. West, Edwin Lemare for Gerontius, all being anxious to arrange the Prelude for organ. Novello's have agreed to publish 'Dorabella' (score, parts, and pianoforte arrangement) separately, and offer £21 for Chanson de Matin and Chanson de Nuit, which Jaeger asks Elgar to complete in score. There is also reference to the possibility of Elgar's taking a large number of Hedley's medallions (see p. 75) and selling them at a profit to his friends.

The Italian programme referred to below was sent at the request of Elgar's father.

On 12 December Elgar was in London to conduct at Lloyd's 'Farewell Concert'.

[*letter-card*]   Sunday a.m.
                              [*postmark* Malvern, 2 December 1900]
My very dear J.
    Thanks for programma d'Italia. What larks.
    'K'ere I wrote a long – (I think) letter to you asking you to put Op. 19 to Froissart – everything of it you print. A young lady[1] took the letters (among others the one to you wasn't stamped – she was going to stamp 'em) and she came back full of tears to say she had lost 'em or yours or some of 'em. Anyhow it's disappeared. No time to write more.
                              Yours E.E.

[*W.P.S. paper*]
                                                      Malvern
                                                      Dec 6 [1900]
My dear Jaeger:
    Only time for this: don't you think
                              Dorabella
looks foolish – I fear it – wouldn't it be better to knock it out of the separate issue. if it's necy to make it sell then I step aside and you must do as you please.
    Urgent[2] – send *as soon as possible* a copy of this to H. Plunket Greene
                                                      34 Kensington Sq
                                                      W
he will belike get someone to play it as P.F. solo.
                              Yrs ever
                              Ed Elgar

[1] 'Dorabella'
[2] twice underlined

(urgent.)

37. Drawing the Trombone.

WACH' AUF!

WORCESTERSHIRE PHILHARMONIC SOCIETY

Malvern

Dear

My dear Jaeger:

about that C# D

at [144] — I think 'best

is in Violin thus

that will do

yrs ever

Edward Elgar

[*W.P.S. paper*]

Craeg Lea, Malvern.
Dec. 7 [1900]
Später

My dear J.,

Enclosed is an attempt at muddling the finale. It brings in all we want I think: try it carefully and *don't* play the original first! take the Prelude as it stands & slur over the last theme

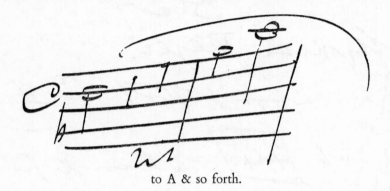

to A & so forth.

I'm to be in town on Monday p.m. for a few days, so if you haven't made up your mind about it before then let it wait until I call or see you.

prestissimo

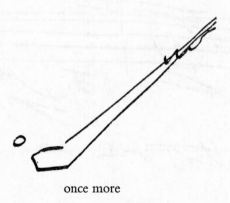

once more

Yrs ever
E.E.

I shall have to (rather) reorchestrate it.

at Langham Hotel
London
Thursday a.m.
[13 December 1900?]

My dear Jaeger:

Borwick is anxious to see the Intermezzo ["*Dorabella*" *pf. score*]
Could you send a copy at once to
Plunket Greene.

If the separate thing is not yet ready could a complete copy go turned
down at the page or otherwise marked.

Do something there's a good angel.

Yrs ever
E.E.

[*W.P.S. paper*]

Malvern
Saty [15 December 1900]

My dear Jaeger:

I did not gather from your pattes de mouche that you wanted the
opening dignifieded. I don't know how to do it – would it do to put
a chord

then the band parts will want altering if they're ever used.

I'll see what I can do about the end of Gerontius – but it makes too
much work! – I wish Pitt wd. do it! Confound the magpies.

I was awfully busy[1] and had to come home midday – I intended to

---

[1] On 10 December Elgar had travelled to London and met H. C. Embleton;
the next day he lunched with Mr. Boosey and on 12 December conducted at
Edward Lloyd's Farewell Concert. On Thursday he dined with 'E. Lloyd etc.',
and returned to Malvern on Friday.

stay until this day in which case I wd. have seen you again. Well it can't be helped.

Much love to you all,

Yrs ever

E.E.

I saw Wd. Davies on Thursday.

By pcl. post I send everything I [possibly *deleted*] have back corrected *can* you alter the date to 1901

[*W.P.S. paper*]

Malvern.

Dec. 31 1900

My very dear Jaeger:

One word to close the century. *All good things* to you 3 from us all, now and ever and ever Amen.

Thanks for your letter and Xmas good wishes! I have given up sending cards, so sent you the score of the miserable Mal de Mer. I forget what quotation I put on – from Piers Plowman's Vision I expect – that's my Bible, a marvellous book! I had a lovely present from Schott: full sc. of Meistersinger "als Freundschaftgruss zu Weihnachten'. I *have* enjoyed it. I was afeared you cdn't come here and told my wife it was no time to ask you; but *any* time you can be spared we shall be only too glad to see you. It is very good of you to mention my works as you do but I take no interest in 'em – if they were to be had in score I shouldn't mind.

Now don't worry about what you said – above all don't recommend me to the firm. They are I know dead sick of me.

I am going to write to you re the prelude and *tack* 'on' Gerontius – I don't think t'will jump quite.

Yrs. ever,

Ed: Elgar

1901

At the beginning of the year Elgar was preparing the Prelude *and* '*Angel's Farewell*' *from* Gerontius *for separate publication, and also revising the score of* Froissart *(Op. 19), of which a score was to be issued. The motto to which he refers in the letter of 12 January (?) is from Keats:*

when chivalry
Lifted up her lance on high
(*Lines to Georgiana Augusta Wylie*).

The Worcestershire Philharmonic Society Concert on 17 January consisted of Stanford's Last Post, *Sullivan's last songs,* Tears, idle tears *and* O swallow, swallow, *two of Mozart's* '*Epistle*' *Sonatas, Parry's* The sea hath many a thousand sands, *Grieg's* Landerkennung, *Cowen's Symphony no. 6 – 'The Idyllic', Lee Williams's* Twilight, *Walford Davies's* Hymn Before Action, *two part-songs by Schumann, and Percy Pitt's* Cinderella *Suite.*

Craeg Lea
Malvern.
Jany 6: 1901
8–30 p.m.

My dear Jäger:

I hope to send my darling child to it's wicked uncle to-morrow – please be kind to it – the house will seem empty to me without it!

Now: I've added small notes for the missing *solo* voice & also for *female* choir (the men's voices were already sufficiently represented in the orch.) & the thing cd be done

(1) as *orchl.* only

(2) with solo voice only,

(3) or (of course) in the original, Chorus & solo, form.

The only thing to note is about the clarinets – they are, for some low notes especially – in A in Vorspiel & originally in B♭ (to save 'em the trouble of changing) in the finale – now there's no time to change, so I've written in the pts in red ink somehow or somewhere for the B instrs all thro' the last movement, it had better be *printed* for the B anyhow.

All else I think you'll twig.

I wrote to you this a.m. as I had friends coming & my brain (?) has been a fog of Horse talk, Hound jaw Fox gossip & game chatter: so you must forgive any stupidity on my part.

Ever yours

Ed: Elgar

[*W.P.S. paper*]

Craeg Lea,

Malvern.

Jan 12 (?), [1901]

My dear Jaegerissimo:

I am sending you all the Froissart I have – what jolly *healthy* stuff it is – quite shameless in its rude young health! deary me! was I ever like that?

'K'ere – if trombones I & II are not engraved let 'em both go a third higher into

clef. it won't really matter a d—n but it looks very *naive*. Now as to the *blue* marks, put in all you can, but here again, it won't kill anyone if they can't be done: if dear Brause – to whom love & a nice New Year – grumbles, tell him he will do only what he likes & I'll come & play the trombone to him while he does it.

There are two passages in Vio 1mo (*div* in 8vi), those are marked in red ink – '*in full*' I don't think it necy to knock it about – its quite plain to the *conductor* & that's all that's wanted.

In haste & joyful (Gosh! man I've got a tune in my head) oh!

Here's your letter.

I think *Prelude* & *Angel's Farewell* much best.

So this angel takes present farewell of the best of souls, i.e. A.J.J.

Yrs

E.E.

Your score engraving is *nice* but *do* you think the heading on 1st page of music *good*, look at some other pubrs & twig.

Put the Motter where you darn please – I wanted it everywhere.

[*letter-card*]

[*postmark* Malvern, 16 Jan. 1901]

My dear Demon (?)

Thanx: I'm awfully busy to-day so will only say do what you can about the *Froissart* improvements – *no* new plates though for 'evin's sake – & never mind that one Trombone passage if it needs a new 'sticherung' (that must be a real word – I made it anyhow). I'll write soon. Foxes, birds, pigs, golf, hares, rabbits – anything except Music.

Yours ever
E.E.

I am not taking it EEsy (!) but am working at the W. Phil. Concert.

In replying to a letter to her from Jaeger, of 19 January, Mrs. Elgar, in hers of 20 January, wrote: 'When are we going to hear those wonderful sounds [Gerontius] again, the sooner you can tell us so, the better for my dear Dr!'s spirits & consequently for his work. I think there could be no *nobler* music than the symphony. I *long*[1] for it to be finished & have to exist on scraps – Do write & hurry him, it always does *some* good –'

Although Elgar claims to be avoiding music he tells Jaeger (there is no existing letter to this effect, but the inference is clear from Jaeger's response) of a projected, but never completed, chamber music work. On 28 January Jaeger wrote: '. . . String Sextet – eh? Good boy! Let me find you six players & we will try it over *here* [*at his house*] next time you are in town . . .

Look here! Prof. Buths will play the Variations in Düsseldorf on Feb. 7 . . . First performance in Germany in Nimrod's native place! I'm *so* glad. Won't you go over? . . .'

Craeg Lea,
Malvern.
Jan 27 [1901]

My dear Jaeger:

Only time for a scrawl. I don't think the Chorus need go in to the extracted score: it wd be well to put a *note* at the beginning of the Schluss saying the Chorus can be sung – or better that the score does for performance with chorus if desired.

I have turned on the Bradford people to the firm re concert Feb. 16. Do what you can!

Yrs ever
Bikily
E.E.

[1] twice underlined

Much love
God save the King![1]

[*W.P.S. paper*]

Craeg Lea
Malvern.
Jan. 30, [1901]

My dear Jay:
I am so glad about Düsseldorf – I would like to go & hear if it could be incog. but I fear to be known.

I enclose titles of full sc. Froissart – I wish it didn't look so like the newspapers' borders over the death of our beloved Queen – but I suppose it's all right.

I should like a Knight in full armour with gonfalons all round & shields & trumps of war. The Russians wd. give a nice coloured title like the Munich Kalendar.

We are proposing a *selection* from Gerontius for W.P.S.[2] we shall do much except the

nick's chorus.

Yrs ever
Nickely
Ed. E.

While at this time Elgar was consolidating his position in the larger world he was pursuing his local interests with fervour. For some perhaps this was excessive as when, following the example of the London Bach Choir he persuaded the W.P.S. to adopt this resolution: 'Performing Members shall be elected for *three* years only, at the expiration of which period they shall become non-performing Members; but on passing a test of efficiency they shall be entitled to re-admission as performing Members for a further period of three years.'

[1] Queen Victoria died on 22 January, and on the next day Edward VII held his first Privy Council.
[2] on 9 May

*At near-by Madresfield a Competitive Festival had been inaugurated by
Lady Mary Lygon. This included, however, two concerts by combined forces.
At the second of these in 1901, on 29 April, Elgar conducted Bach's* Blessing,
Glory, and Wisdom *and Parry's* Blest Pair of Sirens.

[*W.P.S. paper*]

Craeg Lea,
Malvern.
Feb 6, [1901] 12–15 p.m.

My dearie Jay:

Thanks *thousands* for the *facsimile.*

I'm sending as I sd. at ten o'clock as quickly as is possible for any
human being to do.

There is no soloist at Bradford for the Farewell only orchl. so I
suppose it's all right.

The Bach is for the Madresfield folk who have no money to spend
at all poor things!

Look here, if there's any difficulty send to me *& to Bradford* & say
they may do *only* the Prelude. I don't care a tinker's damn about Q's
Hall or London at all *only you*! so do what you think best.

Bless thee

E.E.

From Jaeger to Elgar, 11 February: 'Many, many thanks to Mrs.
Elgar & yourself for the charming photo of Craeg Lea, & the trombone
Exercise on back & the Fugue subject & Mrs. Elgar's explanation, and
last not least, (as they say in Germany) for Mrs. Elgar's kind letter. . . .

Now as to D'dorf[1]. The Variations seem to have been a great &
genuine success & Buths wrote to me a post-card & a letter & sent me a
few critiques which I enclose. . . . Buths wishes to repeat the work at
once with the municipal orchestra & I have told him he may use the
same score & parts, though another Society will use them. I hope &
believe this will be the beginning of the Variations tour through Germany. I was glad to see & hear that the D'dorf audience did not let
its political bias[2] darken its judgment of an English work of art.'

In the same letter Jaeger said that Henry Wood would play the 'Geronti us
Prelude and Finale' *on Ash Wednesday (at Queen's Hall).*

---

[1] on 6 February

[2] Colonial issues in general and the conduct of the Boer War in particular (a
German telegram of congratulation to Kruger after the failure of the Jameson
Raid in 1896 had proved exacerbating) led to strained relations between Britain
and Germany, which the Emperor's attendance at Queen Victoria's funeral did
little to assuage.

After going to Bradford to conduct on 16 February Elgar, accompanied by his wife, went on to London for Wood's concert on 20 February. During this visit they went to a performance of Henry V, *to the National Gallery, to lunch at Schuster's, where Lady Charles Beresford, Mrs. Beerbohm Tree, and J. F. Raffaelli, the French painter, were also guests. Jaeger was entertained to tea, and there was a supper-party at the Trees' house.*

[*W.P.S. paper*]

Craeg Lea,
Malvern.
Feb. 11 [1901]

My dear Jaeg: I sent off the sc & wind of Gerontius prelude etc to Bradford this a.m. early.

I think I'll cut out of the arrgt 2nd Ob. & B Clar. but will mark anything that strikes me in delicate pencil on the lovely score – Dodd is an angel, so is A.J.J. – so am I, but a d—d black one.

Yours ever
Ed. E.

It is so good to hear of your little one – we often talk over you.

At the Bradford concert on 16 February the programme contained the Prelude and 'Angel's Farewell' (here coupled together for the first time), Froissart, and four of the Sea Pictures (*Muriel Foster*). *On 1 March* Caractacus *was given in the city, and on 9 June the Hallé Orchestra, under Richter, played the* Variations.

[*W.P.S. paper*]

Craeg Lea, Malvern.
Feb. 12 [1901]

My dear Jaeger,

Many & various thanks for the papers & programme. I'm really glad they did not hiss Buths. We have a long letter from him this a.m. which my wife will answer in due course.

Bless you for sending the news & doing so much for a duffer like unto me.

I shall conduct the whole concert at *Bradford* & am coming up to London on Sunday & will bring the required parts *myself*. There's a train from Bradford arrvg. at 4 on Sunday. Will you tell Wood I'll send the parts across to Queen's Hall on Monday at 10. He won't want to see me so don't let him think I want to bother him.

Blessings on Brause: give him my love & say I'm going to be good
in future & write no more 'stuff' (and nonsense)
                        In mighty haste,
                           Yours ever,
                              Ed. Elgar

[*W.P.S. paper*]

                                                    Craeg Lea,
                                                    Malvern
                                                    March 20 1901
                                                    private

My dear Grosvenor:
        Gros veneur:
        Great Hunter:
        Nimrod:
        Jaeger:
        Bless him!
        We have had an awful time: I'm out again – certain I got
a fresh chill yesterday – Babbity (Carice) is practically all right &
my wife just creeps about the house.
                        Louse Deo!
as to that bar: I don't think it need go in. I'm sorry the score is to be
copied – ask the firm what a Geidel engraved score wd. cost. I might
think of it – I expect it's what Boosey wd. call 'a trifle' & I also think
the red bars shd. be snuffed. Is any *other* score of the "Prelude &
Farewell" available – I could draw Richter's attention to it, but it is
useless to expect him to do it unless he has the material at hand for
good so that he can rehearse any time.
    I cannot say anything to the composer you name – even to save
English music from an "exposure of ineptitude". – look at the Gloucester programme!
    I suppose [J. E.] West[1] is put in so that Brewer's new thing[2] may pass
easily! I hear from Davies that he is asked for Worcester[3] – so I feel
I'm some good in the world. otherwise I *do* hate it so very much
                        & the next
                           Yours ever
                              E.
P.S. Thanks for returning the 'Arms'. they're not my own. they're

[1] Anthem, *Lord I have loved the habitation of Thine house*
[2] Cantata, *Emmaus*
[3] 1902, *The Temple*

'W.N's'[1] as a matter of fact. Bless you! don't you know I'm quite a small authority on Heraldry – but you don't know me at all – yet!!

[*letter-card*]

[*postmark* Malvern, 29 March 1901]

Dear Duke:

I fear from your silence that something troublous may be going on, my sympathy is with you if that is so & my love always

Yours

E.E.

March 29.

Cockaygne on June 20[2] – you *must* be there.

On 24 March Elgar had finished Cockaigne. *A week later Henry Ettling (see* Elgar O.M., *p. 106) came to lunch. Ettling was a native of Mainz.*

[*letter-card*]

Private.

Ap 2 [1901]

My dear Jaeger:

Is anything going on or being done with the German version of *Gerontius*? A friend (Ettling) tells me it will certainly be done in Mayence if the Deutsch version is available & I understand Dr Strecker[3] (Schott) is sufficiently interested to help a performance. This is quite private so I have not written to the firm until I've asked for a little more news: this I can't do until I've something to say about the translation.

Yours ever

Ed. E.

You might send (*later*) Froissart score to Richter – not just yet – I'll write.

[*W.P.S. paper*]

Malvern.

Ap 7 [1901]

My dear Jaeger:

I told my wife you wd. spend your holiday writing letters & away came two – you had better have come yourself for the weekend &

---

[1] Winifred Norbury?

[2] at Queen's Hall, Philharmonic Society Concert

[3] Dr. Ludwig Strecker (1853–1943) was the owner of the firm of Schott: he was succeeded by his sons, Dr. Ludwig and Herr Willy Strecker.

jawed—gosh! I could talk sensibly into a German vacuum! I mean a receiver.

Thanks for news of the German of Gerontius: I hope it's not at a standstill – if so, we might ask the *Sea pictures* man – you never told me *how* that adaptation was done – well or ill – musically it's well done but poetically?

I know nothing of *any* festivals & fully conclude my countrymen do not want me any more – they want something which they can do without having to see the score & they can't read mine!

Many thanks for the 'Schattenbild' which I keep for your sake but the humour is too German to *enter* an English mind – there are differences one can't explain.

I *haven't touched* 'Sursum Corda', in fact I think the score you had made was for printing. I won't forget your singing birds – "Jaeger's cherubim" when I have a chance. I'm glad you like Brahms – you're getting on – you'll arrive at Ed: German etc etc soon.

You old Mosshead, go to bed & don't sit up playing the Nimrod Variation in the wrong key with pen & ink.

Oh! I wish I could see you for ½ an hour but it's 120 miles & that's a d—d long way.

Much love to you all

Yours ever

Ed: Elgar

My wife joins me in thanks for the Strauss pixter: it was awfully good of you to send it – my only Pfingsten not that Östernfest geschenk. Dame Alicia is very proud to have a letter from you all to herself.

[*W.P.S. paper*]

Malvern.

Ap 28 [1901]

My dear Jaeger:

It was 'awfully' jolly on Saturday morning & to see your dear old mug smiling approval on this idiot's hefforts. we shall be up (all *three* – Carice for the first time) this week & shall meet. Look here! this 'Chanson de Nuit' does not *do* for p.F. I have, I'm afraid, made a sad mess of the proof: just play it thro' & see if anything can be done to make it *look* clearer. The average pianist is a prize Ass: I gave it casually to an amateur (a poor one) & he could make *nothing* of this arrgt – couldn't see the tune. If the accpt. chords R.H. cd be in *small* type occasionally, leaving the theme big, the p. A. might nibble his carrot in peace & not get mixed up with the leaves – this is allegorical which,

as it's Sunday morning & allegory is the great prop of the Xtian
religion – (I'm not going to church it's raining but my wife has borrowed a shilling to go) is all right.

See if your young man can make the thing clearer to the

Yours ever
Ed. E.
which is a fool

*The Elgars were in London for the Queen's Hall concert on 4 May, when
the* Variations *were again played with great success. Jaeger was there, and
Elgar arranged for him to see Dr. Greville MacDonald, the E.N.T. specialist.
Elgar took Carice to see the sights of London in the intervals of entertaining,
being entertained, and correcting proofs of* Cockaigne. *He returned to
Worcester for the Worcestershire Philharmonic Society Concert on 9 May,
and was back in town ten days later. He attended the Richter Concert on
20 May, and on the next day went with Jaeger to the doctor and then to see
Mrs. Jaeger.*

[*W.P.S. paper*]

Malvern.
May 18 Saturday [1901]

My dear Jaeger:

We are so very glad to hear your eyes are better. I do want to
persuade you to see a specialist about the other matter. I am writing
this on the point of starting for London but I fear I shall be so busy
that I cannot promise myself the pleasure of seeing you this time as I
shall be with friends: I *ought* to come home on Monday but may stay
for the Richter concert on Monday & flit on Tuesday.

I never bother about papers now so I fear Lessmann's loquacious
angel must remain unread.

If I *can* get away I shall wobble around to Margravine Gardens on
Sunday but I fear me nay.

Yours ever
E.E.

I retd. the titles proofs to the firm.

at 8, Gloucester Terrace, N.W.
Monday [20 May 1901]

My very dear Jaeger:

I have fixed up to-morrow Tuesday at *11.15*

Dr Greville Macdonald, 85, Harley St. & will meet you at *eleven sharp* at Queen's Hall say about the Box Office. I cannot say how I thank you for promising to come & I hope for the best results.

Macdonald saw to my (supposed) hopeless throat six years ago (about) & I have never had any trouble since.

Greet your wife & 2 bairns from me – their wicked uncle – & turn up to-morrow without fail *on time* as the Yanx say.

Much love
Yours ever
Ed: Elgar

[*W.P.S. paper*]

Malvern.
May 22 [1901]

My dearie Jaeger:

Thanks for your note: good:

Now I hope you have arranged to come here to-morrow or Friday – to-morrow for choice & stay till Tuesday: as to trains: the best train (corridor) leaves Paddington at 1.40 & comes to *Great* Malvern: you can book to *Malvern Wells* & change at Gt Malvern. Let me know in time & we'll meet you. I am looking forward immensely to seeing you here & hope Cockaigne will be here too.

As to paying: yesterday was my wish & I am grateful to you for going with me to Macdonald & there's an end of that matter. Selah!

As to the next expense we'll talk later: I never borrow anything but have powerful friends & can borrow any amount & will sell my last book, stick & golfball for you, if necessary. Now only say *when* & then all will be settled to meet you.

Yours ever
Ed: Elgar.

Jaeger came up to Malvern on 24 May and was met at Great Malvern Station by Mrs. Elgar. He returned to London on 28 May and went into hospital (as also did Alfred Kalisch) the next day, when Elgar recorded a headache. On 3 June he came back to Malvern for a few days until Elgar left for Cambridge, on 6 June, to stay with Alan Gray and to conduct a performance of Sea Pictures *at which Stanford was present.*

[*W.P.S. paper*]

Malvern.
June 24 [1901]

My dear Jaggs,

No time to write! I returned Froissart at once (good boy!). This a.m. I return Prelude & farewell Gerontius strings: I don't think we need kick out that final bar for Prelude, especially as it's already engraved.

I send to the firm three *choruses* from 'it' – boiled down to S.A.T.B. (I hope you will see them).

The finale of the 'first part' wd be a fine thing for all funeral performances that ever were or ever will be. Why not start an Elgar society for the furtherance of

I'm very well but working hard. Oh! my string Sextett – & I have to write rot & *can* do better things.

I say! there's acksherly a steam-roller at work under my window. We killed four (4) (IV) foces (is[1] that the plural of fox?) on Tuesday.

_____
[1] twice underlined

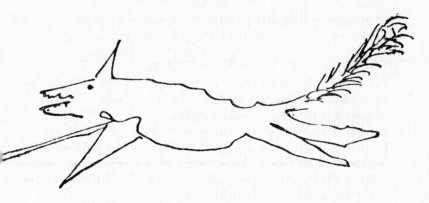

Bless thee & God save the King!
Yours ever
Edward Elgar.
★ a halo, not a Bug.

[*W.P.S. paper*]

Malvern.
June 26 [1901]

My very dear Jaeger:

I send some proofs back in anr. envelope. – *don't* send it me again: it's more bother than it's worth & takes me hours to worry over – Schott's give the arranging to a practical man & don't bother me at all – unless to send me a cheque for reading proofs – which No. 1 never does. Never mind about Cockaigne – I think you'll find it all right some day.

Now – I am wearily distressed about your ideas as to your nose etc. etc. You really must not let your nerves worry you & go at once to Macdonald & make him tell you things: I should think probably your symptoms are the natural sequence of affairs – I fear you brood over C. Woods[1] or whoever it was, & this is not good for you: now I feel I am a wretch all through & you feel I ought to write yards of sympathy – I *do* sympathise with you most deeply but I still trust it is chiefly worry & fret that causes you discomfort now: anyhow, go at once to the doctor & don't go on fretting over it. – let me know everything.

I am arranging with Brewer about taking some of the orkestration[2]: & hope it will relieve his mind & perhaps his wife's – oh, these wives

[1] Charles Wood?
[2] of *Emmaus*

of musicians – what they go through – & *suffer* – my heart bleeds for them sometimes, we MEN can buck up & fight; but the others——

Much love, yours ever

Ed. Elgar.

P.S. Brewer always says how can he '*repay me*' & you said '*pay me*' – I don't want any pay or return – I only want *them* to sleep a little in peace instead of lying awake o'nights.

During this time Elgar was working on incidental music for Grania and Diarmid (*Op. 42*), *which play, by W. B. Yeats and George Moore, was to be performed at the Gaiety Theatre, Dublin, in the autumn; the orchestration of Brewer's* Emmaus; *and – to the extent that he was* 'thinking about them' *– his* Pomp and Circumstance *Marches.*

Malvern.

July 1 [19]01

My dear Jaeger:

The parts of the extract from Gerontius must correspond with the score. P 3 'Cello part must be printed from the new plate: the old arrgt, which is not plain, was condemned long ago. The other string pts cd be altered with a pen – the stock on hand. The Grania *score* is now corrected & the *parts* must correspond as regards expression & phrasing with the M.S. parts – some slurs unaltered etc.

The piano arrgt I do not like in many places but really cannot go thro' it – why not have got Singer to do it or somebody used to the work.

In great haste, yours ever

Ed: Elgar.

Craeg Lea,

Malvern.

July 4, 1901

My dear Jaeger:

I have looked at the Analysis [of *Gerontius*] with much joy – I have not read it *all* but have looked at the marked passages & have noted some things. I say, *need* you call it a *Sacred Cantata* on the Analysis – that is of course the *trade* description but it occurs nowhere on the title I think, so don't perpetuate that dreadful term unless we're obliged. If it would not cut up your remarks too much I think I wd like the term 'Ruin' cut out – the idea is quite right – but the word is *heavy* – too direct–the 'sense of ruin' is the thing & that's too long a title–but I fear the outsider will scoff inwardly & outwardly at that little theme being supposed to represent RUIN.

I intended (see Ex. 34) all this peaceful music to be the 'memory (remembrance) of the soul' – an utter childish (childlike) peace – as described in an unset portion of the poem – the word *flight* wd lead the ASS to think of *rapid* movement – rapid movement *did* (or rather) *was* taking place but the Soul was not conscious of it exactly. Twig? Now let me thank you for your wonderful work: it makes all clear & is really the best analytical work I have ever read; what Heintz [?] is in German I don't know but it is nothing to yours for acute insight as I read it in English. Bless thee!

I note with joy & tears Dec. 19th. My devotion to Buths.

We go to the cottage, D.V. on Tuesday & hope for peace.

I have nearly finished Brewer's Emmaus & have taken much joy in doing it. I only fear one thing: & *it troubles me* – have I done Bell out of a job? If I have, tell me & he must be recompensed. I felt so much for Brewer's worries & thought if a week's work of mine could give him & his wife *rest* – I do know what it is to *want* it myself – I wd gladly give the week & more! Of course – though he offers, very kindly, to pay – I shall not – cannot accept anything for a friendly act but I fear I have done somebody out of a job & feel I ought to pay every incipient scorer all round for being allowed to help Brewer for nothing.

Oh! Lord (Oh! Jaeger) help my conscience.

We are better – I've had a cold.

Much love to you all

Yours ever

Ed. E.

P.S. Some of Emmaus is really beautiful & it *lends* itself to scoring in a ready & exceptional way. I have not made what I call an elaborate score but I hope it's artistic. You *must* hear it if only at rehearsal. You will *like* Brewer's Nos 1—7 & 11 tremendously.

BIRCHWOOD LODGE,

NEAR MALVERN.

July 11 [1901]

My dear Jaeger:

One line to say we arrived here & are in the intense quiet & solitude which I love.

Our colds are better & we live slowly.

I want a few of that Analysis; please make 'em cheap to me.

I can't afford the Bayreuth trip (or anything else)

I wish you would send me a copy of that Mazurka (pf *solo*) I began making a Vn solo of it & left it behind at Craeg Lea where it's safely (?) locked up.

Mr [Henry] Clayton[1] writes asking for more Ladies' trios which I am going to (try to) do.

Yours ever

Ed. Elgar

Birchwood,

Malvern.

July 17, [19]01.

My dear   :

Sorry to hear of Mrs Jay's illness & trust she's better now: my wife unfolded a wild scheme about you & yours having Craeg Lea & Buths &c &c – the scheme wd be nice if you cd all be *dropped* there without any preparation.

Bi*zz*i*ne*ss. I return the 8vo score with some slurs. I can*not* add passages without a lot of (*unnecy*) labour & a sight of the score – I *don't* think it worth doing either as I've lost all interest in my Music & the limbnation thing looks well enough as it is. It is really too good & delightful of Buths to have taken so much trouble & to have produced such an artistic result. As to the C. Bassi; we are of course accustomed to more in this country but I don't think we should say anything about it. I *hope* it will be a success for your sake and Buths' but it (being English) cannot be & will only be another millstone round the neck of me – for which I shall be expected to write polk*i* or something to pay for the blasted expense.

[1] Secretary and Director of Novello's: he joined the firm *c.* 1890 and died *c.* 1930.

I'm awfully busy just to-day – & cross – & have something (a bruised nerve Doctor says) in my foot. Damn everything especially – ah!

Yours ever

Ed Elgar

While the Elgars were at Birchwood the Jaegers and Professor Buths and his daughter came to stay at Craeg Lea. Jaeger was grateful for this holiday – he could hardly afford any other – for he was expecting further surgical treatment for his nasal complaint. At the same time he welcomed the opportunity to discuss the forthcoming Düsseldorf performance of Gerontius, *over which the Elgars organized several tea-parties. During this period – on 23 August – the second* Pomp and Circumstance March *was finished and posted to Boosey's who had received the first at the end of July.*

'That we shall', *wrote Jaeger on 18 July*, 'take the greatest care of your house & all that is therein I need hardly say. We are no vandals but more or less civilised Teutons.'

On 31 July Mrs. Jaeger wrote to Mrs. Elgar, commenting that 'The Professor remarked that he had never imagined the place would be as beautiful as it is, & he keeps ejaculating Ach! wie schön! so ruhig!'

Birchwood,

Malvern.

July 26 [1901]

My dear Jaeger:

My wife will have allayed your worries over our house: there is no bother at all, at all: but in the hurry of writing & telegraphing my wife was in doubt if she made it *quite* clear to Buths that we were away; but that's understood all right so where's the trouble?

As to Olaf: (*why* is it not printed?) a break has been made after the little bird chorus in performance, but as far as I can remember the work that's 2/3 of the way through.

As to the vocal score of Gerontius: by all means add the things you name, i.e. the little notes after No 9. If I could have the *full score* for a few days I wd add a Violin passage or two if you *really* think it worth doing. Remember (Private) that your countrymen never approach an English work with even a semblance of interest or respect – it is only something 'pour rire' after all & I cannot hope that my work will fare better than Sullivan's etc. *Don't* put in the Vio passage p.3 voc sc. line 10, bars 3 & 4. I should really like to do anything useful or helpful to a good appearance – but cui bono?

Now once more I hope you & Buths will settle down all right at Craeg Lea & be assured there's really *no* bother.

We are in the midst of fourteen (14) separate thunderstorms all blazing all day round these hills & I'm tired of the row: it's as loud as Cockaigne.

Yours ever

Ed. E.

P 110 Gerontius: I could add the string & harp passages for 6 bars if I had 'em. What would a scarlet cloth copy cost unto me? I want to give the Squire[1] one if I can.

On 15 August Elgar went to South Wales, to stay in a cottage taken by Miss Rosa Burley. Miss Burley's account of this holiday runs as follows:—

'In August I took a cottage at Llangranog in a little corner of Cardiganshire. It is a little cluster of houses in a small land-locked bay. Boats could only come in in good weather because of the huge rocks. My mother and sister came with [me] and nieces and a nephew from S. Africa, and a pupil Joyce Crane who was homeless for the time being. There was good bathing in the bay and sometimes the children could go out in the boats with the men after the lobster pots. Our cottage was next door to the one and only pub and the steep road down from the hills ended here and made a little quay with a low wall to which high tide came up, so that sometimes, causing great excitement, a little fishing boat would sail right up to the door. We were very happy here. It seemed like a foreign country with all the people speaking Welsh. The young people had a wonderful time.

I had a very melancholy letter from Edward who was in one of his black moods of depression and was unable to do anything. I thought he was needing a change so I asked him to come down to this remote place. We could find him a bedroom in the village and [he could] come to meals with us. There was nothing he enjoyed more than making a complicated journey. He had a great taste for conundrums, enigmas, cross-word puzzles and the thing he loved best was Bradshaws Railway Guide. This journey to Llangranog was after his own heart.

The nearest station to Llangranog was fourteen miles away & we ordered a farmer's cart to meet him. He appeared at Carmarthen station and asked for a ticket to a little station halfway up the line. The Railway Clerk said "No train stops there today."

Sir Edward [*sic*] – "Oh yes! it does and I demand a ticket."

The Clerk – "Well! I can't issue one unless I receive special instructions."

Sir Edward – "Who can give you special instructions?"

Clerk – "The station master could."

[1] Mr. Little, of Birchwood Lodge, landlord of Elgar's summer retreat, friend, and sometime (honorary) bicycle tutor

Counterpoint
for a piece
for strings

Gregorian melody for *The Apostles*

Sir Edward – "Well! fetch the station master."

After a time the station master arrives wiping froth from his moustache.

Station Master – "Now what's this fuss about?"

Clerk & Sir Edward both explain the position.

Station Master – "Oh yes! I know it used to stop at little station, but it *doesn't stop now.*"

Sir Edward produces New copy of Company Timetable on which it stated in small print 1.15 will stop at little station on Wednesday & Thursday by request. "I make my request for a ticket to little station and to go on the 1.15 train."

Station Master to Clerk – "Now issue a ticket for little station to this gentleman. Send a telegram to the Station Master at little station to say the train will stop there and send another wire to the driver[1] to warn him to stop the train at little station."

Sir Edward gets into the train and seats himself comfortably. The train starts and proceeds in such a usual manner that the driver forgets all about stopping at little station until he catches a glimpse of the Station Master and the only porter standing stiffly to attention.

The Station Master & porter stand together on an otherwise deserted platform. They stare in amazement as the train goes rumbling through. The engine driver being a man of great resource and being reminded of his telegram by the sight of the station master & entire staff puts on all the brakes he has got and pulls the train to a standstill about half a mile from the platform. He then backs the train to the platform & pulls it up exactly in the right place, a perfect example of timing and execution. Sir Edward opens the door himself and also closes it before handing his ticket to the astonished staff. The engine driver sounds a blast on the whistle and goes on his way. This was part of his adventurous journey. He was too nervous to drive down the steep hill road which simply dropped into the bay, so he got out and walked. By the time he arrived he was in the highest of spirits.

He had never stayed at the seaside in his life and knew nothing about it but he was very happy.

We rigged up a bathing suit for him out of an old pair of pyjamas and he did not mind when my little niece told him that he looked like a monkey!

We were in and out of the water all day. The children went off in the boats after lobster pots, and they often got shrimps in the bay. There were mussels and winkles on the rocks. Edward was quite

[1] An extension of fact into fancy: the station-master at Carmarthen would have told the driver.

unrecognisable – He shouted with glee and played about like a little boy.

We had to walk about and forage for vegetables which we bought from the cottages. Mushrooms grew in plenty in the moist valleys.

In the evenings a little company of men used to collect on the little quay in front of the pub. They used to talk & smoke and then someone would hum a note and they would all sing a hymn or song in four part harmony. It was so natural and beautiful. One day as we looked across the bay we saw a party of folk on the hillside & wondered what they were doing. Presently we heard them singing. It must have been a choir or choral society out for a holiday. The music as it came to us across the bay was quite entrancing. Edward was entranced and he [brought something like it into the Welsh Overture *deleted*] when he wrote the Introduction & Allegro for string quartet & string orchestra he translated the effect of the hillside singing and used it as the second subject of that work.

We went for a day's excursion & met a man walking with a coracle on his back and a fine salmon which he had caught in the Teify. We bought the salmon from him & took it home in triumph. We often waded out at low tide to the little island of Inys Lochtryn [*sic*]. There were a few sheep on it, but the views of the beautiful coast were lovely.'

That Elgar had a Welsh Overture in mind is indicated by the suggested scoring of the 'Welsh' melody in his sketch book, which is also inscribed 'Ynys Llochtryn' [sic].

Birchwood,
Malvern.
Wednesday [14(?) August 1901]

My dear Jaeger:

Glad to hear of you! You will have received my note of enquiry. I have returned a week from *Llangringoggywoggypygwgssill*.

Bless you I have not touched Gerontius neither will I do much but I enclose on a sheet one or two points. I don't know how to join the 'Allge Deutsche M.Verein'; surely this is not the obscene society that men like Dr Maclean etc belong to? Tell me more & see if I am worthy to jine.

I will D.V. be at Brewer's rehearsal & hope you will sit with me during Emmaus & lend me a copy – that's put down for 2–30 on Wednesday.

Sorry you are not going to Glo'ster – you really couldn't well work your criticising from Hasfield (eight miles) I shall probably go to no performances at all.

It is pleasant to think that you & yours enjoyed Craeg Lea. Buths writes to-day but his letters require prayer & fasting before tackling.

Hope your wife & bairns are well.

Love, yours ever
Edwd Elgar

Birchwood
Malvern.
Aug 31 [1901]

My dear Jäger:

Good: I'll bring the Skourghowrore[1] (that's the best yet!) with me in my Bag: it's difficult to get it to rail or post.

Sorry to hear you talk of your nose – I must see about this when I come.

I saw Prof. Sanford last year but it's never any good: these Johnnies only talk-alk-alk-alk-alk- with a blasted twang. Anyhow I'll be amiable & *nice* (fancy me!)

I don't want any novelties xcept Emmaus.

Much love
Yrs ever
E.E.

[*W.P.S. paper*]

Malvern
Tuesday October 1, 1901

My dear Jaeger:

The Vars will be rehearsed in Leeds only Saturday morning & Tuesday if necy.

I've been awfully busy writing & have finished the short incidental music to that Irish play: there's a funeral march which you wd. like & it sounds big and weird – not deep in the orchl. whirlwind sense

Much love
Yrs ever
Ed E

The following is copied at the end of this letter by Jaeger:
'Ich lese mit wachsender Freude die Partituren von Elgar, der

[1] German vocal score of *Gerontius*

wirklich ein interessanter famoser Kerl ist. Die Overture [Cockaigne]
ist ein prachtvolle . . . .[1]

*The Variations were performed at Leeds on 11 October, Elgar conducting.
After returning to Malvern Elgar went north again, to rehearse the Marches in
Liverpool, to dine with Richter and to attend his concert in Manchester, and
to hear the first performance of the Marches on 19 October. The next day the
Variations were given in St. George's Hall. Because of some confusion Elgar
missed Wood's rehearsals of the Marches and their London première on 23
October. On 24 October he was again in Manchester to hear Richter's
rehearsal of* Cockaigne.

*A letter from Jaeger, of 16 October, shows a new appreciation of Elgar in
Novello's, and also indicates a commission – for the Norwich Festival (of
1905 presumably) – which was never completed and of which no traces
remain:* 'When', *wrote Jaeger,* 'are you going to send us your Norwich
Cantata? Now, you will send *that* to us won't you? You *ought* to
anyhow, seeing what we are doing for Gerontius here & in Germany;
& we shall pay you just as well as Boosey & Full Scores won't be any
difficulty in future, I guess. I have had another long talk about you to
Messrs. A[lfred]. & A[ugustus]. L[ittleton]. & you need fear no worries
in future. They have had an eye-opener over the Leeds Festival & I'm
sure they'll meet you in every way in future. You know when they
have taken to a man they'll do *any mortal thing* for him as in the case of
Sullivan & Stainer. Only understand each other a little better & all will
go like a house on fire & you can't deal with a better firm. . . .'

*Fame, however, was unremunerative. When Elgar had conducted in
Bradford at Cowen's request he was offered expenses* 'and even a small fee'.
On 7 November a Diary entry tells its own story: 'E. to the Mount [Miss
Burley's school in Malvern] to arr. orch. class.'

Craeg Lea,
Malvern.
Sunday Oct. 13: [19]01

My very deary J.

Here are some proofs – most lovely to see – so beautifully set out &

---

[1] cf. undated letter from Jaeger, previous to Elgar's visit to Leeds: 'Did Ettlinger
tell you what Weingartner wrote to him. . . . If not, I can give you the exact
words . . . which I copied from W.'s letter . . . "Ich lese mit wachsender Freude die
Partituren von Elgar, der wirklich ein interessanter, famoser Kerl ist. Die Ouver-
ture ist ein *Prachtwerk*".' ['I am reading the scores of Elgar with increasing
pleasure. He really is an interesting and excellent fellow. The Overture is a
marvellous work.']

engraved – my thanks to the firm & to you & most of all to dear Brause & his Men. – the engraving is better than the music. I need not refer to the corrections I have suggested. Tell me, isn't it *'grammar'* to say Allo *di* molto (p. 28) I forget. p. 31. Shall we add those demoniacal *fourths* small – please decide: there's no room for them in the *second* group of semiquavers – but perhaps the *first five* wd suggest the passage.

Do. do. p. 32, but here the whole lot can go in without re-engraving nicht wahr? – of course *if you*[1] *decide* to add 'em. p. 34 Buths' note is of course best.

p. 35. I don't think the *col. voc.* need be in – it's superfluous anyhow & if in shd, I think, be in the plural.

p. 45. Geistes, eh?

p. 52. the whole thing looks so lovely that I cd not help querying the position of the slurs. Yes! the sound of the Variations was splendid & it was a great triumph. They are down *zum ersten Male* Mainz, Wiesbaden. Weingartner is taking Cockaigne on tour with the Kaim orchestra! The Overture is also down at Boston, Chicago[2] & Pittsburg – 3 different orchestras! *Things is humming.* Much dear love from us to you all. We are so very glad to hear good accounts.
Schuster *wept all thro Nimrod.*

ever yours
Ed. Elgar

From Jaeger to Elgar, 18 October: '. . . I say, your Black Knight, which is spanking fine stuff, doesn't move much for some reason or other, chiefly no doubt, because the subject is a bit gruesome & the music ends poetically pp.   I have thought that if we could do something with the work for orchestra alone, we might make it better known, & it has struck me that the Banquet music (Menuet etc) might be done in a short orchestral Suite. Do you think there is anything in the idea? . . .'

66, Huskisson Street, Liverpool.[3]
Saturday [19 October 1901]

My very dear Jaeger:

Everything has gone to you now – I've really 'bucked-up' & kept nothing longer than a day except the odd sheets.

I fear a letter I wrote answering many points has never reached you – the one in which I replied re dedication inter alia.

---

[1] *you* three times underlined
[2] For Boston and Chicago performances – due to the interest of Theodore Thomas – see *Mus. T.*, February 1902, p. 117.
[3] Rodewald's house: see *Elgar O.M.*, pp. 108–10.

Yes. A.M.D.G. etc etc as in Eng. edn, please.

I note all you say & *when ready* will certainly come to 1, B[erners]. St. *Say so.* The Irish play music I am having *copied* out for Wood as I may (silentium) utilise it for an opera later. I wish you wd do something with the poor old B[lack]. K[night]. – I haven't time. Why not communicate with the Johnny who did Sursum Corda – I'll find his address & write again – a good chap for selections, small orch. arrgts etc etc. Alas! we have no Britisher who does that sort of thing, they're all for *great* original work.

We can't get to London for Tuesday I fear. We're doing the Marches here to-night.

Much love to you all 4.

Yours ever
Ed. E.

at 66 Huskisson Street,
Liverpool
Home on Friday
[24 October 1901]

My dear Jaeger: *private*

Mr. Ernest Newman is anxious to write in one of the reviews articles on modern English music – you know his writings I expect[:] he lives here & was talking over the project. I understand the idea is to write an introductory article & then take different men, one to each subsequent article – beginning with E.E. as the 'Leader of the revolution'!!!

Now he wants to see scores. the *printed* ones he has at his disposal if not his own property but my big M.S. scores are necy for his work – will you bring this before the firm? He's a responsible person & you need not fear to lend them to him: if it can be done he shd see *everything*. I won't write any more now just off to Manchester – orchestra the finest I ever heard not so big as Leeds but gorgeous. I conducted Cockayne at Rehearsal yesterday at Richter's request!

I have heard that those cocky marches went well.

Yours ever with undying affection
from us both
E.E.

at 66, Huskisson Street, Liverpool.
Home to-day Friday.
[25 October 1901]

My very deare Jaeger:

Many abundant thanx for your telegram. I cannot possibly come up – Wood asked me to rehearsal this a.m. at 10–12 – but I only recd the letter at 9.15 so couldn't come in time to be of any use & I ain't much ornament nohow in giddie London town.

Thanks for your very kind thought (p.c. &c) – I don't get papers here – London papers I mean save fitfully & late in the day or days old – & I feel – or rather felt – in the dark at Q's Hall proceedings[1]. Now I understand that they played two badly scored marches without any tune & that they were hissed off: nicht wahr? I come up next Friday & shall smite you under the 5th rib, but hope to find you well before I do it. Cockaigne was *golorious* last night under Richter. I don't think any of you London Johnnies know what orchestral playing is until you hear the Manchester orchestra (*in Manchester* that is, in their own room). Coriolan was colossal & Brahms' No 3 Sym. overpoweringly fine.

Much love
Yours ever
Ed. Elgar.

The eight sketch books for which Elgar asks are now in the Elgar archives. No. I is dated 19 November 1901, and the opening pages contain material (headed 'Ynys Lochtryn') which would appear to have been intended for a 'Welsh Overture' (see p. 142) but was transferred to The Apostles (Part I).

Jaeger to Elgar, 26 October: '. . . Wood tells me he hopes to do your Symphony at the Festival if it's ready. Now I don't suppose it will be ready unless you have an inspiration for the slow movement yet. But let me tell you now that Nimrod relies on your offering that Symphony to your old original publishers as in duty bound, (ahem) . . . The Marches are worrying me into an illness. The Tunes, damn them, keep buzzing in my empty head, & the orchestral effects, harmonies & all your monkey tricks dance about & within me. The things are splendid & will make your name known everywhere. Send *us* Nos 3, 4, 5, & 6 of the Series, pray . . .'

In a postcard (23 October) Jaeger had remarked: 'Your splendid marches were the greatest success I have ever witnessed over a novelty

[1] Promenade Concerts (24 August – 8 November)

at any concert. The hall was only half full alas! (though the Promenade was pretty crowded) but the people made such a row & kept it up for so long that No 2[1] had to be repeated in toto. What a pity you were not there. That tune in No 2 is glorious . . .'

In fact Wood gave a double encore to placate an enraptured audience. See My Life of Music, Henry J. Wood, pp. 203–4.

Craeg Lea,
Malvern.
Nov 6 1901.

My dear old Jaybird:

We arrived home last night & found this place overwhelmed with *fog*! it has, we learn, been buried in it since Sunday: this evening it is clearer – & so am I.

'Kere! I've told Ernest Newman (quite a young man) 54, Grove St, Liverpool to write to the firm about the scores & have written to them also about it.

I *wish* you would do some thing for me! My sketch books are rotten – I know the sketches are & so do you "& *Mrs Barnett*[2] *says so too!*" Now I want some new ones: do get for me 12 quires of *oblong* [12 stave – *deleted*] paper (B. & H. No. 23, 6, 7, 9, sizes which see 3 quires of each) & have each 3 quires bound in buckram or art linen or some decent coloured cloth (*all different colours*) & send 'em down to me within *3 daze*[3]: with your vast machinery I know you can do it – I'll give you a week to do it in. Do be a good angel (for once) & send me these otherwise many

noble (?) thoughts!

mean (?) cabbages!

will be lost to the world & to YOU.

Yours as you demean yourself
E.E.

P.S. I hear strange things about that letter but I have not seen it yet – it never came here if sent.

4 different colours of binding, mind you, & no beastly colours either – something artistic. The paper need not be B. & H's of course – only something near their size – your own will do. I pray thee let one sketch book be bright scarlet!

---

[1] Jaeger means No. 1, in D major.

[2] a myth of Elgar's invention, see illustration facing p. 161, *Elgar O.M.*

[3] *daze* twice underlined

[*W.P.S. paper*]

Malvern, Nov 9 1901

My dear J.

I say I'm knocked over: Rodewald came last night & announced to me the great surprise about the Robes – I don't know what to make of you all & am in a fit of the *blues* thinking of the kindness of you all for which I have done nothing to deserve – it's very odd & dreamlike & I don't know who I am; or where we are, or who's who, or anything – perhaps in a week I shall realise the thing.

Now as to the sketch books: you are a duck. 1 inch will be too thick so please make 8 books 4 limp & 4 stiff – I hope it's no trouble to you *really* if I give the order in an ordinary way it would take *weeks, – weeks, weeks.* Yes oblong is right; 10,000 thanx.

I am *awfully* stunned about poor Jacques[1]: *do*[2] be kind to him – I trust & hope something may be done to make matters smooth. Oh! dear, these quarrels.

As to the Symphony – we did talk of it & *if ready* the festival shall have it, of course, but there's not the slightest chance of my doing it I fear – there's the Norwich work – a real paying commission – to complete – (for you to see) – & 100 other things to come first.

You are *quite* wrong about Manchester: oh! you stupid Cockaigners.

I am so very glad about Pitt's Suite[3] & want to see it: give my love to him – but I forgot I have to write to him about another matter.

Send oh! send those sketch books!!!!!!!

Yours ever
Ed Elgar

[*W.P.S. paper*]

Nov. 12 [1901]

Dear old Moss-head:

I know this is only a half sheet. YAH!

Many thanks for delaying my sketch books – how proud (& tidy) I mean to be when I get them – but you are so slow & I shall have ceased holding the pen by the time they come. Now. there are to be *eight* books, nicht wahr? Well then, by all that is colourable let's have eight tints. I have *sewn*(?) – tied I think I mean 8 together & if that's

---

[1] presumably Edgar F. Jacques (1850–1907), editor of the *Musical World* (1888), *Mus. T.* (1892–7), music critic of *The Observer* (1894) and author of Queen's Hall programme notes

[2] twice underlined

[3] a *Suite de Ballet,* entitled *Dance Rhythms,* played at Promenade Concert on 7 November

the correct number please, in the esteemed mossiness of your 'greiser Kopf' use those. In any case use the four you, in the esteemed mossiness of your 'greiser Kopf' chose, 'cos I shall like 'em better'n what I choose myself.

You, in the xtra mossiness of your head (less esteemed) have a woful idea of the Symphony. Manchester as you say can & will wait – not so Coving Garden & *several* 100 other things – which, in the extra esteemed mossiness of your greiser Kopf you will *not* mention please deary. Raining cats & dogs.

Yours mossily, moodily, merrily & melancholy
E.E.

The Robes have not come yet. I'll let you know – I *want* 'em now to appear at Court.

The reference above to Covent Garden (Festival?) led Jaeger to observe on 14 November: '. . . *And* have you a good libretto? . . . Don't set impracticable stuff to music, for Heaven's sake. So much good music has been ruined through silly, ineffective, preposterous, dull, unimaginative, etc etc librettos . . .'

Craeg Lea, Malvern.
Nov. 13: [19]01

Pig[1]:

I wrote ages ago about that piano arrangement [of *Gerontius*, Finale] – I told you a letter or two must have gone astray – or you have, or – anything has.

I think you had better omit the little notes – & would it not be best to cut the Finale from 129 to 136: we played it so at Gloucester. If you want it *all* – the piano pt wants some amplification in places (see 132).

As to those Sketch books – I'm wearying for 'em – *no* lettering. If room on the back I should like

I
II
III

etc, only large.

If no room on back then on the front middle as big as this *at least.*

I do hope poor old Jacques will not be worried: I don't know anything about it but I imagine no one can say anything bad enough about that paper.

Now, if those sketch books don't arrive in one day from this I shall be ill – nothing to write on.

[1] three times underlined

Looke here: If I tear things – 1st sketches I mean – up, you say I'm a fool. If I send 'em to you you say I'm a conceited ass. So I send you one or two scraps: if you do not want 'em my little wife does.

E.E's M.S.S. = pearls?
Jaybird = Swine?
D'ye see.

                                    E.E.
Tell Pitt I sent him an important letter to Q's Hall – I have lost his new address for the moment.

                              Craeg Lea,
                              Malvern.
                                    Nov 14 [1901]
My dear Jaeger:
    Look here! Here's some rot & you can jeer at my conceit if you like – but if you don't want these sketches keep 'em for me 'till I fetch 'em: I hope the new sketch books will be leading me to superior tidiness
                         Yours ever
                         Edwd Elgar

[*letter-card*]   [*postmark* Malvern, 17 Nov. 1901]
                              Sunday
My dear Jaeger:
    Oh! those books are lovely & I have been using one cruelly hard – I will not write too fast I promise you – I don't *publish* fast whatever I write anyhow. I want a sketch book bound in *Human skin*[1] to write some of the things I am doing now. I am *not* doing an opera yet you antique papagei. Tell me if you have any human skin handy.
                         Love
                         E.E.
10,000 thanx for all the trouble you took: & to the stitchers & binders etc etc.

    The notion that the trio of the first March *should go into the* Coronation Ode[2] *prompted Jaeger to write thus, on 6 December:* '. . . I say, you will have to write another tune for the Ode in place of the March in D tune (Trio). I have been trying much to fit words to it. that drop to E & bigger drop afterwards are quite impossible in singing *any* words to them, they sound downright vulgar. Just try it. The effect is fatal. No, you must write a new tune to the words & not fit the words to this

───────────

[1] twice underlined
[2] Correspondence with A. C. Benson over this work began on 21 March 1901; the first draft of 'Land of Hope and Glory' was dated 10 December.

tune. Consider this carefully & give no Choir a chance of scooping down. It will sound horrible. Try it (no extra charge) . . .'

Craeg Lea,
Malvern.
Dec 9 [1901]

My dear Jaeger:

I haven't time to answer all your *impertinent* letters, Yah!

I've sent a line to Godfrey[1].

Have been correcting proofs & parts for two days and my eyes are not good. Here's Godfrey's letter.

Have had charming letters from Buths – have not decided when to start yet. My wife has been sorely laid up with an awful cold & we fear the weather for her – *and* my eyes. The doctor wants me to give up as much music writing as possible! so do the publishers & the critix – and the public – and the other composers & so does

Ed: Elgar.

P.S. I'll write to the firm about my things when they're ready[2]. I don't want them to buy any 'pigs in Bags' – I was delighted to find the gown etc on Tuesday & hope to wear 'em to the credit of the profession; it is awfully good of everybody & I am much touched & overcome. Thanx.

On 9 December Jaeger returned to the theme of the Covent Garden commission referred to on p. 150. 'Don't', *he writes,* 'cook up Caractacus for Covent Garden. It will never do. Write a real opera, & wait a year or two. I cannot imagine Englishmen or Englishwomen, however operatically fashionable & blasé enjoying Britons being shown on the stage under the conqueror's yoke. . . . I have studied Caractacus again & cannot see anything operatically effective in it, except the Love Duet & the March with Britons tied captive to the conqueror's "wheels". DON'T!!!'

On 16 December Elgar arrived in Düsseldorf where he was met by Buths. Gerontius *was performed on 19 December (see German press reports reprinted in* Mus. T., *February 1902, p. 100, and a report from* 'Our Special Correspondent').

He also visited Mainz where he was entertained by Fritz Volbach.

---

[1] Dan Godfrey, conductor of the Bournemouth Orchestra?

[2] 'Funeral March' from *Grania*, and *Concert Allegro* for pianoforte (Op. 46), written for Fanny Davies, but never published. The latter was played by Fanny Davies at St. James's Hall on 2 December.

1902

*Having reached London on New Year's Day Elgar lunched at Pagani's
with Mr. and Mrs. Henry Wood and Percy Pitt, and attended part of a
Promenade Concert. When he reached home he settled to* Dream Children;
and a hymn (Oh mightiest of the mighty), *after some protestation, for
the forthcoming Coronation.*

Craeg Lea
Jan 3 [19]02

My dear Jäger:

Thanks for the p.c. re Düsseldorf. I am in the midst of awful epistolary confusion – a whole *sack* of things came up in a cab from the
Mount & I have had to sort 'em out & answer what I can.

That Hymn is all 'wrong' – hymns always are – look at the accents
in the first lines – then the words [require a *deleted*] pause [or long note
deleted] at end of third line in every stanza *except* 2 which requires to
go on at once. That's the reason I never write hymn tunes – they are so
ghastly inartistic

I'll try.

The horrible musical atmosphere I plunged into at once in this
benighted country nearly suffocated me – I *wish* it had completely

Yours ever
Ed. Elgar

P.T.O. Urgent.

Private. I am hoping to do *Prelude & Farewell* on Feb 1 after all in
London (Clara Butt) & *Angel's song* (Alleluia). Can the parts be had for
that? – you have strings but how about woodwind & horns – you have
a double set of wood but the horns wd. (might) have to be copied for
the concert. More when I've breath.

Craeg Lea,
Malvern.
Jan 9: [19]02

My dear Jaeger:

As to the Hymn Tune I thought £10/10/– but as it's for a special occasion it may be worth less on that account or more! The firm I think always treat me fairly & they must say please & I'm silent & satisfied. If there should be anything due to me (Mazurka, Violin arrangement for instance) I should be glad to have it as it is an awkward time of year financially.

I was going to write to the firm about this but you can shew it: also I wanted to ask them if someone might, on their behalf, hear the Funeral March (Grania) at Q's Hall[1]. I want £100 for it & have not *offered* it to anyone, although it has been enquired for by other publishers on the production of the play in Dublin.*

Yours ever sincerely
Edwd. Elgar

* The March wd. arrange in every possible way & there's now room for a new dead march I think.

Craeg Lea,
Malvern.
Jan 13, 1902.

My dear Jaeger:

Many thanks for your long letter: you know the one I mean. I am ill & have only crept out of bed to scrawl a few very necessary lines to 2 or 3 folk.

I am glad to hear about Gerontius at the Fest[2] – more for your sake than my own. I am dead to these wonders – About the strings used at D'dorf – if there is anything *written in by the players* worth notice I had better see them. I *hope* to be up on Friday for Wood's rehearsal at 12. *Come in.*

Percussion received – I await the full score. Oboe & Cor.A. also received. Now that's business.

I'm awfully distressed to hear you are again ill & terribly disappointed that our operation was not finally successful. I wish you all the good things & only wish I could put this right for you; do tell me what can be done & how & when? I think hourly about you & worry about it till I'm sick – which is human but not poetic. As to your long

[1] on 18 January
[2] at Worcester

letter: my things are successful among musicians but the public don't buy them [.] Boosey's (to whom I went owing to that unfortunate business connected with that New Brighton concert) – are very good but I know that they don't make a fortune out of me, *except* the Sea-pictures. My music does not arrange well for the piano & consequently is of no commercial value. If I had a free mind I shd like to write my chamber music, & symphony etc. etc, on all of which forms of art providence has laid the curse of poverty. Bless it! So I don't see how any publisher cd. be persuaded to endow an *artistic* writer: why should they? If I write any stuff at all somebody is bound to publish it – & they all say it's no good – they are proud to do such stuff 'cos it's in all the high class programmes etc etc. But providence, as I've often told you, is against all art so there's a satisfactory end.

Yours ever
Ed. E.

I shd. be glad to consider anything you have to say of course & thank you a 1000 times for thinking of it.

Jaeger's letter, to which the above is a reply, does not exist. Letters from him dated 13 and 15 January are concerned with the engraving of the parts of Gerontius *for Germany. At the end of the latter, however, Jaeger reports a fine notice of the Düsseldorf Concert in the* Münchener neueste Nachrichten *of 30 December.*

Craeg Lea,
Malvern.
Feb 3 [1902]

My dear Jaeger:

No time for kompoliments – that sextett will not be ready for years – trade my boy, trade before everything – every damn thing.

Now. I want you [to] tell me this: the poor competition folk are doing Bach's (so-called in English Novello edn) 'Blessing glory and wisdom',

      661, 8vo choruses.

I suppose it's intended to be unaccompanied? we did it *with organ* last year & this year are doing it again but *in Malvern*, here they have no organ & the simple villager is no good with one rehearsal unless he has a fair buzz going on. Can you tell me if any *orchl* arrgt has ever been done – London is the hotbed of all such atrocities – in the country we are much too artistic unless for a special object like the present, when we want the proletariat to have a good, healthy, honest & (at the same time – very seldom they all go together – (sarkazzum) Xtian

Shout! Do tell me, otherwise I must suggest the thing being arranged –
not by E.E. for strings.

Hope you are all well.
Yours ever
Ed. Elgar.

Craeg Lea,
Malvern.
Feb 6 1902.

My dear Jaeger:

By this post came Mr Broughton's M.S. of the transposition – I have
only had time to look at the *alterations* & find it all right & of course
exceedingly well done – I have only altered *one* place – last bar p.6 et
seq: so as to give the C.Bi their original 'entry' which always gives
me a nice fat feeling in the tummy.

I don't know Mr Broughton personally or I wd. like to thank him
for doing it so 'friendlily' & well, but when I have thanked some of
these young composers they have sat upon me wearily & called me
names – so I am shy – but, through dear Kalisch, I wish him well
always & in this case I thank him: tell me, shall I send the fee to him
direct or what?

Oh! 'drop your eye' on my green ink 'die Böse Farbe' (Schubert). I am frantically busy & take no joy in my work.

In the excessive mossyness of your head I salaam

Yours ever,
Ed. E.

I keep my M.S. score *for the present*, to refer to when Geidel's proofs come – that will be best, won't it?

Craeg Lea,
Malvern,
Feb 7 [1902]

My dear Jaeger:

It was perfectly criminal of me to let this go by – the thing is this – in the original where the Cho[ru]s sang the *same note* it is better to have the final syllable ⎰ -- er ⎱ on the *second* bar of ¾ – *but* in the appx. I
⎱ dich ⎰
didn't like the (unavoidable) drop of a 5th *slurred*, so I put the above syllables on the *first* bar of ¾. Now – when the German proofs came they had put the syllable on the second bar – this seemed to me to save confusion & a lot of explanation to the chorus, so *please* let it go *on the second bar* as at first: after all the voices will not be heard much & endless confusion will be avoided.

I have sent the two pages of score corrected to Geidel direct.

This is my ink! I've *no* commission for Bristol & wouldn't take one. Bless thee! Don't you fidget.

Pomp & cirkumstance have been out in various editions for a fortnight I believe; do you want any? & if so, what?

I think all your acquaintances are well, including the lovely 'Betty'.

I've hurt my finger & cut myself in 3 places shaving & have sciatica.

YAH!
Much love.

Tell me if Broughton is a 'nice' decent chap.

Yours ever
Claudius Monte*verde*[1]

Craeg Lea,
Malvern.
Feb 15 [1902]

My dear old Jaeger:

We are so dreadfully sorry to hear you are laid up & hope you will be soon all-right again.

[1] four times underlined

M.H. must have puzzled you extremely – it means Moss Head, no less. So you see you *are* a M.H. after all!!!! Yes: allright about Muriel Foster.

I can't tell you anything about Worcester yet. Pomp & cirk not out for piano *duet* I think yet: the *solo* has been out for a fortnight (?) I believe – do you want full score or what. Miss Vipan ('cello) here today you met her at 'Hasfield' We all send best wishes.

Now dear old Jay get better at once or we shall all be lost

Yours ever

Edward Elgar.

Now I'm in forty frightful fits as to the *Todesengel* – I *wish* it could be sung as intended for once

My poor little wife has a bad eyelid & is shut up in the house.

Craeg Lea,
Malvern
Feb 19 [1902]

My dear Jaeger:

Many thanks for your welcome card saying you are better etc etc. I hope you will not be rash in going out too early.

I note what you say about proofs & the entire staff shall be turned on. Bless you! I don't see any music scrawls & don't want to.

I suppose you can assist the German Johnny (whose letter to you I return) to a full score soon enough – his scrawl had better be allowed to appear unless he wd. translate *your* unapproachable analysis. This wd. please me but perhaps it wd be better to have another hand in it. I *do* hope either Lessmann[1] or some other paper will have something like a preliminary analysis.

Keep well & in good spirits.

Much love,

Yours ever

Ed: Elgar.

Scores of pomp etc shall reach you soon. E.E.

P.T.O.

My wife is much interested in the letter & thanks you for a sight of it.

[1] Otto Lessmann, editor of the *Allgemeine Musik-Zeitung*, who was present at the first performance of *Gerontius* with Buths

Craeg Lea,
Malvern.
Feb 26, [19]02.

My dear Jay:

Kalisch tells me there is, or are, a par: or pars: in the papers one line
to say *I*[1] *know nothing of the announcement.* I've heard from Mr Clayton
about things in general.

Much love
Yours ever
Ed. Elgar.

On 28 February Jaeger asks Elgar to put in a good word with the Worcester
Committee for his 'old friend' Madame Sabrino. He also speaks with
enthusiasm of a new string quartet by J. B. McEwen – presumably No. 3 in E
minor – and some pieces by W. H. Bell. J. Pointer, a 'new man', is checking
Elgar's scores in Novello's. There was, as Jaeger says in his next letter of
4 April, much to be done: Gerontius and the Grania music, with the
Coronation Ode (finished on 1 April) in prospect.

Craeg Lea,
Malvern.
March 20 [1902]

My dear Jaeger:
Everything conspired yesterday to prevent any letter writing by
me or by my wife.
I don't quite understand what you say about something at No. 1[2].
but as it's blown over, all right – you can tell me anything when we
meet. I hope you are better – I have been laid up with a wretched cold –
just about again & glad of it.
I keep my readers (W[inifred]. N[orbury]. & C.A.E.) going with

1 twice underlined
2 i.e. Berners St.

the proofs but of course *I* can do nothing until that score comes – I don't see how it is ever to be ready. I can't tell anything about vocalists at Worcester, not my business at all.

You *must come* to Düsseldorf. Many happy returns of the day.

I must now go on with my score – that paper is a boon & saves much worry as to getting the chorus onto 2 lines instead of four & a 1000 other troubles.

Much love.

My wife wants to enclose something she tells me & I am to put this in a long envelope

Yours ever
Ed. E. . . .★

★ ELGAR I think you will like to see this. If no use to keep wd. like it back – some time Many best wishes for yr birthday [*added in pencil*]

Craeg Lea,
Malvern
Ap 11: 1902.

My dear Jaeger:

Thanks for all your notes on the proofs.

re *Appendix* note

on p. 39

   put simply

'For transposition of this solo into A♮ see Appendix & put *fuller* directions on our proposed Note (preface, page.

also, on the preface page put about the *semi-chorus* ceasing to sing before 64 I send a separate sheet with these things on.

At 50 the Celli in score are not clear – I've put a lucid mark in the proof – please compare it with the *part* (orchl) & make 'em correspond – that is to say I think the "*II* tutti" begin at 50 – & "*I* Tutti" two bars later.

Bar after 59 Pt I, 2nd Vio (demisemiquaver passage) shd be f not p. *Please put in orchl pt.* I don't think we can overhaul the organ part – I could if I had the whole score at once. The only thing to do wd be to put full directions in the preface.

I   Sw. (Oberwerk)

II Gt (Hauptwerk)

III Ch (Positiv)

& then use the numerals all thro' with 8, 16, 32 etc as now, omitting '*ft*'. If this can be done thoroughly it wd. be nice but I fear it's too much.

This is interesting – Fr Bellasis, a friend of the Cardinal, writes "The passage 'My soul is in my hand' is from the 118 ps & is correct as it stands according to the Vulgate from wh: the Cardinal wd. be sure to quote. There are other readings which have "thy' & much discussion among commentators on this subject but there is no reason to make any alteration or to suppose that "my" is a misprint. The phrase is indicative of security in the midst of danger.

No time for more

Yours ever
Ed. Elgar.

[*W.P.S. paper*]   Malvern
Ap 21 [1902]

My dear Jay:

Thanks for enclosed advt. – the things were down also at Glasgow (twice I believe) also Birmingham Richter

Liverpool (Rodewald)
do.   Richter
Blackpool Richter
New Brighton E.E.
Worcester Festival E.E.
Middlesboro Richter

I can't think of any more offhand

Oh! Halifax

I hope your home affairs are well. you don't say: BRUTE.

must go now
Yours ever
E

I think it wd. be best to say, as you suggest, by the Richter and Halle Orchs. (orx)

good word

Do look at the enclosed it seems to me to be just the thing required to explain Olaf: – take care of it & if you could get people performing the work & print it (that is if the author wd. let it be used) do.

Yrs ever
E.E.

On 12 April the Committee of the Worcester Festival expressed doubts as to the propriety of performing Gerontius in the Cathedral. The principal objector would appear to have been the Bishop, who, however, was prompted in the matter. Elgar took the matter up with Canon Claughton, and wrote also to Father Bellasis, of the Oratory, to inquire whether alterations of the text would be permitted to meet the episcopal requirements. On 29 April Jaeger *wrote to say that Mr. Littleton had no objections to slight alterations so long as the work was done. In the same letter Jaeger observed:* 'Mr. Littleton is dreadfully disappointed about the "High Tide" & very sorry indeed to hear of the cause of the mischance. What will Norwich do? . . .'

Novello's (not Jaeger) wrote on 8 May with further reference to proposed alterations in Gerontius which included the omission of the passage between 29 and 32 and a general substitution of 'Jesus', 'Lord', or 'Saviour' for 'Mary', to which it was thought no Roman Catholics would object. Dealing at the same time with Elgar's new arrangement of the National Anthem they said: 'We altered Clarionets for Clarinets in our ignorance of the fact that Clarionet is the English way of spelling the name of the instrument.'

Craeg Lea,
Malvern.
May 9: [19]02

My dear Jaeger:

I return the proof of God save the King: I wanted in this particular score everything to be 'plain English' – it would be best to ask Mr Littleton to settle the names of the instruments – they look *very nice* in English I think & *Kettledrums* is a good Handelian-looking word: see West's query as to *Haut-boys* – I feel that Oboes wd. spoil the whole thing – but I don't want to be faddy or silly, only English – which after all may be both! I am sending the old proof to Mr Rogan as directed with my remarks.

As to Gerontius pt II (120) the Harp direction is all right only it's divided in the Score

     1mo R.H. 8va.

I think it must have been plain in the part or I shd. have noticed it.

Now as to Gerontius libretto: what is proposed is to omit the litany of the saints – to substitute other words for Mary & Joseph – & to put 'souls' only over the Chorus at the end instead of 'souls in purgatory' & to put 'prayers' instead of Masses in the Angel's Farewell. The point is that (quite unfairly I feel) Atkins etc expect *me* to take the responsibility & I promised to enquire for *authority* for them to do it as they wish. So far I have only said I have no objection to the alterations or that I concur – permission *I* cannot give.

The Bishop has written to me a very kind letter thanking me for making the performance possible & I don't see that I have done this! What I *feel* is that Fr Bellasis ought to be asked his opinion (for instance) & see if he cd. arrange that the Worcester folk are not troubled in the matter. It's a dreadful mix-up &, as usual in these petty things they all seem to hide somewhere & expect me to 'play the man!'

I am only anxious to do what is sensible & of course absolutely & completely candid & honest. I quite *see* all you say about no Catholic
raising objections but in my view of the fact that the whole objection
now is manufactured by one man with the express purpose of (as he
thinks) ruining the work & me I wd. like everything to be quite
square & understood.

My eyes are bad & I must write no more

Yours snly

Ed: Elgar

*On the following day Elgar conducted the Worcestershire Philharmonic
Society in a concert which included the two* Pomp and Circumstance
Marches *and Volbach's* Reigen. *In the programme note Elgar wrote:* 'By his
conducting and literary work in connection with the Handel Festival,
held at Mayence, he has made a great reputation . . . . The . . . work
given today forms a cheery introduction to the music of an important
modern composer, who is also highly cultured and estimable as an
artist, and lovable as a man.' *Six days later the Elgars set off for Germany
for the triumphant production of* Gerontius *in Düsseldorf, and Strauss's
notable tribute, described in* Elgar O.M. *pp. 104–5.*

*From Düsseldorf Elgar went to Kassel to see the fine Picture Gallery,
thence to Eisenach to visit Bach's (reputed) birthplace. He then went across
Thuringia to Leipzig, south to Dresden, where he saw* Lohengrin, *met
Eugen d'Albert, took a boat up the Elbe, and then back to Leipzig where he
spent some time in the Hotel Sedan[1] in which he had stayed on his first visit to
the city nearly twenty years earlier. Back in London at the beginning of June
he again met Strauss and heard* Die Meistersinger *at Covent Garden. He
heard Melba rehearse the* Ode, *of which he was by now busy correcting
proofs. On 12 June he had to go to Sheffield for a rehearsal.*

Craeg Lea,

Malvern.

June 11: [19]02. 5.30 a.m.

My dear Jaeger:

I am up & at work vainly endeavouring to persuade myself it is
summer: but it is frightful weather, so cold & grey.

I am coming to town via Sheffield, arriving on Friday or Saturday &
shall be with

Mr Ramsden

8, Gloucester Terrace

Regent's Park

N.W.

for a time.

[1] at present Blücherstrasse 1

My wife is in bed with a bad chill but is better & will D.V. join me next week. I hope to see you when I come within range. I must however thank you for your M.T. article[1]: I will read *nothing* now but I made an exception of course for the genial mossheadedness of you – bless you.

What a fuss about Strauss' speech! too ridiculous & nobody seems in the least to understand what he said or meant. I always said British musicians were several kinds of fool & ignoramus – but this is worse than usual from them.

Alas & alack!

I hope you are all well at home & shall hope, if I stay all the time in town to come down. How about that new house?[2]

Give my love to the Angelicals

yours ever
Edward Elgar.

Craeg Lea,
Malvern.
June 17: [1902]

Dear old Mosshead:

I had hoped to have seen you in town but all our plans were spoiled by my wife's illness. I hope she is getting better, but I had to hurry up my business & come home.

We are dreadfully concerned to hear about Mrs Jaeger & hope it is not so serious as you said in your hurried note. Anyhow our hearts & best wishes are always with you all – *you know* how much.

I am not wanting to talk of business: but will you send me a full score of 'God save the King' & send to Covent Garden

7. 6. 5. 6. 6.
strings
& wind etc

addressed to the Librarian. I had a good rehearsal & all goes well.

Dorabella is here & is seeing to my wife charmingly & skilfully.

My eyes are not good & I must not write more than necy.

Much love & good wishes for your new home

Yours ever
Ed: Elgar.

I replied to Busoni that I can't go to conduct – was Strauss going to

---

[1] 'Morecambe Musical Festival', 'by one who was there', June issue
[2] Jaeger moved from 16 Margravine Gardens W. to 37 Curzon Road N.

play the extract? Busoni spoke to us about it you remember long ago –
will you settle it all sometime about parts etc.

Malvern
June 22 [19]02

My dear Jaeger:

I fear Dorabella did not get your message as she was leaving as the
letters came in. I'm sending her a note.

My wife is at last much better & will soon be able to travel. I'll
call at Berners St. about those corrections.

I *hate* coming to town – shall miss the hay-making I fear. Had 50
miles ride yesterday amongst the Avon country – Shakespeare etc etc.
Oh! so lovely but solus 'cos I can't find anybody here foolheaded
enough to eat bread & cheese & drink beer – they've all got livers &
apparently live in the country 'cos they can't afford to be swells in a
town.

Oh! lor.

Hope your wife is better & that the move is over successfully. Send
me your new address.

Yours ever
Ed: Elgar.

*The Coronation was due on 26 June and Elgar was to have gone to London
to conduct the* Ode *on the previous evening.*

'We went for a bicycle ride', *wrote Miss Rosa Burley,* 'and had tea at
an inn. People were already going up to London in great numbers.

E. was in a good mood and looking forward to the next day.
While we were having tea I suddenly said to him, "Don't be disappointed if there is some hitch tomorrow. I can't believe that the
King can go through such a programme. Think! He goes down to
Spithead & reviews the Fleet in the morning. Salutes being fired all
the time. Sunshine blazing on the sea. Then in the afternoon he comes
up by train to London – Then dinner, eight courses remember. Then
he goes to Covent Garden and has a long affair to listen to and pre-
sentations to be made. I can't see him doing it all."

We had just finished tea and were preparing to go when the landlady
rushed in saying "Oh! Sir. The Coronation is put off, the King is ill
and is to have an operation at once. The news is just in at the Post
Office."

This was consternation indeed, but Edward was very calm and said,
"Well: I shall have a few days bicycling that's all".'

Craeg Lea,
Malvern.
June 24 [1902]

Deary Jaeger:

I think it will be best to send anything here: I am going to a quiet farmhouse to work for a bit. D.V.

Don't for heaven's sake *sympathise* with me – I don't care a tinker's damn! It gives me three blessed sunny days in my own country (for which I thank God or the Devil) instead of stewing in town. *My* own interest in the thing ceased as usual, when I had finished the M.S. – since when I have been thinking mighty things!

I was biking out in Herefordsh: yesterday & the news reached me at a little roadside pub. I said "Give me another pint of cider". I'm deadly sorry for the King but that's all.

Hope your house settles well – I *fear* they are going to build in front of us. If so, we're nomads once more. I think Wales or the sea will have to endure the follies of your affecte

Ed: Elgar

directly the scaffold poles arise.

The Apostles *is now on the stocks and Jaeger hopes on 27 June that this work is not going to go away from Novello's. As a dissuader he observes that Stanford has quarrelled with Boosey's. Elgar goes again to Germany, to Mainz and Bayreuth (for the Wagner Festival).*

Malvern
July 10 [1902]

My dear Jaeger:

I have been biking far away & now return to work for a little.

I quite forget if the dedication to Henry Wood is in the Grania music – if not already in as on the M.S. score it might run thus:

"Dedicated to my friend
Henry J. Wood,
London."

How are you all? I trust well. I go to Bayreuth next week & shall hope to have a day or two in town with my wife (who is better Deo gratias) we shall in that case see you & talk.

No more now as I'm frantically busy.

Yours ever
Ed. Elgar.

Langham Hotel,
London.
Friday p.m. [July 18, 1902]

My dear Jaeger:

Here's the proof, the two lines look odd being exactly the same length: but it will do if any difficulty arises in altering it.

I cross on Sunday night – to-morrow (Deo gratias). I am to hear 'Don Giovanni'[1] (after a fashion) this even Strauss* cannot shake in the depths of the heart & soul of your friend

Edward Elgar

* The Wagner shaker.

Craeg Lea,
Malvern.
Augt. 3 [19]02.

My dear Jaeger:

We are so very much relieved to hear your dear wife is through the operation safely & can only hope & pray that she may continue to improve & arrive quickly at good health.

Pooh! to you over my photographs – you have grumbled at them all in turn some more & some less, & you have grumbled at the original more than all put together.

Go to!

My eyes are better I think & I'm working at the Apostles – which you will not like – it's too philosophical for your *cheap publisher's side* of your mind, but just the thing for the *real* A.J.J.

No more now only good wishes to you all, & *do* have your eyes seen to & anything else that wants patching up or revising in your dear old body.

Much love,
Yours ever
Ed: Elgar

The Cottage
Saughall
nr Chester
Monday [*sic*] Augt 12 [1902]

My dear Jaeger:

When I asked the firm about the original M.S. Score of Gerontius, Mr Alfred asked you to say it was a pity to put the score in an in-accessible place – I shd. like to give it to the Oratory in Edgbaston

[1] at Covent Garden

where the good Cardinal lived, worked & died: wd. the firm approve of that? I shd. like to know before making a formal offer – it wd. be in the Library.[1]

We hope you will come to Worcester. It is very nice & restful here but the weather is awful.

Yours ever
Ed. Elgar

We are dying for news of you.

[*W.P.S. paper*]

The Cottage
Saughall
nr Chester.
Aug 18 [19]02

My dear Jaeger:

Many thanks for the Skoughrze which look very nice & will sound nicer (?) What about the P.F. arrangement?[2] I don't know nuffin about it, do I?

As to Cologne[3]: I wd. go & could of course do it all right – I don't know the date & might be already engaged – but that's scarcely probable. Wood wd. be splendid granted sufficient rehearsal.

We hope your wife is progressing as well as you could reasonably wish: it is a sad & great trial & we deeply sympathise with you all. I *wish* you wd. get your eyes seen to & other things: I shall have to rush up & seize you again – I trust with better results than before.

Yours ever
Edward

I should naturally prefer to go to Köln myself.

letter-card]

[*postmark* 29 August 1902]
Malvern

Dearie Jäger:

Tharnx! about that cut.

Of course you're a good-natured fool otherwise you wouldn't be Nimrod or A.J.J:

Look here you must come to Worcester & hear what Gerontius

---

[1] On 9 August Fr. Bellasis had said that the Fathers would be pleased to have this score, where it is now to be found.

[2] by McEwen of the *Grania* music (reference in Jaeger's letter of 19 August)

[3] Wüllner is anxious that Elgar should, if possible, go to Cologne to conduct *Gerontius* (ibid.).

might be – the building will do it. I may see you in the next few daze but am not sure.

yours ever

Ed. E.

Don't write 12 pp to anyone except me!

At the morning concert on 2 October, at the Sheffield Festival, Gerontius *(with John Coates, David Ffrangcon-Davies, and Muriel Foster deputizing for Brema who was seriously ill) was performed under Elgar's direction, Henri Verbrugghen (1873–1934) leading the orchestra. The opening was almost disastrous, the chorus taking fright at their entry on p. 12 with the result that the whole of their first entry was a semitone flat. Afterwards, it was reported, they sang superbly. The afternoon programme included the Prelude to Act III,* Lohengrin, *Beethoven's Violin Concerto played by Ysaÿe, and Elgar's* Coronation Ode. *The Sheffield Choir should, of course, have taken part in this in London. For that projected performance Elgar had laid down that the composition of the choir should be: 44 sopranos, 34 contraltos, 42 tenors, 40 basses. All but five members (who resigned) allowed their names to go before Coward, the chorus-master, who nominated the best singers and then selected the rest by ballot. The disappointment of not singing in London was at first mitigated by Coward conducting a 'private' performance for a meeting in Sheffield of the Incorporated Society of Musicians, before the official first performance at the Festival under Elgar. The* Sheffield Telegraph, *3 October, gives this picture of Elgar:*

'Dr. Elgar, standing on the conductor's rostrum, gave scarcely any indication of his own fervour. He was like the conspirator who, having carefully arranged the plot, stands calmly watching its development. Dr. Elgar is more fiery in his music than in his conducting, for although he is a man with highly strung nerves and of a sensitive temperament, he seems frigid as a conductor when compared, for instance, with Mr. Henry J. Wood, who inspires so much enthusiasm.

'But the Sheffield chorus know Dr. Elgar and his works, as Dr. Elgar is familiar with the Sheffield chorus and their merit. They know exactly what he requires, although on one occasion he asked for too much when he exclaimed, "Ladies, if you must rustle your leaves in turning them over, I do wish you would do it in the right key." This was a case of nerves when deeply absorbed in music, but such an outburst from a man with the charm of manner of Dr. Elgar is easily forgiven. The members of the Sheffield chorus have great affection for the eminent composer, and a very pretty, though pathetic, little story was going around the Hall yesterday, after the performance of "The Dream of Gerontius."

'The critics will probably tell of a slight failure in the opening of the work which marred the choral effect. After the laurels won the previous day, and the earnest desire to do full justice to the doctor's work, the defect was such a source of grief to some of the lady members of the choir, and, after the performance, a soloist found one of the more emotional members in tears. The grief was unnecessary considering the perfect way in which all the other parts of the work had been rendered. The soloist, being a man, of course could not understand this little weakness in human nature. When he was told he burst into laughter, and exclaimed, "My dear girl, I am older and uglier than you are, and I shall never hear better singing than that to which I have listened to-day until I get to Heaven."

'As a matter of fact, Dr. Elgar was delighted with the singing of the chorus, and immediately he was able to tear himself away from the host of admirers who besieged the small artistes' room, he made his way to the chorus. Every member of the choral body was anxious to express their regret at the mishap which they made at the opening. But there was no necessity for sorrow. Their perfect choral singing in the other parts of the work, as well as in the Coronation Ode, had more than atoned for the defect. Dr. Elgar soon put the choristers at ease, and he congratulated every member on the success of the performances. "You know my opinion of you," said the genial doctor. "It is not altered." He made a slight reference to what he described as an"unfortunate event" in the opening work, but when he added that, if he had again to choose a chorus to sing the "Coronation Ode" he should not hesitate to come to Sheffield for the voices, he raised the enthusiasm of the choir to a high pitch, and singers and conductor parted on the best terms.'

Sheffield

Sunday Oct 5 (I think [1902]

(In bed with an awful tooth
My dear Augustus darling:

I am so sorry I saw so little of you in London. I rode (Bike) to Ridg[e] hurst[1] on Saturday after the St Jas' Hall rehearsal & knocked a Man off en route. bad tea at the '*Bald faced Stag*'
– then this toothache began. I came into London on Monday & had it temporarily seen to & now it's really awful again.

I have at last got in Macpherson's Psalm (on which I have had my eye for a long time) at Worcester – we will do our best to make it go – I hope the score & parts are all right – I told Miss Hyde to see about 'em but have not heard yet from her[;] however the Psalm is in the printed

[1] Hertfordshire home of Edward Speyer

scheme so I conclude the details have been settled all right. I want some particulars of Macpherson for the Book of Words also about the Psalm – where has it been done etc. etc? I don't know, I think, the composer although I have probably met him. the Psalm is a fine piece of work & a serious one – the only thing I can't 'follow' is the repetition of the words 'Sing us a song' – all else is right. I hope there's an organ part – if not I shall suggest one & if a *small* one exists I shd ask for as full a one as Macpherson will permit. You will be sure to know him so I tell you all this. Oh! this tooth is awful.

I've lit a pipe now so I can't swear without sacrificing some smoke (Sanford's tobacco) So a more Xtian atmosphere prevails. I wish you had been here for Gerontius. some of it was worth hearing

We are supposed to go to Bristol tomorrow, tooth & all if it isn't lugged out today

Much love to you all from us both

Yours ever

Edward.

The Bristol Music Festival, directed by George Riseley, took place in the new Colston Hall between 8 and 11 October. On the second day Elgar conducted the Coronation Ode, *and at the final, Saturday, concert,* Cockaigne.

Craeg Lea,

Malvern.

Oct 18 [19]02

My dear Augustus:

At 130 the 2nd Violins have the D (=A in Cor 1°.) so the parts can stand just as they are. It is more 'bedeutend' if the first Horn takes that bit of solo & the A doesn't matter. Any decently conceited 1st Horn wd. strike, I shd. think, if any other *Cornist* had the solo.

We were very glad indeed to hear from you: it is terribly sad to hear of Wood's illness[1] – I hope & trust it is not serious.

I may send you a scrawl in a few days but I'm working hard & 'it' looms big.

Yours ever

Ed. Elgar

[1] *Jaeger to Elgar, 16 October:* 'Isn't it sad about Wood? I'm not surprised though. Two years ago I told him he would be an old man before he reached middle age unless he gave himself more rest. He has been burning the candle both ends & in the middle too & now he is a wreck & has to be massaged every day to get rid of his (partial) paralysis in his legs. They give out here that it is influenza, but it is much more serious than that . . . . Who, I wonder, will conduct the Symphony concerts? . . . What about you?'

[*typewritten*]   Craeg Lea,
                                                Nov. 1st, 1902.
AUGUSTUS DARLING!

I have brought this infernal machine down home to try if I can make head or tail of it so I think I can't do better than worry your dear old Moss-head with one of my first attempts.

BIZ — The Hanley people ask me if [g *deleted*] Gerontius can be done with one Oboe & one Cor-Anglais: I seem to have a vague remembrance of a M.S. [& *deleted*] part; do you happen to know? Don't worryabout it if it's gone out of your knowledge.

(How's that Augustus dear for afirst — no, a secondattempt?)

I practised this giddy jamboree in the train on the way home this afternoon, & this is the dire result! Much love, Augustus, from us both to you all.

                              Always yoursaffectionately
                                    EDWARD ELGAR

On 5 December Elgar went with Sir Walter Parratt to Kensington Palace to meet Princess Henry of Battenberg. Then he and Mrs. Elgar went to Edward Speyer's house at Ridgehurst to dine with Strauss and other notabilities. On the next day Strauss's Heldenleben was played at Queen's Hall and was described in the Diary as 'very astonishing'.

                                                Craeg Lea,
                                                Wells Road,
                                                Malvern
                                            Dec 10 [1902]
My dear Augustus:

Here's the reprinted '*praise*'.

If you *like* knock out the Voc pts of score I sent [?].

There's no time sig: but perhaps that doesn't matter.

Can you put *Cardinal* instead of J.H. – it seems evading something – but p'raps it's done for a reason.

I might see the *last* page only if you like, but my alternative improvement is quite plain.

Yes! Heldenleben is there; but I can't write – we can talk sometime.

                                    Yours ever
                                    Ed. E.

We rushed off to Ridgehurst immediately: Strauss tore himself out of the crowd & said to me 'Freund, sind Sie zufrieden?"

                                        Ja! gewiss!

On 16 December Jaeger wrote that he had had a letter from Strauss's father, whom he described as 'another such grand old man as your sire'.

NANCY. (?)

ncy (?)

Alassio

Craeg Lea,
Malvern.
Dec 17: [19]02.

My dear Jaeger:
Here is the corrected *Praise*. Will you cause to be sent (Volbach asks for it) a copy of the German 8vo Gerontius to
Herrn Landgerichtsdirector *De Niem*[1]
Vorsitzender des
Cäcilen Vereins, Wiesbaden.
Volbach tells me they are arranging a performance with the combined choruses of *Mainz* & *Wiesbaden*. He says also they are giving the Variations again in Mainz, in Wiesbaden & in Frankfurt!

I wrote about the partsongs last week but find the letter has not gone, so I write to-day. I have *liver:* you know what that means!

I hope Macpherson's fine Psalm will now go on. Do see Edwards about the M.T. Notice. I have caused a B'ham Gazette to be sent to him & am sending the one decent local paper.
Yours ever
Edward.

Craeg Lea,
Malvern.
Dec 21: [19]02.

Dear Augustus:
This is the shortest day so I set forth on the longest letter I ever wrote (to you) a regular Yule-loggy puddingy, Brandy-saucious letter. Christmas, my Boy! Law!

Think where we were last year: Düsseldorf no less – & we smoked cigars at 15 pfg *pour la Noblesse* in the streets of that city.
12 months ago!
Well! well!

We hope you are well & flourishing both businessily & domestically.

I'm no hand at writing letters requiring invention. I can only run on & say evil things weakly: as thus: – I have had Xmas presents – all Wagner's prose works (translated) 8 vols & & & & & & the Encyc. Brit. & the bookcase!!!! a present (£42). ¯ = ≡ ≡ ≡ ≡ ≡

Behold in me a learned prig: *prig*[2] mark you – I know the height of Arrarat (But don't know how to spell it) & all sorts of japes. Look 'ere: *I'm learned*[2] now & no base Nimrodkin (Hebraic plural) shall look down on me: is not my learning vast in 35 volumes & in a revolving bookcase – my head too revolves with delight.

I can tell you who was Aaron's mother-in-law's first cousin's bootblack & infinitesimal Calculus etc. etc. I charge 6d to enter the study now.

I say, I have a lively fine specimen of a Vanessa – pish! I shd. say to one unwise a peacock butterfly who is helping the Apostles & lives in this study. I feed him – no, drink him on sugar & water & he lives in a Chrysanthemum – it's all lovely & Japanesy & pastoral – I'm sure the beast is a familiar spirit – Angel Gabriel or Simon Magus, or Helen of Tyre or somebody: just fancy sitting in this study surrounded with flowers & a *live* butterfly at Xmas – this music's going to be good I can tell you.

Much love to you all (I must read up Love in the Ency:). A merry Xmas to all at Curzon Rd (limited to No 37)

Your austere & learned friend (34 vols & a bookcase)

Paracelsus Elgar.

(with a pain in his stomach) Mince pizon.

Craeg Lea,
Malvern.
Dec. 30 [1902]

My dear Jaeger:

Many 1000 thanks for the photo[1], which is fine – I prize it & hold it tight. I am much pressed for time & must go on to Biz: I have had to give up the Phil. at Worcester as I cannot find the time – I am only sorry about *one* thing, that is Macpherson's psalm, whether they will give it or not I can't say: do tell him I am endeavouring to get several serious-minded people to do it & he shall hear results.

One other thing: that *Grania* music goes well & made a tremendous impression again on Saturday in Liverpool[2] – *When* is it to be published? Score & parts I mean – it is wanted badly. I will write in a day or two about the TTBB things[3] but am only just home & have heaps to do.

Yah! this is not so good as the typewriter.

Yours ever
Ed E

[1] probably one of the photographs sent by Strauss's father to Jaeger and mentioned in his letter of 10 December

[2] Elgar had previously conducted *Grania*, the March from *Caractacus*, and *Sursum Corda* in Liverpool on 29 November.

[3] On pp. 21 *et seq.* of Sketch Book I are various rough ideas headed Op. 45 'Greek for Men'.

1903

Although he had not been well in December Elgar was reported as better on New Year's Day, and 'keen on his work'. *He was absorbed by* The Apostles, *which brought Jaeger to Malvern on 4 January. A few days later Johnstone came over from Birmingham to discuss* 'Novello's terms', *and on 12 January Richter was a visitor. Having heard parts of the new oratorio and of the* Coronation Ode, *Richter, according to Mrs. Elgar, said* 'Ach, grossartig, eine so heilige Stimmung, aber er ist ein ganz famoser Mann, und es ist so wunderbar (or something like that) ein so lebenvoller Mensch.' *Coming on the heels of current copies of* Die Musik *and of* Die Neue Musik-Zeitung, *both of which contained enthusiastic articles, this was more than gratifying.*

Craeg Lea,
Malvern.
Jan 1: 1903.

My dear Jaeger:

A happy new year to you – this is the first word I've written in this Ann: Dom. & it goes to you with complete affection & I thank goodness my first scrawl is not a business letter.

It's not a letter at all really, only to cover this weird epistle[1] which I've not answered – do send the enquirer a p.c. I don't know & don't want to know what to say. He could fiddle at it himself if he likes.

Yours ever
Edward Elgar.

[typewritten]

[4 January 1903]

This is to Certify that Augustus is a trumd — no, I mean A Trump of the deepest dye.

[1] not extant

Augustus honoured this humble dwelling with his august(us) presence on Jan. 4, 1903. Deo gratias, Gott sei dank.
Signed, Edward Elgar. Mus. Donk.

Ode to the Ency. Brit.[1]
I know the height of Ararat,
    Specific gravity of fat,
And heaps of other things besides, —
    As what makes vermin scratch their hides!

Craeg Lea,
Malvern.
Sunday 25/1/[19]03

My dear —— Jaeger:
(I'm saving a sheet of paper – hence this dash.

Here is a bit more [of *The Apostles*], & upon my — *corazza*[2] (that'll do! for a fustian oath) it's the best bit of music I've wrote up to the present.

I had hoped you would have engraved the thing *exactly* like the German Gerontius – which is better than *anything* I've ever seen & beats all that Röder[3] etc. etc. turns out in that line. So you had best do it as I send it to you & let Buths have a final proof to work from & send me always two or three proofs.

Yours ever
Ed:
the false Apostle.

Troyte[4] is *architecting* this church here & proposes to call it "the Holy Apostles' & wants me to go & write in the Crypt so as to give it, or imbibe from it, local colour.

Oh! Augustus, if you had only been an Apostle, what a brute I'd have made you.

[4 February 1903][5]

[*on reverse of letter from Mrs. Elgar to Jaeger, dated 'Wednesday'*]
Dearie Augustus

I shall be sending you 'some more' this week so buck up. Send me

[1] *Encyclopaedia Britannica*, acquired on 20 December 1902
[2] twice underlined
[3] engraver in Leipzig
[4] A. Troyte Griffith, subject of the seventh of the '*Enigma*' *Variations*; see *Letters of Edward Elgar*, p. 344
[5] Elgar received a letter the day before with an invitation from Strauss and Mengelberg to contribute a work to the proposed Strauss Festival (see p. 177).

some proofs. Sorry the binding music got mixed

Much love

Yrs ever

Ed Elgar

Strauss & Mengelberg both have asked me to let a piece be done at the Strauss Festival, so I have said *Grania*.

[*W.P.S. paper*]
[*typewritten*]

Craeg-Lea, Feb: 6th 1903.

Lieber Augustin (!)——

Pluck ye by the ear & mark:——

I am changing my Bike for a free-wheel (never mind if you don't know what that is) & my old machine is no longer of any use to me: my wife remembers that you said something about riding this next season — that was during our happy days at Worcester — now, will you accept this Bike, that is if it's of any use to you for your own use? I forget if you know anything about bikes, but I send full des-cription (that word's divided wrongly) on the other side from wh: one of your expert friends could tell you if the size & general hang of the thing would fit your lengthy, wiry, athletic & weary carcase.

Now, guck [*sic*] up, & tell me if you're going to take this scheme on.

Yours ever,

Edward Elgar. E.E. *m.p.* [*handwritten*]

(Professional Trick Bicyclist, annulatory Equatist etc. etc. etc. etc. etc. etc.)

To be disposed of as a GOING CONCERN!

Bicycle – (not a Free-Wheel, but a free Bike.

Royal Sunbeam, Third season, in good condition, nary a scratch. Frame 27 in.

Brakes:—Front plunger tyre

Back wheel, Bowden rim brake fitted

It has never been 'down' & such wear-marks as it shews are all railway porters' mementoes.

I'll bring it up if you will accept it.

Gosh! Augustus darling! you might write some music on it!!

[*typewritten*]

MEMORANDUM

from

Edward Elgar, BICYCLE & ORATORIO MONGER,
Craeg Lea, Wells-road, MALVERN

To

Augustus Sherlock Johann Holmes Jaeger, esq:

Please to receive by rail, safely packed in Case (which please return) ONE aged BIKE, warranted sound in wind & limb, & be good enough to acknowledge safe arrival of same.

All sorts of machines in stock or at short notice, — any sample forwarded carr: pd: against remittance: – NO connection with any other Cycle dealer in the world.

YOUR KIND RECOMMENDATION respectfully solicited. February 15th, 1903.

Craeg Lea,
Malvern.
Feb 16 [19]03.

My dear Jaeger:

Please accept the Bike with our love. I hope it will carry you as safely & as exhilaratingly as it has done me.

I enclose a book about the oilbath – some people scoff at it – but it's a real good thing I'm sure.

Yours ever
Edwd. Elgar

The machine – known affectionately in the family since its birth as 'Mr. Phoebus' goes to-day – packed by experts.

On 19 February Jaeger sent Buths's translation of the Part Songs *from the Greek Anthology. He also said that Buths wished to see the proofs of* The Apostles *so that he could estimate whether he had time to translate that as well. The first proofs of this work had arrived on 17 February. Three days later the MS. of the second scene,* By the Wayside, *was sent to Jaeger.*

[*W.P.S. paper*]

Malvern
Feb 21: [19]03.

My dear Shylock: (rather Sherlock)

Here is or are Buths' translations many copies – send your type-writing to this establishment for elegance & dispatch. The translations are fine we think. Buths is[1] a clever Kerl!

In No 5 my wife wants to understand, line 6, what does – '*es weis*' mean?

---

[1] twice underlined

Hope the Bike is with you & that you are safe from Manchester.
Much love

Yours ever

Edward

To

Augustus Henry Sherlock Johann Slater Holmes Pollaky Jaeger, esq:

*The following letter is apparently in reply to one from Jaeger which is
lost. Jaeger's general concern for young English composers was, however,
stated in his letter of 8 February, in which he quoted the claims of Bell,
McEwen (who had promised to teach him to bicycle) and Cyril Scott. But to
gain the favour of Novello's they must all write anthems.*

Craeg Lea,

Malvern.

Feb 22 [1903]

My dear Jaeger:

Of course put the clefs in as they come *most conveniently* for Fag &
anything else. I thought Mr. Dodd in making the first copy had
probably done so: in the hurry of scoring – which must be done red
hot or *not at all* – one doesn't think of clefs & notes but only of the 'mid-
glory' – the *Mss.* scr shd. make it clear. please tell Geidel therefore to
make the part *sehr praktisch*. What he calls the violin-schlussel is
probably used for a high C or something tasty.

I can't *think* why you worry about what's written in papers – I
never see any & don't miss them. You will now have to write eight
pages to all your friends explaining that Bell is better than Holbrooke
about which nobody wd. have been in doubt until you call their attention to a foolish article in an unknown paper etc. etc. etc.

So you all go on except your calm country life friend
Ed Elgar

After all what you quote is *not* more foolish than the Times (e.g.) often
has said, is it now?
So where are you?

I return Geidel's wail.

[*W.P.S. paper*]

Malvern

Feb. 26: [1903]

My dear Jaeger:

I am awfully sorry the Bike is so long on the way: it was removed from here *last Monday week*, ordered to be packed in crate & forwarded at once. I learn to-day that it was sent on *Saturday* last & now you say it wasn't packed. Oh! Malvern tradesmen.

I don't think it can be too high – but your friends can lower the saddle & handlebars to suit you – if the thing is really too high (the scale usually advertised is 27 in frame, which Mr Phoebus is, for anybody 5 ft 11in) just use it to learn on & charge it away. Don't expect to do too much at first, & *above all*, don't give up under a month's hard work at it.

Bless you
Yours ever
Edward.

[*W.P.S. paper*]

Malvern
March 1 [1903]
Private

My dear Jaeger:

Many thanks for Mr Ould's[1] platitudinous letter which tells us exactly & fully – what we knew before: a valuable person – (does he really think I set Gerontius without knowing where *every* word came from!)

Following up his argument (on Extract 'C') you will have to cease singing Magnificat in the Catholic Church & e.g. Nunc dimittis in the English Church, etc. etc. etc. The man is *too* stupid: anything can be sung reflectively.

The extracts might well go in the 8vo. choruses I think, but I would prefer the firm to decide whether they may be worth the commercial risk: I think the words will be all right – at any rate they are as 'apt' probably as Dvorak's 'Fac me vere' in the same series. A dear, giddy old pirate to suggest sending 'me' (!) texts – as if I didn't know my own liturgy & everything else connected with it.

re Chanson de Matin. as to the score or conductor's part – I don't *mind* the score appearing – it looks a neat bit of small orchestra work but I would prefer the *most useful* thing to be done – nobody wd. ever buy the conductor's part for fun, but they might procure a score –

---

[1] Edwin Ould was a double-bass player in the Philharmonic and other orchestras. His son Percy had been at St. Andrew's College, Grahamstown, since 1893 (see *British Musical Biography*, J. D. Brown and S. S. Stratton, 1897, Birmingham).

see? Then, on the other hand, the expense of the score may be infinitely more than the conductor's sheet, all of which is in your practical mind already.

I've had influenza & am only just up.

Yours ever
Edward Elgar.

Craeg Lea,
Malvern.
Monday. [9 March 1903]

My dear Jaeger:

I hope Mr Phoebus behaved well & that you rode Feierlich u. Ritterlich.

I detest bothering you & if it's any trouble – stir not: I don't know how all that egregious binding goes on – but, if you can, put in a plea for the *Liszt scores* – I don't want to study orkistrayshun but only the markings the compozer used for Rall &c &c as aforesaid.

Probably the whole lot of books will be coming soon, so the skoughghrze need not be sent first; if that's the case – that ain't grammar! Never mind.

M.S. to p 161 sent by this post.

*Yours ever
Edward the Elder,
Knight the dracons.*

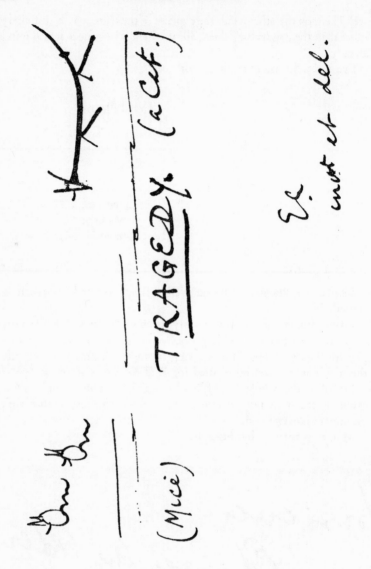

On 10 March Jaeger wrote noting that, according to Elgar's score, 'Peter, John etc. are to be deprived of their sanctity in future.' He also expressed satisfaction at performances of Gerontius *at Danzig on 11 March,[1] at Manchester on 12 March, and at Hanley (Stoke-on-Trent) on 13 March.*

[1] Actually 23 March, see p. 187

[*W.P.S. paper*]

Malvern
Mar 11 [19]03

My dear Jaeger:

Many thanks for the page – retd with more M.S. (to p. 177 incl.) –
the rehearsal figures shall go on all right now.

If anything is posted to me to-morrow (Thursday) or Friday,
address:—

N. Staffs Hotel
Stoke-on-Trent.

The Saints must be removed (only two or three) from the early pages.
If you could send me copies of Stainer's things I shd. be glad to see how
his parson friends managed the names & you might ask Mr Alfred if
he has any views or, better, *feelings* in the matter.

As the thing is not for *service* but is an oratorio I think from every
point of view *Peter* etc without prefix is best & right – on looking at
'S. Paul' I see Mendelssohn says simply Paul:* none of them had been
sainted at the time they are speaking (– or singing?)

Mil. Band 'Lux Xti *looks* all right but I don't understand these
things – I marked the score in pencil at one point where something
seemed to clash. By all means if you engrave the score of the Meditation
let it be ready (in same size) for the complete edition of full scores of
all my things which will come some day.

Now: I beg of you to arrange with a *Bike teacher* to give you an
hour or two, lessons – the cost is trifling & you wd. be getting on – I
wd. defray the cost of six lessons if you'd let me! You wd. find a good
strong professional better than ½ doz enthusiastic friends I think

Yours ever
Ed. E.

Send on anything you can as I can correct there.
* I think this settles the point without further thought?
I have only just looked at S. Paul, so don't trouble further.

North Stafford Station Hotel
Stoke-on-Trent.
March 13th, 1903.

My dear Jaeger:

I have looked over the German of Buths – i.e. the altered notes &
don't think anything could be better done.

Manchester must have been something extraordinary from the
news given me[1] & the telegram recd.

[1] by Adolf Brodsky and Rodewald in particular

I think the titles of the Greek things shd run, on each
"Words from the Greek Anthology (Anonymous)
or
(Marcus Argentarius)
etc & not as copied in this M.S. – see?

Don't trouble to write a long letter to me until you can ride your bike.

Yours ever
E.E.

The Chorus here is A.1.

In the middle of reading proofs (the first of which arrived on 17 February), and completing the third scene of The Apostles (*finished on 23 March*) *Elgar lost his new bicycle. Jaeger offered to return 'Mr. Phoebus'.*

Craeg Lea,
Malvern.
Mar 19 [19]03:

My dear Jaeger:

I don't want to worry you about the proofs – but you promised me I shd have plenty (of copies that is): you know I am not a *proper composer* & I know I ought not to try – but! well I must. Now–I prefer *revises* of course & I like to send 'em to three or four friends whose judgment I rely upon* – vocalists & *sich* – that takes one copy. My wife wants one for *scoring* purposes, i.e. making the skeleton for me – that takes another & I like to have one by me to refer to, phrasing etc. Now, if there's any *difficulty*, don't trouble & don't *laugh at me for my silly ways* because I'm clever at some things but *not* at composing.

You ought not to have been let fall. I'm very angry with your teachers. Squire Little never let me down *once*, bless him! No: you keep that Bike – I must stick to a free wheel.

Yours ever
Ed: Elgar.

* for phrasing etc. etc.

[*W.P.S. paper*]

Malvern
Mar. 19 [19]03.

Mosshead!

Don't be a ————————

Here's your precious note about the percussing things. The note about Timpani must not be too long.

Cheer up, you old snorter. You ought to be ashamed of yourself

to write to me like that. I have lumbago & am stuck in my chair,
percussing violent, & my fountain pen has gone to nought.

Alas.

Goodbye. stick to that Bike.

Yours ever contentiously

E.E.

[*W.P.S. paper*]

Malvern

Friday [20 March 1903]

Dear old Jagpot!

No '*composed*' for me: I can't compose 'as she is taught' – as the
words – (bless them!) were from the Scriptures I feel bold to put like
dear old Handel

The A——————

an Oratorio

by

E.E.

Op. 49

Send along revises – anything else. Lumbago better, rheumatism bad,
temper evil, disposition venomous, mind, – vacant.

Your affecte ass,

Edward

I'm afraid p. 28 means a *new plate*! so you will be sad & dyspeptic all
day. I told you I wasn't a proper music monger. This pen is broken,
D—M!

Craeg Lea,

Malvern.

Mar: 22 [19]03.

My dear Jaggernaut:

Ride roughly over me if you will. Anyhow I'm not upset[1] – except
over & by reason of my Bike.

I want *three* clean revises – that's all! My wife has used the *single*
proof we have; – you *did* send me duplicates (or rather triplicates – one
to return corrected) of the first 10 pages or so. Now I want the blamed
thing to refer to as I go on, & my wife has it making the score as
aforesaid.

I explained to you how erratically I work. I'm an ass – a duffer & all
that Paul says to Titus of the Cretes chap. I v. 12, especially the '*slow
belly*' part of it.

[1] at not having received sufficient revised proofs of *The Apostles*

Ja! I was coming to hear Wüllner[1] but this rheumatism settled that & many another promising scheme as well.

In referring to a coming artist you shd. write plainly: but *unkuncizly* [*sic*] you tell the approximate truth – your scribe's writing looks like "a new terror" meaning *tenor* Ja! it's mostly the same thing. I *was* coming to see you.

Address the Box to *Malvern Wells*.

In haste, yours ever
E.E.

The best way to learn to Bike is to have a good strong strap round your waist & let your coacher grab that: that's how I learnt.

The Liszt scores are beautiff*uly done.

* that's meant to be one F.

Craeg Lea,
Malvern.
Mar 31 1903.

My dear Jaeger (Moss).

On p. 179 please put f instead of B (Ger, voc. sc. *Apostels*) Buths put the B as the note was *tied* in the original.

This 'bogen' of 16 pp was stuck in at the end of my advance copy accidentally. By post I send full sc. of "*In the South*". I cannot suggest anything about arrangements for P.F. Simrock used to do

> piano solo
> piano duet
> 2 pianos

at once & one thing advertised the other: I have craved (for other people who write to me 1000 times) for Variations P.F. duet but it's not done.

As to preface in German by all means leave it out except about the Augener's tune.[2]

The 3 stave sketch of the overture is of no use to anyone & there are only a few bars here & there readable.

Some wretched paper has announced that I am in Bournemouth – haven't been & am not going – but I am inundated with begging letters from there! Life is not all joy.

Much love
Yours ever
Ed. Elgar

[1] Ludwig Wüllner gave a recital on 20 March, in which his singing of Wolf impressed (see *Mus. T.*, April 1903, p. 249). In May he gave weekly recitals at the St. James's and Queen's Halls.

[2] see vocal score p. 21

On *23 March* Gerontius *was performed by the Apollo Music Club, in Chicago, under Theodore Thomas. There was an enthusiastic audience of 4,000 (see* Mus. T., *May 1903, p. 311). Three days later it was given under Walter Damrosch in New York. On the day of its performance in Chicago the work was also being given its first performance in Danzig, by the Singakademie, conducted by Fritz Binder. So far as England was concerned the scheme to produce* Gerontius *in Westminster Cathedral, on 6 June, was by now more or less settled. The choir would be that of the North Staffordshire Choral Society. On 4 April Jaeger wrote:* 'They want you to conduct 'cos they are proud of you, I daresay.'

Craeg Lea,
Malvern.
Monday [6 April 1903]

Good old Mosshead:

Preach away – my liver is better now & the new Bike is friendly.

Look here: *do* send me all you can revised or not before Easter – you *are* playing slow over it. I have a lot more ready for you but must – or rather humbly wd. like to see the end of III.

Hope you had a ride.

Do you want to see U.S.A. papers – they have sent me about 2,000 which my wife has – I sternly refuse to read anything.

Buck up!

I hope you really can balance yourself.

Much love, yours ever
Edwd Elgar.

[*W.P.S. paper*]   27-4-[19]03

My dear Jaeger:

Wüllner will of course want to sing the low version of 'Sanctus fortis'[.] Is the alternative bit for chorus in the Sol-fa? Do, there's a particular angel – write to Hanley or Stoke or wherever it is, & prepare their minds for the change – they will do it all right – I wd. write but I don't know if it's in the Sol-fa.

Yours ever
Ed. Elgar.

Craeg Lea,
Malvern.
Sunday 2 3/v/[19]03[1]

My dear Jaeger:

I'm glad you're glad! Although your expressions are as difficult to

---

[1] For once realizing a characteristic error in dating, Elgar added the current date (3) but did not delete the incorrect 2.

make out as your namesake's in Dante; yours because of your writing,
his because – well (see Carey, Hell **XXXI**, *62* etc etc).[1]

As to the printing or rather engraving – I don't think you'll manage
to do it in one *engraving* & I should have thought the necy (?) difference
in the German & English *prices* wd. have made it imperative to have
two copies.

I hoped you would have gone on eng[ravin]g piecemeal – but if you
must have a M.S. copy made, well you must! but it seems a lot of
trouble.

Yours ever
Ed. Elgar.

Jaeger to Elgar, 5 May 1903:
My dear E.

Splendid! that's a capital afterthought introducing the Earthly
Kingdom theme at that point where 'Satan entered into Judas' vocal
score p. 132. It illumines & elucidates much 'darkness'. I say, *do* give
us a less jolly tune for Christ's 'The Keys of the Kingdom', p. 102.
The words themselves *jingle; do* make the music a little more stately
dignified & monotonous (in the true sense of the word), & on p. 83 at
'Ye shall lie down' you have the *notes* of 'God save the King'. Don't
sneer at me; these things will jar on one. Simply take out the E on 'lie'
& there you are. I call that [quotation on] p. 5 etc (over the Gospel
theme) the Preaching & Teaching theme. But, where it should be *writ
large*, on p. 101 last 2 bars, *it don't turn* up!!! though the Apostles do,
largely. Is the 'Preaching' in the orchestral score or can you add it?
Cheek, E.E.? Your work grows on me tremendously & by leaps &
bounds. It's great stuff & quite wonderfully original & beautiful. Bless
you, this is your finest work so far & your greatest. I fancy I can do a
decent description for the poor amateurs who have to study the work
(so very original!) before a concert. It wants 'getting at' certainly but
all pains & labour are amply rewarded.

Once more, bless you & thank you for this superb stuff.

ever thine
A.J.J.

*On 15 May Jaeger wrote again to say that to substitute 'Blessed Virgin' for
'Mary' in the score of* The Apostles, *which Elgar had suggested, was
unnecessary in the firm's view. He also said that he was going to the Duisburg*

---

[1] see XXXI, l. 77f.

Nimrod is this,
Through whose ill counsel in the world no more
One tongue prevails.

Festival in Germany with Parry, and asked whether he should remember
Elgar to Buths, Strauss, Steinbach, Volbach, and other friends. To this Elgar
replied in pencil on the back of an undated letter from Mrs. Elgar:

Love to all friends. Duisburg isn't a Lower Rhine Fest. after all – I
suppose you'll all try to make out it's a bigger thing. I'm sending you a
Bike stand
                                   Yrs
                                   E.E.

Having returned from Germany, Jaeger reported, on 27 May, that Parry
had enjoyed greater success with Blest Pair of Sirens *than Strauss with* Tod
und Verklärung. *He also reported that the engraver, Brause, was upset at*
Elgar's having sent 17 pages of a new chorus for The Apostles.

Craeg Lea,
Malvern.
28/5/ [19]03

My dear Jaeger:
I am glad you are back & rejoice that dear old Parry had a good time
with his 'Sirens'. Now: it is really & truly a great deal too bad & *too silly*
(I must say it!)

Brause shd. have gone on as I said: it wd have made no difference to
his 'laying out'.

– I said go on '*without* paging & omit rehearsal figures' – I have been
obliged to recast on acct of the difficulty in finding a Judas to my mind
& particularly wanted these sheets as I have to travel & try vocalists –
now here I am, through confounded stupidity, without any copy at
all. Even if the Judas sc: cd not be proceeded with – I suppose everybody layed him down & wept & forgot all about such things as revises.
I am absolutely vexed! for once.

Tell me is Messchaert[1] singing well?

Now: will you *analyse* this thing as before: I am authorised to ask
you & can arrange decent terms I think – I have sounded the way for
that but say 'yes' first there's a dear.

Yours ever
Ed.E.

I *had* to insert two pages voc. sc. near the beginning of another work:
I telegraphed to those printers "two pages to come in between 19–20 –
move paging two pages on pp 20 – 99 & rehearsal figures also". I sent
them the M.S. & had a full proof whole thing next day. I wish to
goodness you did not print for yourselves.

The old wooden stand comes to you now: it is good for the Bike's
tummy to rest on it I believe.

[1] see p. 286

[*W.P.S. paper*]   Thursday [28 May 1903]
My dear Jaeger:

I wrote hurriedly this a.m.

Pt. I ends with the new Chorus & the Chorus pts can be printed to the end of that number. First I want to see final proofs to p. 67 – 2nd proofs 68 & on as far as I've been allowed to see p. 108. Also I want revises of Chorus parts.

Surely *some* of this might have been seen to.

I conclude you will not print from the score, or whatever it is, for the conductor & pianist – two of the proofs wd. do for them, if we can only let the Chorus have copies up to end of Pt I – which you now have.

There's an awful storm going on just now – & it would frighten you & your men into fits – I wish it would

Buck up!
                                   Yours ever
                                   Edward Elgar.

                                                    29/5/[19]03

My dear Mosshead:

You are an angel not to be angry. I hope to have a rough copy of Judas in time to catch (*private*) van Rooy[1] next week.

As to the Analysis, *you must* do it. I want you to come down here & talk it over in a week or two. It's all quite simple I assure you & the theological parts can be made plain even to an old Heathen such as *you*[2]

r's truly   Ed. E.

[*letter-card*]   [*postmark* Malvern, 4 June 1903]

---

[1] see p. 288; van Rooy was expecting at this time to read through the part of Judas. Jaeger warned Elgar of his 'foreigner's English'.

[2] twice underlined

What book is that you have with Musical terms in all *lingos* in? My new score is sadly unbesprent with terms descriptive &c. & I've no book: if you publish the book & it's within my means – or my *meanness* let me have a copy to Westminster.

Yours ever

E.

For the rest of this month Elgar was extremely occupied. After Gerontius at Westminster Cathedral and consequent entertainment by distinguished persons he went home and worked at The Apostles *so that on 21 June Mrs. Elgar entered in her Diary:* 'Finished – all but the very end'. *After that Elgar was again in London, where he talked with the King, who told him how much his music had meant to him at the time of his illness. On 3 July the Elgars went to Wales. The letter from Jaeger referred to in Elgar's second of 1 July is not extant.*

private strickly[1]!

Craeg Lea,

Malvern.

July 1: 1903.

My dear Jaeger:

My eyes are bad – but sufficient – this (new) pen is worse – drat it! & the ink will not flow.

I was bothered in town by a heap of people – principally trying to find singers *with brains* – now I have to put up with a ――― caste of English – I won't go into the disappointments – oh! these singers – *where* are their *brains*?

Now: Mr Johnstone will send the firm a list of the *authorised vocalists.*

I have some full score ready for you but will hold it for a space.

Do you know any *clean* wholesome young man who wd like a couple of months in the country to copy my score as fast as I do it: he wd have to be in a lodging near & be able to write clearly & decipher my blind work – any *musician* can do that with prayer & fasting. I could not pay *much*. The Johnny might also – under my direction – make out the band parts with proper cues etc. You will find no difficulty with the Analysis.

Much love

Yours ever

Edward.

The only way out of the singer business was to omit 'Peter' – who shines forth in Pt III & let Black do Judas – It's pitiful but there are really no *good* singers beyond three & one (Bispham) we can't have!

[1] *strickly* twice underlined

Craeg Lea,
Malvern.
July 1 [19]03

My dear Jaeger:

Your very dear letter came this a.m. *I'm not ill*[1]! & it is of no use to postpone the work as I shall *never* get English vocalists – a complete caste that is – to do my work. Pt III was written first & most of it is ready to print – but I can find no singers. My eyes are not good.

You are a bonny boy to talk of my career. I know nothing of any such thing. I only know that my things are performed – when they go as *I* like – elastically & mystically people grumble – when they are conducted squarely & sound like a wooden box these people are pleased to say it's better. It's a curious thing that the performances which I have hated & loathed as being caricatures of my thoughts are the very ones held up as patterns!

Ffrangcon Davies' address is:—

> c/o Messrs Alexander, Watriss & Polk,
>   Attorneys at Law
>   32, Nassau street,
>   New York.

Let F.D. have his pages soon. My address on Saturday will be

> Minafon,
> Bettws-y-coed,
> N. Wales.

Now don't go pouring out your dear old heart to me, 'cos I'm not worth it. I want to do things well but I want power! I *can't* think why you preach to me about my career (once more). My career, to me, is this:—

I live on a pound a week.

I receive applications for autographs.

I receive applications for subscriptions.

I don't read about myself but I invariably get sent to me anything people think I don't like to see!

And I try to write music & don't like that either! A damned fine *"career"* – wot ye well!

Mustn't write any more now.

Yours ever
Edward

---

[1] *ill* twice underlined

Minafon
Bettws-y-coed
July 6, 1903.

My dear Jaeger:

Many thanks for your note[1]: I am sorry about the amanuensis – but it's too late to be of any use*. Here come 48 pp full score – a score to do *your* heart good to see! Please let there be any amount of cues – sensible ones – & don't print anything until I've seen it – only to be of any good I must check the parts (M.S.) with the full score. Send me proofs of title of the Men's voice things

Much love
Yours ever
Edward Elgar.

Love from all here. Rodewald asks you to *come here* as soon as you can & as long as you can – bring your bike & we'll do analysis. You will be *heartily welcome* Rodewald says & there are no Blackbeetles (clergy) here! (his message, not mine!) Tell the firm it's necessary for you to come.

* my fault, I ought to have asked sooner.

Minafon,
Bettws-y-coed.
[*c.* 9 July 1903]

My dear Jaeger:

Thanks a thousand times for your letter: Now: you *must* come up on Saturday – it shall *cost you nothing*.

It is quite free & easy here – you dress as you like & do exactly what you please – no formality or any nonsense.

I hope you will have had my wire.

I am so glad you like my stuff but come.

Yours ever
Edward.

Please ask Mrs Jäger to let you come, we'll meet you either at *Llandudno Junctn*[2] or at Bettws. The journey is via Crewe, Chester & Llandudno Junct. There's a through carr: to Llandudno & you change at *Llandudno Junction*

On 8 July Jaeger wished that he could accept the invitation to Wales. But

---

[1] of 4 July, in which Jaeger said that he had found an amanuensis. Two days later he sent more proofs of *The Apostles* and also a military band arrangement of the Prelude from *Lux Christi*, to be performed at a massed bands concert in Queen's Hall.

[2] *Junctn* twice underlined

he could not afford it. 'I . . . must', *he wrote,* 'work *like the D— on that Analysis to make a few pounds for my expensive Bairns, bless them.' At the same time he would like to discuss his Analysis with Elgar. As to the music, which was now going into full score, he said:* 'I shall be surprised if Buths doesn't do this work at the Lower Rhine Festival in 1905. I have just sent him a copy of Pt I. I can see him quizzing it, close to his nose, glasses off, twisting his moustache, grunting and saying 'ei! ei! . . . That opening! & that there "Temple stuff" with Shofar, antique cymbals, colour most gorgeous & new, effects most astounding & bewildering, organ etc. etc . . .' *This letter concluded thus:* 'Have you seen Graves's "Life of Gore" & the lovely tale of the German Governess who thought there was such a nice, appropriate English prayer for people of her calling, viz:—the prayer "for all women labouring with child"! That made my wife & me roar. This morning one of our workmen (stock-keeper) came to me, wondering whether Stanford's Oedipus music was for male voices. When I told him, "of course", he said that's a funny turn-out, seeing as all the confab is about a woman & a baby. There's a description of a tremendous Greek tragedy for you.'

However, the renewed invitation brought Jaeger to Minafon.

He was back in London before 29 July – the Elgars left Wales on 31 July to prepare for the visit of Canon Gorton who was advising on theological points in the oratorio – and wrote to complain of 'dirty, filthy, stuffy London after a delightful holiday in a *clean air'. On 1 August he wrote again, with proofs. Examining* The Apostles *in detail he was surprised by a* 'fearsome progression of the voice parts in bars 3 & 4 page 109 (second stave) . . . It sets my teeth on edge. If I found that in a work by a beginner I should laugh & say "poor chap, how crude".' *This Elgar found amusing.*

Craeg Lea,
Malvern.
Sunday Aug 2 [19]03.

Dear Mosshead:

Sorry you are not well – what a fellow you are! it's only liver of course. I wish you wd. let me doctor you – I could have set you up at Bettws. We are *all* right & I have my work well in hand & everything goes well. You are a perditioned old Moose: p. 109, 2nd sc. bars 3 & 4 are all right – & you were good enough to admire them a fortnight ago! – I played 'em to you several times: try it ppp & dolce – I fear your heavy thumb & melodious forefinger are rather stiff, old Boy.

Tomorrow I send ye

    I. Some of Dodd's work corrected.

    II. a section of score

III. last pages voc. pts
    Alto
    Bass
      corrected
IV. Title proof
 V. M.S. of Title page etc.
VI. 8vo. copy of pt I with corrections
       Gosh!
Let me know if the whole lot arrives.

I hope all your dear ones are well – the weather is now lovely. I am off to Elg[1] (can't spell it yet) Eglwys, that's right.

        Yours ever
        Edward of the *crude* (you old toad) progression.
I think you said all the vocalists had their copies of pt II? Ffrangcon Davies?

              Craeg Lea,
              Malvern.
              Augt 5 [1903]

O Glorious Moss!

Eglwys is Welsh for church!

You are a brick not to grumble at my correction: it's very important because I'd clean left out the 'Earthly Kingdom' motive at the important temptation point[2] – copied from the early sketch instead of the complete one: that comes from having note books: I did better when I cd only afford scraps of paper pinned together. The alteration will not affect the Solisten. p 32 & 33 meek twice over is right. Before Mr Dodd gets on to the wind – or if he *has* begun it I want again the section of f. score containing pp. *71. 72. 73.* I enclose a letter from Buths – which please return when read.

It *is* fine to have a fellow or two in the world to understand one. You might read it to Mr Alfred if opportunity occurs. I don't want it for a few days.

Glad your bairnies are well.
            Yours ever
             Edward of the crude *progression.
*You *infernal* old toad. Canon Gorton has been here[3] – he is a fine man so jolly & clever.

---

[1] deleted

[2] see p. 132, vocal score, also p. 188 above. This letter was in reply to one from Jaeger, dated 4 August. In this Jaeger conceded that the effect of the 'crude' progression was quite different to the ear than to the eye.

[3] 3–5 August

Craeg Lea,
Malvern.
Aug 6: [1903]

My dear J.:

p. 102. The 'keys' are all right, if sung intelligently – the *Keys* do not want emphasising – but the result in the next two sentences – no one but you wd try to sing it in time, Moss. p. 83. Shan't alter it on any account – put a pause over the $\hat{e}$. I should not call that theme (?)

anything. It only adds to the sort of 'life of the passage' – gives it more sort of "movement". It cannot possibly occur on p.101 where
the Gospel and
Apostles are combined
I must get to work.
Try again.
Yours ever
Edward.

Craeg Lea,
Malvern.
[*c.* 7 August 1903]

My dear Jaeger.

Accidentally I have called you by your right name! No offence!

First you had better do just as you *feel* about the xplanation of Judas & if you say too much, which I don't anticipate in the least, we can suggest curtailment regarding the theological side.

I think Canon Gorton only *refers* to the view I have adopted – which view is perfectly well known by any serious student etc, & he does not *apologise* for it – see?

Thanks for proofs of Band parts, fine! I like the look of 'em much.
I enclose with them a green page of direxshuns. Thanks for arranging
about proofs. Pointer's a jewel – but!! his tobacco! Do tell me what he
smokes & I'll send him some.

Return the enclosed (from Rodey) when read – amusing! Stanford is
here & came & talked (contra) Strauss to me – rather on the brain, I
think.

Much love
Yours ever

Edward the Crude.**✗**

Can you spare me another *complete* copy voc. sc. of Apostles; you
have most of mine for correction.

✗

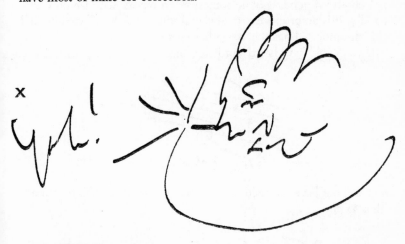

Weather bad
P.S. Please say to David 'not possible'. I have sent him a p.c. saying I
have sent to Messrs N. – not ready yet.

Craeg Lea,
Malvern.
Augt 9: [19]03.

Dear Moss:
    Smell this!
        It's scented!!
            Gosh!!!

p. 132 put in *Cl. & Fag* if you can possibly (at [150]) I know there's
no regularity about the instl. markings – in many cases they're unnecy
– but this passage could (& *is*) played by any group or family of insts.
All else answered in the proof

please put this – I decline to alter the notes.

There is no objection to the repetition of cometh 3 times – if done with any dramatic instinct as a good actor would do, & as a chorus, to be considered good, *must* do someday. To repeat 'with lanterns' wd. be silly. It is unfortunate that all choral music shd. be affected by dull church music & by comic opera but so it is.

If you could have heard van Rooy sing

you wd. not have criticised it – it is useless to try & explain to you my ideas so put

Well go on & find some more.

I am awfully annoyed about Johnstone & have said as much to him. Curse the Festival!

I hope my letter may do some good. I had no idea you wd. work so hard at the thing! Oh! dear what a nuisance I am to everybody & I wanted to do so much good.

Curse the Festival!

Yours ever
(ohne Moss)
Edward

Thanks for pp 71–73 of score. Bless you I'm methodical & keep, in my copy, a register. Method, my boy, is everything. I apologise for the extra moss.

[*W.P.S. paper*]

Malvern.

Aug. 9 [19]03.

Oh! Moss!

What a crop of moss is sprouting.

I asked (I *believe* for f. sc: containing *pages* 71–73. In a mossy letter you say you send me *pages* 71–73 & you actually send me rehearsal figures 71–73 – really *pages* 121–144. Oh! Moss, live for ever!

All right, let me have pp 71–3 & I'll drop you in another leit motive. Serious.

Do tell me about Johnstone & the terms – I am furious if they propose low terms after my request – I really think the more one has to do with the practical side of music the more awful this life becomes. I am so sick of it all!

Birmingham is the worst Festival programme I have ever seen I think (Talk about the 3 Choirs!)

Elijah!

Messiah!!

Legend!!!

I *can't* invite any decent folk to such a week.

Yours ever

Edward of the crude (you old badger!)

progression.

Keep Buths' letter for a bit.

In a letter (or letters) which have not survived Jaeger raised further critical points. On 10 August he wrote: 'I wouldn't alter anything in your Apostles for the world if you think your original idea is quite O.K. I only draw your attention to things that strike my critical eye & ear & appear to them as little specs on the Sun (or moon). But I do not dare to write until I have *got quite used* to the things that worry me, for I know your stuff is so confoundedly original & unconventional that they *require* getting used to. But as I have said I won't alter a thing if you ain't willing . . .

'. . . All right: "Cometh, cometh, cometh". You are in good company: Mendelssohn's Walpurgis night: "Come, come, come, come with torches" etc. Yah! I *can* imagine an artist like van Rooy & Wüllner singing "Hold him fast" with A.1. effect. Alas, where is *your* van Rooy & Wüllner amongst English oratorio singers! If Black *can* do it as you *imagined* it leave it for Gawd's sake. Perhaps he can be taught *not* to be comic. That Judas part is superb & worthy of the biggest artist living. Younger fellows want educating up to it, unfortunately. Perhaps your Apostles will be a liberal education unto them. *Don't* worry about Johnstone. I'll tackle him. He "trades on my poverty".'

[*W.P.S. paper*]

Malvern.

Aug 10 [1903]

My dear Jaeger:

I think these are the last corrections or alterations. I fear it may upset your analysis a *very* little. I meant to suggest the Earthly Kingdom on p. 36. Here it is (see score also) – the germ –. I really meant to make it feel as if it *grew* out of Peter's first speech (1st bar p 35) or rather first tune – the Apostles first ardent feeling. You will find a weak (very) version of the theme (in small notes viola) at ⟨185⟩ & on p 163 (small notes) by which you learn that the Earthly Kingdom turned out rather badly. See corrected copy sent with the score to-day for alteration, which I hope makes the allusion clearer

In haste,

Yours ever

E.E.

[*W.P.S. paper*]

Augt 11: [19]03

Dear Moss:

Go ahead: tell me anything you like only don't think I haven't a reason *always* (probably a bad one) for what I do – virtue or crime. You had better put in those emendations now, markings because some of 'em I have put in orchl pts.

I am sorry you are copying out the (or rather that Mrs Jaeger is taking that trouble) Analysis.

I saw Mr Johnstone here yesterday: I understand they give you five gns for the right to use the Analysis for the 1st perfce – he says from Bennett etc. they have the *copyright* for that sum; this they have with you. He says they have never paid more than ten gns. (Grove) which also included the copyright. But I won't interfere (Ignoramus!)

Much love,
Yours ever
Edward.

I went for ride 6 a.m. this morning. Cold to the tummy!

[*W.P.S. paper*]

Malvern
Aug 12: [19]03.

My dear Augustus:

I must try & be sensible for two minutes:

Look here!

In a few days, D.V. I shall send you the last pages of full score: Dodd sends me portions of sc. & string parts as you know – which I revise *with the score*. Now I want to be *quite free* for a little time – Bike touring belike – & could not undertake to do anything, *except* to revise Dodd's M.S. pts with the score.

This is the point – I always get Austin[1] to play thro' *everything* with me & we generally manage to turn out the parts pretty correctly: will it do if I do the *whole* of the string parts at once, i.e. when Geidel has engraved & sent proofs of the whole shoot or must I go on in driblets. We have plenty of time I think & it is difficult to get Austin at a moment's notice & I don't like to ask him to come for less than a day.

Perhaps you can't say so don't trouble to cudgel your brains. Proofs of TTBB[2] recd. I *don't* see how any English chorus is to make anything of them if they have to sing from these scores – & they are too much spread out – all turning over beautifully engraved. *Do*, for your own sakes, have a type edition done in the usual style. I hope you received *all* my huge package.*

Yours ever
Edward.

* 1 new sect. 2 old. 1 Dodd with pts.

[1] John Austin, of Worcester, who helped Elgar in reading proofs
[2] Op. 45, dedicated to Sir Walter Parratt (see 17 August below)

[*W.P.S. paper*]

Malvern
Augt 12: [19]03

My dear Analyst:
Here is a book about the Apostles: read anyhow *Judas* & return to
me – it's all interesting & won't take you long.
Look here on p. 180 "Son – & of the *Holy Ghost*". I have not made a
new theme for the 'Holy Ghost' but have used the 'Spirit of the Lord'
theme (I don't know what you have called it). But it must not be
thought that I have confused the 'Spirit of the Lord' (prologue etc)
with the Holy Spirit. I have used the theme here as representing the
whole Spirit of God.
"God (in the Old Testament) when influencing persons is called the
Spirit of God. The Spirit of God is not something less than God, it is
God."
Rev. Professor Davidson[1]. Introdn. *Isaiah* (Temple Classics).

Yours ever
Edward

You will probably, in writing of the passage, say I have used the *Lord's
prayer* chorus for 'The Father – the Xt theme for "the Son" & you
might refer to 'the Holy Ghost' as above.

[*W.P.S. paper*]

Malvern.
Sunday [16 August 1903]

Dear old Jagpot:
Thanks for analysis which looks fine. I'll read it later & tell you my
feelins.
The enclosed note will do – *you* or somebody less can see to the one
alteration – 'will be' for 'are'. Don't trouble to send it me again.
Delitzsch[2] enclosed.

[1] The Rev. Professor Andrew B. Davidson (1831–1902), of New College,
Edinburgh
[2] Franz Delitzsch (1813–90), a German theologian, who wrote commentaries
on the *Book of Job* (1866), the *Song of Songs and Ecclesiastes* (1877), and the *Psalms*
(1871). Delitzsch was inspired by the necessity for converting the Jews to Christian-
ity: he also spoke out against anti-semitic attacks. The missionary seminary
which he founded in Leipzig was subsequently known as the *Institutum Judaicum
Delitzschianum*.

The Rev F. N. Cohn[1] [*sic*] gave me much information – I enclose his notes – please *save* & return.

It might please him & be a good thing if you quoted the Tekia & Tera exactly as he gives it, mentioning his name?

Much love

Yours Crooder than ever & within 6

pages of the end.

Edward

C r u u u u u u u d

X

these

are *u*'s

[*letter-card*]

[*postmark* Malvern, 17 Aug. 1903]

My dear Augustus,

Thanks a 1,000000 for the first pt of Analysis, it looks jolly: I'm going *into* it to-night. By this post comes some revised strg parts & corresponding portion of score.

& two sections *completing*★ the work. Alleluia! Dear old Mosshead; the pleasure you take in it repays me for some labour.

In haste

Yours ever,

Ed. Elgar

★ Send me a wire to say you've received it, there's a dear. *Parratt* does want his part songs. Can I have the M.S. *p.F. score* to keep?

On 17 August Elgar completed the score of The Apostles. *The next day Jaeger wrote of the work as follows:*

'I'm steeped in your music just now & have no thought for aught else . . . The beauty of the music moves me to tears & the longer I study the work the more & the greater beauties I find. The Apostles are certainly your maturest & greatest work; the certainty of touch & style displayed throughout is wonderful, & the feeling of the most touching, heart-searching kind. But it is all so original, so individual & subjective that it will take the British Public 10 years to let it soak into its pachydermal mind; unless, of course, the story, being known by everybody, will carry the work along, assisted only by the prima facie

[1] The Rev. F. L. Cohen (1862–1934); a considerable authority on Jewish music. An essay by him, *Music in the Synagogue*, had appeared in *The Musical Times* in September 1899. Earlier essays appeared in the *Magazine of Music* V, 1888 (see also *Bibliography of Jewish Music*, Alfred Sendrey, Columbia University Press, 1951).

effective parts of the music. As for the poor critics (the dullest among them I mean) they will be bewildered I fear. But all this can't affect you. I believe that by the time you have completed Part III [i.e. the trilogy of oratorios intended] you will have given to the world the greatest oratorio since the Messiah, though this seems a rash statement to make, & time alone can prove the accuracy or futility of such a guess. Anyhow I know (in oratorio) nothing in which consummate mastery of technique is allied to such deep feeling, pure & holy; such mystic rendering of hidden truths, such chaste beauty of thought as I find in the Apostles. And then the strength & manliness of other parts, the convincing force of your proclamation of the Faith that is within you are superb & astounding. So you will believe I sent my congratulations this morning with a full heart overflowing with gratitude to the master to whom I owe so much of beauty & of inspiring, ennobling thought . . .'

The German translations of the Part Songs from the Greek Anthology *were expected back from Buths. It is to this work that the following letter refers. The English words of the first were by Alma Strettell.*

[*W.P.S. paper*]   Malvern
                                                                 Aug 18: [19]03.
Dear Augustusus:
    Sorry to hear about your tooth & hope relief follows the sacrifice.
    About this pt song title – will it be right to have the German *sentence* in the mid of the page: I think it shd. be in paren: anyhow – will this title do for the German edn – if *not* you had best put in English 'German translation by Buths, & leave the German wording for the German title if one is to be done. I think we ought to put the Johnnies' names *alphabetically* on the title page to save any ructions.
                                            Great haste,
weather awful   Yours ever
                                                    Edwd
Place aux dames! Miss Strettell must come first! Men in order as marked.

[*W.P.S. paper*]   Craeg Lea.
                                                                 Augt 20: [19]03
My dear friend:
    Your letter[1] touches me extremely & I feel I can only say 'non sum dignus'. Never mind the B.P. – they must wait; so long as my intimate friends – friends I have gathered round me because of their hearts and
    [1] of 18 August

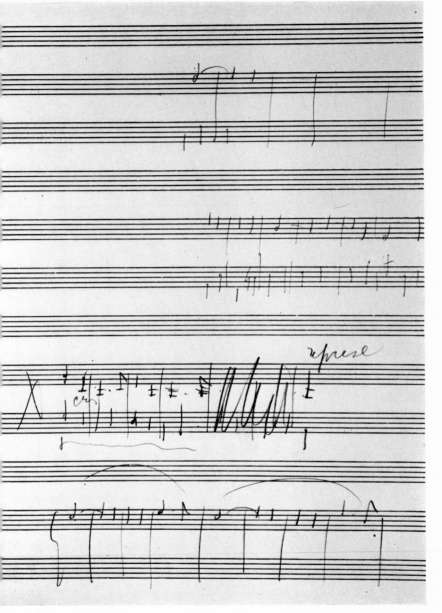

beginnings of a symphony (1)

The beginnings
of a symphony (2)

brains – are satisfied, nay even only *interested* in my work, I have my reward.

I have read through the portion of the Analysis & now return it: it is *superb* as a piece of informing dissection & you hit off every idea & feeling of mine. perhaps you use the word 'Elgaresque' too many times but that you will see in proof & can take out.

I don't deserve the adjectives & you will prune it in that respect freely I expect before it sees light: Now as to copying the themes: I would do it gladly (but I don't know what you have already done). I am *hoping* to come to town tomorrow (Friday) & will come straight to you to see you – if I come. The weather is awful & has upset all plans for rest & change – deplorable & nearly *fatal* I fear – I can't even get outside the door on acct of rain.

Atkins was here two nights ago, full of Apostles bless him! & yesterday dear old Bantock also. Bless him likewise! I played heaps of it to both – but where the 'change of mind' & rest are for me is more than I can tell. I *must* get out of it somehow!

As to the *shofar* – I think in the Analysis wd. be the place to say what it is or was – look at Stainer's Music of the Bible & compare with the M.S. notes I sent you by [F.L.] Cohen

Much love
Your groping old crudity
Edward

[*W.P.S. paper*]

Malvern
Aug 22 [19]03.

My dear Jag.

I did not start as the weather was too wet to walk into a cab.

I never was better but the impossibility of getting any exercise – and I am so active – is telling on me dreadfully – the weather has killed everything for 12 months.

p 73 6/8^1, you're about right – I meant a 'rhythmic memory", slow Eastern dance if you like – *then*, unconsciously perhaps, M.Mag. sings the saddest part of her soliloquy to a reminiscence as it were – this becomes more tangible in the Chorus A & B at 87 Now, Moss, nobody can do it like unto you, but you must not do too much.

p. 71. leave all that chromatic passage ending at 81 to take care of itself – say it is only carrying the feeling of excited sadness. p.76 bar 4 etc has really nothing to do with the last-named – the insistent *A*'s

---

[1] 'As to that ritornello (in 6/8 p. 73 etc) is it perhaps intended for a suggestion of a slow graceful Eastern Dance?' – Jaeger, 21 August

hold one down to the unwished thoughts of past vanities while the chromatic harmonies shew a feeling of struggle to shake off the memory; you need not say a 10th part of this – it's what I feel. The whole idea means roughly that "temptation is not sin". M.Mag: comes triumphantly out of it by sheer force of prayer.

I *did* drive the Buzzer[1] after you left, it was only my fear for *your* safety that kept me from it before.

That's a good one – the last part I mean.

I cannot for the life of me understand your view as to that Mercy & forgivenesses. Now you quote the iteration – surely you know that it is impossible to write varied chords to the last 3 syllables of such a word as forgivene*sses*[2] – the point of the word is forg*ive* – the remainder is nothing & it wd. be awful art to write a 'passage' for it – really it is

with a drop in the Tenor to prepare for the next chord. But you are beyond me.

Glad your tooth is better.

Just off to the forest.

Yours ever
Edward.

[*W.P.S. paper*]

Malvern
Augt 27: [19]03.

My dear Jäger:

Sorry for your head & hope it's better.

Oh! Moss!!

Shall be glad to be rid of those TTBB. *Heaps* of people want them – can't you put a short advt. in M.T.? too late, I forgot.

The enclosed rubbish was going to be torn up with 1000's of other things.

Throw them away: only you saw my dear place[3] & I hate having to give it up. My life is one continual giving up of little things which I

---

[1] the motor-car used in Wales. The end-note to the next letter alludes to Jaeger's letter of 29 July in which he thanked 'M. le Shover for the gentle pastime of shoving without accidents to fellow, fowl or female on the road'.

[2] twice underlined

[3] Birchwood

love, & only great ones, I'm told, come into it, & I loathe them. I do
like my *little* toys.

Yours ever

Ed:

Poor shover!

In answer to a letter from Jaeger, dated 28 August:

[*W.P.S. paper*]   Aug 29 [19]03
My dear Jag:
    Some brilliant-minded soul has written to me addressed
                    Wach auf!
thinking that is the name of the *House*!!!

    Thanks for all proofs &c. Glad the type English TTBB is started – I
am sure the things wd. not 'go' without. Yes: you had better print
Buths' translation with the english – it seems to be the plan now & is a
wise one seeing that *some of us* set better words than formerly.

    As to price – I'm no judge – I think I put in a plea for as low a figure as
possible – (I say! isn't *Apostles* rather high?)

    I shd. *think* 1/6 for the *T.T.B.B.* score.

    I have not seen Canon Gorton's article[1] (he read me his *first* sketch) –
so I do not know anything of its present length. *see other sheet.

    As to the separate edn of libretto – I think that must *wait* a little: I
shd. like it set *exactly* as in the 8vo edn only *one col. to a page & references* on same page. *notes* on the opposite page. example

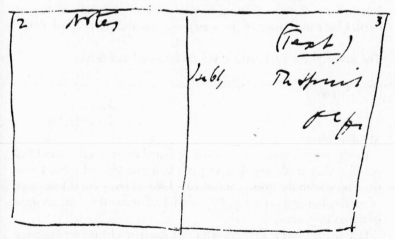

but I'll send my *copy* which I can complete now I have the *reference
copy* back.

[1] published in *The Musical Times*, October 1903

I don't think I wd. move the A -   -   - ⌐¹ etc note to end of libretto:
does not your copyright "These words etc" come there?

Yes, the A.M.D.G. will come before the libretto this time.

As to Birchwood: we give it up on acct. of the difficulty of keeping
it aired etc. besides we are almost certainly leaving here on account of
the building which will spoil our heavenly view, so it will be of no use
to think of Birchwood, I fear. All the same, 10,000 thanks I'll enquire
about it. I would like to end my days there – only it's too remote for
my wife & Carice is now growing up! & must be in the loathèd world.
Alas! alas!

Ever yours
Edward

Enclosure 1

* re Canon Gorton's article

I think it *might* be easiest to make it the same size as the Analysis, but
am not sure. I was going to propose a small 8vo. for the separate edn
(with notes & references) of the libretto but I may be in town next
week for Hereford rehearsals & will call & see you about it. – Enclosed
I send the original Gregorian tone, Constitues eos, & also the *Solesnes*²
version which I have worked from.

Yrs E.E.

I don't think you need say anything about A -   -   - ⌐¹ etc. it is difficult to express shortly & *ought* to be understood.

Enclosure 2

You will see that the Solesnes version is an amplification of this, as
usual. I have used more of the *amplification* than of the original Tone!

Ed. E.

The stereo in the *M.T.* article wd do for you I shd think.

[*W.P.S. paper*]

Malvern
Sep 1: [19]03

My dear Moss:

I only arrived home yester even & found those much-be-raddled
proofs – they made my delicate paws in a dreadful red mess. I post
them now with the queries answered – I would *bring* 'em if I was sure
of starting to London to-day. Anyhow I'll call to see about the progress
of things in general.

I am so glad you're through with that Analysis – let me see anything
when in print – like you I am slow at M.S.

¹ see *The Apostles*, vocal score, p. iii
² *sic* and twice underlined

I wish you were coming to Hereford – I've just returned from 2 or 3
quiet days with Sinclair & rode home yesterday per Bike.

Adieu

Yrs ever

Ed

The Crwwwwddd (Welsh form)

At the Hereford Festival Elgar was represented by the 'Enigma' *Variations
and* Gerontius. *This work, according to the official record, had* 'in company
with "Elijah" and "Messiah" . . . become (to use the phrase often heard
at these meetings) "one of the pillars of the Charity", and no one has
appreciated this more than Dr. Elgar'.

Herefordshire Club,
Hereford.

Sep 8 [1903]

My dear Moss:

Many thanks for your letter & Contents: I return *all* proofs & have
marked 'out' some of the names of motives. I think too many *names*
are confusing & I had a talk to good Walford Davies yesterday. He is
so nice to see & we persuaded him to come to lunch & tea! & were so
glad. We only want you here – a sad insufficiency of Moss.

I have a feeling that if the *principal* motives are named the others had
better go unbaptised (but not unblessed.

Do talk it over with W.D. who very shyly said something about
casting a fatherly eye over your technical remarx: you have my full
permission (!) to consult him.

These Club pens are vile.

Much love from us all.

Bantock arrived at the 'maternity home' yesterday so I suppose his
case is more urgent than Kalisch's.

Yours ever
Edwd.

Hereford, home to-morrow.
Sunday, 13 Sep [1903]

My dear Jag:

Sorry for delays in answering, we have had a *most* jolly week &
wanted you.

You *dine* with me in Birmingham on *Tuesday Oct 13.*

Now. wind pts *Gerontius* if there's room I shd. like the full vocal
cue to go in wind parts pt 2, 104 to 106. I don't suppose it's possible –
there are about four insts implicated. I'm afraid of those names, *plot* etc.

The analysis is A.1 & you need not be afraid of it's effect I think.

I'm sending all your proofs off to-morrow – no chance to-day.

I *wish* you had been here: we walked to Belmont Minster last Sunday thro' the cornfields – Heavenly.

Next *Friday* send a p.c. to

Brother Rodewald

66 Huskisson St

Liverpool

this question & *nothing* more

"*What is the boon of far Peru?*" I'll explain later; *don't fail.*

We had a festive meeting of the S.T.P.[1] & the Gold works & shall hope to meet in B'ham & include the *Psami.*

> Much love
>
> Yours ever
>
> Edward.

> Herefordshire Club,
>
> Hereford.
>
> Monday [14 September 1903]

Dearest Moss:

Just off home. I send this to Muswell Hill as I think it may reach you tonight. Your 'stuff' is A.1. & I am delighted. I have altered a few places. Don't insist on the Faith part of the forgiveness in Mary Mag. scene (end) – the words of Christ mean a good deal more than mere Faith as interpreted literally by dissenting folk of a low type & your remarks may be understood in this limited sense: I think it's innocuous as I've left it.

Your Judas is splendid – I should have liked a reference to the way a proud sinner at last confronted with the result of his sin is swayed by all sorts of feelings – prompted or suggested by the Psalm he knows so well – ending in blasphemy & despair. I don't like *plot* – it (that theme) figures more the man of action – & it staggers about at the end in a ghastly way.

> Much love, yours ever

[*W.P.S. paper*]   Edward

> 15 Sep [19]03

My dear Jagpot:

Thanks for yours: you must be at Birmingham somehow! I return the proofs of the T.T.B.B.

[1] The 'Skip the Pavement' Society, in which Elgar, Basil Nevinson, Troyte Griffith, and Archibald Ramsden, the piano dealer, were involved. Ramsden was its President. The remainder of this sentence remains an enigma.

As to Apostles. I want the score when I have any parts to correct –
it's about time I had some of 'em to do. If you have a day's work for
me (strings) let me know because I can't get Austin at a minute's
notice. Now as to the analysis: it's all right: if you are in doubt do ask
Canon Gorton. I think it reads well. Let me see a proof with your latest
corrections & we'll see.

I always take Nimrod slower than M.M. in score. Cowen says it shd.
be altered, what do you think? Try it & see.

Is anything being done about Canon Gorton's article? I want to
see it anyhow whether it's used or not.

Much love

Yours ever

E.E.

It is bitingly cold & we have both colds! It was really jolly at Hereford.

Craeg Lea,

Malvern.

16/ix/[19]03

Dearie Jagpot:

In English we always say *"the"* Greek Anthology – I shd. think the
Germans wd. also use the definite article: but there may be some
custom I am not aware of. If it is an oversight (einer) in translation all
right put *der* – but if in any doubt ask Kalisch★ for choice who wd know
the German & the Greek & everything etc.

Yours ever

Ed. Elgar

★ he hath a pretty brain.

I've dropped music now & going at algebra – it's better fun & no
audience! I shall give a lecture on the properties of numbers, come &
hear me!

*On this day Jaeger wrote agreeing that 'Nimrod' should be played slower
than the metronome marking. Hearing that the Elgar family were suffering
from colds he advised sleeping with open windows.*

Malvern

Sep 17: [19]03

Dear old Skittles:

Mark in score "*Nimrod*" IX *adagio* ($\dot{\downarrow}$=52)

As to *fag: 10.* in Troyte's Variation – the part *as printed is correct* – the
marks could not have been added at Hereford but somewhere where
they had no Contrafag.

Bar before ⌐48⌐ is in tenor clef & is correct in my score – anyhow the f should be ♯ (& so should you!) I expect the player only made the accidental *plainer*.

Colds are better: we *do* sleep with our windows open.

Stanford, who heard the chorus rehearse, is *enthusiastic* over the Apostles: telling people all round (Albani etc etc) of its or their glory! Thanks for your rhyme, I'll set it.

yours ever
E.E.

Taylor's work[1] was a disgrace to any civilised country, the utter want of *education* is the curse of this chap. The clergy condemn it as blasphemous.

[*W.P.S. paper*]

Malvern
Sep 18. [19]03

My dear Jaeger:
  Many thanks.

  1st. I fear Buths will be found in error by classicists – there's only *one Greek Anthology* [:] of course there are Anthologies in every civilised language but scholars only refer to one '*The*' Greek Anthology. I will send libretti with notes etc. at once, i.e. Monday. Send me back *Whately now* please for the purpose of notes and Delitzsch.

  I can't score those part songs yet[2], but Wood said March so there's plenty of time. T.T.B.B. I'm sorry for the 'orribul fifths & have knocked 'em out, alas!

  As to that article many thanks. I am writing to Mr Littleton – of course I've no intention of doing anything law-wise & by that means advertise the paper etc – but I wanted good advice as to how to go about a firm contradiction – it is impossible not to resent being called a thief, isn't it★. I'll ask Volkert[3] to look up the date of publication & also (Brit: Museum?) the date of the publication of the other thing.

  In greatest haste. What lovely weather now! & you are sending proofs!
★P.S. All else doesn't matter. Although the man wrote here some time ago & insulted my wife! *I could kill him for that*!!

---

[1] *The Atonement,* an oratorio composed for the Hereford Festival
[2] Op. 26, nos. 1 and 2, performed with orchestra at Queen's Hall, 12 March 1904
[3] Charles Volkert, of Schott & Co, publishers of *Salut d'Amour* (1889)

Craeg Lea,
Malvern.
20/Sep/[19]03

Dearie Jag:

1st. Birchwood is not for sale & we clear out for ever next Septr. Selah!

Please have the corrections made in the Anglo-German Edn TTBB if you possibly can – they at *least* can go in the *separate vocal* parts which you say you must issue. Now. we must have everything ready by Oct. *5th* – first rehearsal on that day – (so look alive) – in Manchester I think but I know nothing official yet.

Oh dear!

Those wind parts. I have carefully (!) marked all thro' score where the double wind is to play. I *suggested* that it might save writing out a lot if only those portions marked *tutti* were duplicated; see?

> Flauti,
> Oboi,
> Clarinets,
> Fag &
> Horns are *all* that are wanted.

There are only *six* Horns in the list but they must have something to do.

All string parts, V.1, V.2, Va, 'Cello & Bass pt 1 recd. & will be returned to-morrow. Hope you're well – We are all right again & going strong.

Much love
Yours ever
Edward

You haven't called me crooood lately – I breathe again – I feel crude in the stummick.

YAH!

I have been thinking over Canon Gorton's article & feel it *must* not go with my edition of the libretto: it's place is with the explanatory portion – analysis: otherwise it will give the feeling we were anxious to avoid, i.e. that he is 'bolstering' me up – I don't want that – but if the 'churchman' objects to the libretto he can see what one of his leaders thinks of it – but his leader may not *introduce* me – only explain me, see?

[*W.P.S. paper*]   Craeg Lea,
                                                        Malvern,
                                                        Sunday
                                                [*c.* 20 September 1903]

My dear Jaeger:
    I'm tired out.
    I return *all* I can correct with score.
    I *must* have wind on Tuesday early somehow or I cannot correct the
stuff – my man – helper – comes on that day. – Wire Dodd & send
Horns & transposing things at least.
    Many thanks for the parcel found on our return. Muffat & Fux & the
M.S.
                                        Yrs ever
                                        Edward

                                                        Craeg Lea,
                                                        Malvern.
                                                Sep 23, [19]03

My dear Jag:
    Alas! I'm so sorry. Party's name¹ is
                J.W. Ibberson
                41, Durham rd,
                Sheffield.
    All understudies are arranged amongst the staff – see programme
book. I told Dodd about picc. part – & will see it's right. If you have
any copies ready (8vo etc) let me know – they shd. be printed I suppose
by this time.
    I shall have to be in town next week but will let you know.
                                        Yours ever
                                        Eddard
Score received (portion), we'll soon get the parts right: no news of
rehearsals beyond the fact that they commence on Oct. 5 as aforesaid.
[*letter-card*]
                                [*postmark* Malvern, 26 September 1903]
Dear old muddle:
    They have a pause & lunch in the Messiah & continue 'Behold the
Lamb'.

    ¹ Reply to Jaeger's inquiry of 23 September: 'Was the razor gent Ibberson or
Ibbotson?' Ibberson (1864–1954) was a cutlery manufacturer, of the Sheffield
firm of Geo. Ibberson & Co., and a Freeman of the Company of Cutlers in
Hallamshire. From 1894 to 1944 he was organist of Wesley Church, Fulwood
Road, Sheffield. His zeal was such that in 1897 he took a long vacation from
industry in order to have organ lessons from Widor in Paris. (See p. 64.)

I am returning all I can. We stay with Lord Windsor first [at Hewell Grange, Worcestershire] and at the Grand Hotel [Birmingham] subsequently. We should be charmed to dine with Mr. A.H.L[ittleton]. I can't get a room anywhere for S.T.P. Japes.

Yours ever
E.E.

Craeg Lea,
Malvern.
Sept. 26¹ 27. [1903]

My dear Jag:

I sent off all strings (remainder) today – so they are finished. I leave for Bir: (Chorus) Tuesday afternoon – then on Wednesday to London. I have an awful *cold* now. I forgot to say that in them 'orns & Clarts my marks were not in.

L· · · ⌐² etc etc. Something must be done about it – put in *rit* or something I haven't really time. In great haste,

Yours ever
Ed.

I hope the Analysis is all right on the way to completion

Craeg Lea,
Malvern.
[*c*.28 September 1903]

My dear Augustus:

Here's all the stuff!

Let me know when *all* the wind is ready & *all* the string pts 2nd proofs as you said. I've answered all your queries & found some green errors. I agree with you that most of the superfluous *axidentles*³ may be left in.

We went biking to the forest & came home in doleful rain. Curse this weather!

yours ever
Edwd

I don't [know] anything of Miss Foster⁴! You can print pt 1 as soon as you like. The caps in the music differ from the libretto, is it too late to alter them?

[*added in green ink*]

---

¹ deleted

² see *The Apostles*, vocal score, p. iii

³ *dentles* twice underlined

⁴ Jaeger to Elgar, 23 September: 'How is Muriel the gorgeous? I am told she looked very ill at Hereford.'

please in prologue (Libretto) have l[ower] c[ase] m [*the letter* m]s put for *me* – *five in all*

[*Craeg Lea paper*]   address Langham Hotel.
                                                        Sep 29 [19]03

My dear Mosshead:

I'm sorry the parts worry you; I can't think *why?* Your men must be jolly slow.

Now: I arrive D.V. to-morrow mid-day. I'm really *very* unwell & my eyes nowhere – a frightful cold I fear. (I must have a fur coat the doctor says.) Now (again) I can't check the parts (really unnecessary) but I *do* like to *play* them all through. I fear this will be impossible – send nothing till you hear (or see) me. I will bring with me the 9/17 of the Full score which I have & it can all be stitched together. You *must come* to Birmingham somehow.

Full rehearsal on Friday afternoon Oct 9:

I'm not fearfully busy at all: I just left this time blank to correct parts & where are they? oh, where?? I don't know how I got this fearful chill, but it is a bad 'un.

Don't worry, take Bile Beans
                              Felsnapthah
                                 anything oily.

preserve Nimrodic calm – it don't matter a straw if the Oratorio is never heard. Yah!

                              Yours
                              Edward

On 1 October Elgar rehearsed The Apostles *with the solo singers in London, and on the next day, together with Mrs. Elgar, he chose the fur coat prescribed by the doctor. Jaeger came to the station as they left for home, with part of the full score and woodwind and brass parts. The next day he wrote, sending additional full score and orchestral parts, and saying that Mackenzie, Parry, and Stanford had all requested early copies of the vocal score. Three days later he wrote again to say that he was delighted to hear of the splendid rehearsal and that he would be coming to Birmingham for the first performance of* The Apostles *on 14 October. He came but collapsed on that day.*

Of this performance The Daily Telegraph (*15 October*) *wrote as follows:* 'The occasion may be described as in some respects unique. It was so in my own personal experience, for through all the years in which I have known the Birmingham Festival it has never happened that the whole musical world, not only in this country but also abroad, has gathered more or less closely around the production of an Englishman. It is a good omen that at last a man of our own race and nation has come to the extreme front, and drawn to himself the wondering admiration of all who profess and call themselves musicians and lovers of the art. There is something impressive in the position now occupied by Elgar. He is not an intriguer. He does not compass heaven and earth making proselytes to believe in his own powers, neither does he trim his sails to catch the varying breezes of popular opinion. Having something to say in the fashion which appears to him best, he says it straight out, and leaves the issue to the fates. Yet, though sturdily independent, courting nobody, he now occupies the position of a man with whom most people are determined to be pleased. There must be something in him much more than common to bring about this result. But what that is cannot now be discussed. Elgar's latest work is one for calm consideration and deliberate judgment. It cannot safely be written, I speak for myself only, while the excitement of a first performance is still seething, and there has been no time to analyse sensations and form conclusions. Besides this remarkable oratorio is worth any amount of care in handling. It is not a work of a mere trafficker in musical goods. Its sincerity is unquestionable, the loftiness of its aim cannot be denied, and its strength must be taken into account, whatever may be thought of its methods. The close of the oratorio was followed by the boisterous compliments which on such occasions no musician escapes. Dr. Elgar doubly deserves them first as a safe conductor, and yet more so as the composer of perhaps the most remarkable work of the present century.'

Craeg Lea,
Malvern.
Oct 20: [19]03

My dear Moss:

We are only just home & my hand is aching with writing letters: such a pile! However if it drops off I must send to ask how & where you are.

I trust, old boy, you are well again – that sort of thing happily often goes as quickly as it comes: I won't say a word about our disappointment over your absence from the performance – it's still too bitter.

I was so sorry I got to the station so late. Mr Johnstone drove me & owing to races or football business we got *blocked* twice: however my will was good & I did see you with an immense cigar. I send you a scrap – you wicked old sinner – cut from a letter from my sweet sister [Helen, or "Dot"], now a nun.

Tell me how you are. I am sending correction for 8vo. vocal score & when you are fit for work we must talk over the score & parts printing etc etc.

I'd better run up to town for a jaw over things I think.
Much love from us to you all,

> Your ever affectionate
> Edward.

I am getting conceited now.
I have asked Coates to call & sign the score if he can.

Jaeger's health was seriously undermined. He wrote that 'it is evident I had
been burning the candle at both ends and in the middle for weeks past.'
*Not only was he ill but also severely depressed by his lack of prospect in the
publishing house. About this, and the ability of some of his colleagues to earn
up to £10 a week by occasional* 'scribbling', *he was bitter. At the same time
Elgar was also in a state of melancholia. On 23 October Mrs. Elgar noted,*
'E. not very well & much worried with finance side of new work &
disappointed at that side.' *However, on 30 October Jaeger sent a more
cheering letter:* 'Good news', *he wrote,* 'Fritz Steinbach (have ye heard?)
wants to do the work (crooood passages, ugly bits, awkward points &
all) at the Lower Rhine Festival (Sunday Concert) Whitsunday, 1904
at Cologne. He is sehr entzückt of the work, calls you einer von den
Ganzen & sends Grüsse to you Meister Elgar.' *Certain points which
Jaeger raised in this letter are answered in that of Elgar following. The
success of Elgar was not to everybody's taste. Jaeger added in a postscript:* 'I'm
told that Mackenzie foams at the mouth when you say Apostles to him.'

[*W.P.S. paper*]   Sunday All Saints (a
                                      Nov 1: 1903 (b
                         a) date for moderate Xtians
                         b) date for heathen Mossheads.

Dear Jaggs:

I *think* I can send the libretto in a day or two. I have permission to
quote Whately at large if necessary now.

I can't think of any alteration for 148 & 149, except to put a *whole bar*
first for orch. – but I think this is *wholly unnecessary* & wd. make a fearful knocking about of plates. Surely there need be no alteration except
a pause over the chords which can be added to 8vo score & full sc.&
parts easily enough. The passage is marked 'Quasi RECIT" & is not
likely to be performed without rehearsal.

I am glad to hear about Steinbach: give him all sorts of greetings
from me. I'll write to him if you'll tell me *how* to address him, is he
still '*General*-[1]*Musikdirektor*"? As to Essen, let me know more. I don't
understand your allusions to critics. I don't read 'em so don't refer to
anything.

[1] *eral*- twice underlined

The effect at 208 is exactly what I want & must stand. I know better than to expect the rf from the voices but they must *feel* it.

In great haste,
Yrs ever
E.E.

Tell the firm I had a cable *reply pd* inviting me to N. York, Nov. 19. I refused. I'm sampling manure now with surprising results.

Specimen Sheet [of paper]   Guy Fawkes his day. [19]03
Dearie Jaggs:

You are right the Bug¹ was not for you & his pretty body is about done for in the post. Never mind, I'll catch another – altho' this year has not been good for flies & stinging beasts. We gave up Birchwood last week for ever! The weather has been too bad really for it to be of use & my regrets, which were bitter, are assuaging themselves.

Glad to hear of Köln etc. etc. only it's sure *not* to come off.

Give my kind regards to your host & my love to your fambly. I *do* want to buy your Angelicals something for Xmas before I leave this clime for ever. I wish *you* wd. buy them something – I shall be sure to give something they don't want or have already got.

Think it over – they are too young for Books yet I suppose. Tell me.

Yours ever
The Bughunter.

Craeg Lea
Sunday Nov 8 [1903]

My dear Jaeger:

Proofs of score recd. I *don't* want any more. I am coming to town tomorrow.

I am writing now to tell you about our poor dear friend Rodewald: it came as the most awful shock to me yesterday a.m. – he is quite unconscious & four doctors say he cannot possibly recover – I had a cheerful card from him on *Wedy* morning last – & now — it is too awful & my heart is quite broken.

On the card he says I shd meet you there on the 14th – alas! alas!

Yours ever
Edwd.

He thought he had influenza & said he was over the fever & hoped to be soon all right.

¹ 'I found this BUG, with letter attached, in my letter. Surely it is meant for *another* boy?' – Jaeger to Elgar, 3 November

North Western Hotel,
Liverpool.
My dear Jaeger: Nov 9 [1903]
   Too late.
   I stood it as long as I could & rushed up here – our dear, dear, good
friend passed away quietly at 12–30. I am heartbroken & cannot believe
it. God bless him.
   He was the dearest, kindest, *best* friend I ever had. I don't know how I
write or what I've written – forgive me. I am utterly broken up
                                   Yours
                                       Edward.

[*W.P.S. paper*]   Malvern
                                                Nov. 11: [19]03

My dear Jaeger:
   Thanks for your letter. Yes, it is too awful. I am glad you *began* to
know the dear, good fellow. I could not rest so went up on Monday:
did not go to the house but called at a friend's in the same street – they
told me – I broke down & went out – *and it was night* to me. What I
did, God knows. I know I walked for miles in strange ways – I know I
had some coffee somewhere – where I cannot tell. I know I went &
looked at the Exchange where he had taken me – but it was all dark,
dark to me although light enough to the busy folk around. I thought
I wd. go home – but could not – so I stayed at the hotel. Now, had I
been less stricken I shd. not have eaten – but in a dazed way I ordered
dinner & wine & I believe ate all thro' the menu – I know not – it
probably saved my life I think – but I lived on as an automaton – & did
everything without thought – then I went to my room & wept for
hours – yesterday I came home without seeing anyone & am now a
wreck & a broken-hearted man.
   Do not send me any more score – yet. I used to pass him every sheet
as I finished it at Bettws & heard his criticisms & altered passages to
please him, God bless him!
   Pointer & Brooke can do it all for the present & perhaps I can see to a
revise later – not now for God's sake.
   I am cold & don't think my doctor will let me go to the funeral.
   Good-bye: I cant say what I feel but I have lost my best & dearest –
I thank heaven we all had that bit of time together in Wales you know a
little of what he was.
                               Much love
                                   Yours ever
                                       Edward.

On 26 November the Elgars left England for Italy, where they spent the
rest of the year.

[*postcard*]   [*postmark* Bordighera, Italy, 5 December 1903]

Dear Moss; All right, I am writing to Richter. By this post, proofs
corrected; there seem to be many errors not marked: tell Pointer & Co.
I have my eye on them although the tobacco here is bad. Don't tell
everybody my address, I don't want to be bothered & what I pay for
begging letters etc etc to be sent on wd. turn you grey. I am going to
buy a donkey: shall go into the Ass trade I think: Much love, yours
ever
Ed Elgar

5 xii 03

[*postcard*]

Villa San Giovanni, Alassio,
Italy.
[11 December 1903]

Dear Moss:
   The above is the address; don't tell anyone – the Hotel Royal,
Bordighera will do for outsiders. p.1. f.score Apostel, 2⁰ vio, last
bar, the *accent* is not required.

We have citrons, lemons, olives in the garden & heaps of flowers:
the weather's again bad but not cold: this is a nice house & we are
very happy with 2 Italian servants – I can't jabber much, it's an in-
convenient tonguage. Love to all, yours ever
Ed. E.

11 xii 03

[*writing paper of Hôtel Royal, Bordighera*]

Alassio.
13–12–[19]03

My dearie Jaggs:
   We have run short of letter paper. My wife writes to you on kitchen
wrapping up stuff. I return proofs – *now* I understand what you want.
Sorry I left some queries unanswered. I think this lot is done *very
carefully*. My apology is written on the back of the last page of proof.
   This place is jolly – real Italian & no nursemaids calling out "*Now*,
Master Johnny!" – like that anglicised paradise Bordighera! pff!
   Our cook is an angel: do come out – it seems *so easy* to come & so

difficult to go back – & have a meal or two. What matters the Mediterranean being rough & grey? What matters rain in torrents? Who cares for gales? *Tramontana*? We have such meals! such wine! *Gosh*!

It is curious burning nothing but olive wood in the open fires – they bring a load with a corresponding number of *fir cones* (dry) for fire lighters – no smoke – no dust – paradise. We are at last living a life. The Mosquitoes are a trial & I am stung because I refused to believe in 'em & wd. not pull down the mosquito curtains at night round my bed.

Much love to you all. I can't believe all these great Germans are doing my music[1]: is it true? I think it's a dream. I hope you are pleased, old boy, anyway.

Yours ever,
Ed Elgar

Villa San Giovanni
Alassio.
27–xii–[19]03

My dear colossal Moss:

This is only to wish you all a most happy New Year & many, many more. I fear you have been overworked or something & we are anxious to hear of you.

I seem to hear nothing of anybody at all! We sit & shiver in the cold – we have had 5 fine days in a month – & wonder *when* the fine weather is coming. Is the Köln affair fixed? I have heard from Wüllner that he is suggested for *Judas* – wishing for a few alterations – we looked at the part in London. He would do it gorgeously, eh? But, as I said, nobody tells me anything & confine themselves to saying 'You lucky fellow! *now* we expect you to really write something'! Don't trouble to write at length if you are holiday-making or resting or busy but just send a *fact* or two about yourself or any other dot on the horizon. My love to the children. I must send them their remembrance of the wicked uncle (ME) when we get back. I fear the village affords nothing worthy.

Much love to you all,
Yours ever,
Edward

---

[1] Regarding performances either arranged or under consideration in Aachen, Köln, Mainz, Wiesbaden, Frankfurt, Danzig, and Budapest, see *Mus. T.*, Jan. 1903, pp. 20 and 100.

The Budapest Philharmonic Society, conducted by István Kerner, performed *In the South*, in the Pester Redoute, on 19 December 1904.

VIII

1904

Regarding this Italian holiday Miss Rosa Burley wrote: 'The Elgars went to Italy on November 25, taking a little villa, San Giovanni. I followed with Carice in time for Christmas. They met us in Genoa and we stayed the night there. Elgar seemed excited and happy. He liked the surroundings, which were lovely, and the change of food, and soon began to want to compose.

He ordered a piano from Genoa and after some delay the little piano arrived, with twelve men (brigands as he always called them), staggering and snorting, taking the piano upstairs. Edward, looked sadly at them, saying "They will all expect a tip"; but they all smiled, seeming very pleased [and] regarding the occasion as a festival, quite in the Italian style.

Edward said: "My father had two men who could carry any piano as though it weighed nothing at all, and look at these men. All of them seem to be breaking their backs!" '

The work on which Elgar was now engaged was the Overture In the South (*Op. 50*), *intended to take the place of the long-promised and long-delayed symphony.*

The first letter from Jaeger of this year to survive is that of 5 February, in which he apologizes for possibly having said too much about the non-appearance of the symphony. By this time Elgar was at home and working vigorously on In the South, *the engraving of the parts being the main reason for Jaeger writing on 11, 16, 17 and 24 February. In the last of these Jaeger asks:* 'Why the Divel have you a *silent* bar[1] in your Coda (Overture). You will play pranks with your Kodas. Foolish boy! ungracious neophite! Weber, Beethoven, Wagner knew better. It's never too late to do the wrong things, however. But that there Overture looks dem fine allee samee.' *He adds a request:*

'I say, *if* the C[ovent]. G[arden]. people give you any tickets which you *can't* do with remember poor "Nim". I really can't afford to pay &

[1] bar before 61, in which the timpani only play.

I *should* like to hear at least the *Overture*. You have no poorer friend than yours ever

Moss'

V[illa] S[an] Giov[anni]: Alassio.
Jan. 3 1904

Oh! most colossal & peculiar Mosshead!

I am very angry with you for writing such rot: I can't think why you think I've written to other people & not to you. I sent a line to Jos. Bennett asking him (so as to save my poor pocket pounds sterling – really – of postages) to say what address wd. find me – which he *didn't* say I believe & I've sent cards to Pitt & Kalisch.

Private Now: there's nobody in my precious confidence more than you: this visit has been, is, artistically a complete *failure* & I can do nothing: we have been *perished* with cold, rain & gales. five fine days have we had & three of those were perforce spent in the train. The symphony will not be written in this sunny (?) land. You must understand that when a wind *does* come – & it is apparently *always* on – it is no bearable, kindly east wind of England – but a tearing, piercing, lacerating *devil* of a wind: one step outside the door & I am cut in two, numbed & speechless: I have never regretted anything more than this horribly disappointing journey: wasting time, money & temper. Our house *is* comfortable & there is a decent English library here. Carice is here – Miss Burley brought her – & we are all happy together & only want weather!

I am trying to finish a Concert Overture for Covent Garden instead of the sym but am writing definitely *tomorrow* to the authorities so don't say a word yet. I really get no news at all – even of the things which concern me; people at home are so curious about writing – a p.c. wd tell what one wants to know: but most people will not start writing abroad until they think they can see time to write a long letter: then they write a lot of envy of sunny skies (which we haven't got) warm weather (which we never feel – or seldom) etc. etc – & then – they put 1½d stamp on it & I have to pay 75c. Joking apart the amt. of excess postage I have pd wd. pay the rent: almost every post brings lyrics, libretti with 1.50 to pay on each!!

Cuss! I'm not stingy I trust but this awful waste of money is wretched. P.S. *Your*[1] *letters are all right!*

---

[1] twice underlined

Glad to hear about Köln[1] etc. etc. you will be there of course – *must* be there.

I've no Violin music, I'm sorry to say, at all worthy of your wife's attention – would I had – I don't think I shall ever write any now – in fact this cold air has completely withered any brains I ever possessed: but it *is* lovely when fine, & the local wine at 3d. a bottle is A 1. But "poor Tom's a-cold" frozen, & it will take months of sunshiny England to unfreeze me.

I had no idea 'Apostles' was to be done in N. York. Don't be *down* about the M.T. – the actual joy of writing I think was not much to you – I know you ought to make some money by coaching people – Lunn & Butt for instance now. Do not bother about anybody's oratorio unless they *pay* you to look thro' it. It is not fair at all & you have been badly treated by too many. Now good-bye & buck up old man & be a little lively & don't fret. If you were in the midst of this icy land you might feel *blue* but not in London.

Our kindest regards – no [–] love to you all.

Yours ever
(with a frozen circulation)
Edward

[*postcard*]

Alassio.
[*postmark* 18 Jan. 1904]

Thanks for the sc: *Lux Xti* which will come anytime during the next 3 weeks[.] So glad a score of Ap. has gone to N.Yk. Richter will want one also I suppose. I wish my friends wd. not gossip about me: Ettling wrote from *Weingartner* asking for first German perfce of Sym. promising Munich Berlin etc. so I wrote to *W*. saying it wd. not be ready for him this season etc. etc. Then apparently Ettling writes off to Pitt! Bless us all! Weather better. E.E. d[itt]o. Love to you all.

Edwd.

[*postcard*]

Alassio
Sunday. 24–1–04.

In with chill, cold, *rheumatism* etc. etc. East winds for a week enough to scarify the D—l! I *think* I return this day week & hope to bring most of the new score for you to go on with: we shall be in good time only your people will have to look alive *as usual*. I return all the Ap. sc.

---

[1] *The Apostles* was to be performed at the Gürzenich Concert Hall on Whitsunday, 22 May 1904, Steinbach conducting.

proofs as they come &, as I hear no complaints from you, I conclude
they reach you safely. Oh! this weather – what a delusion the world is.

Much love, dearest Moss

Yours ever

Edward

I have, *at last*, started an eyeshade & find the benefit, thanks to your
Nimrodic preaching.

[*letter-card*]   [*postmark* 18 Feb. 1904]
Dearest Mosshead.

I wired as you said & return the M.S. score of Singing Bird.

By this post pp. 93–118 incl. of "In the South".★

I am not well – chill – but will write fully to-night.

Yours ever

Edward.

★ The Schluss folgt.

The month following was very full. On 20 February the Elgars saw and
liked Plas Gwyn, the house in Hereford to which they were to move on 1
July, and the next day In the South *was finished. Four days later there was a*
first performance of The Apostles *in Manchester, after which Richter*
rehearsed In the South *in Manchester on 9 March. About the business*
arrangements concerning this work Jaeger wrote a battery of letters at this
time. Bearing in mind the forthcoming Elgar Festival at Covent Garden
(14–16 March, In the South *being given its first performance on the last*
night), and the increasing attention being paid to the composer by the Royal
Family and others of the upper set, he could not forbear to add a cautionary
word:

'Don't', *he wrote on 8 March,* 'let 'em spoil you, you "dear, innocent,
guileless Child" as dear old Hans [*Richter*] calls you in his fatherly
loving way.'

Grand Hotel,

Manchester.

March 9: 1904

Dear Mr Jaeger:

The time has now come when I think all familiarity between us
should cease: the position I now hold – greatly owing to your exertions
& friendship – warrants me in throwing you over.

Yours truly

Now, you old moss, read the other side.

[*on opposite page*]
Dearie Moss:

What an old frump you are! whenever anything of mine is to be done you beg me not to be conceited & not to forget my old friends etc. You are an old PIG[1] & deserve some such letter as the unfinished one on the other side anyhow you always seem to be *expecting* it: be assured you won't receive anything of the kind from me. There is no fear that I shall forget anyone.

That Overture is *good* & the Roman section[2] absolutely *knocking over*. They read it like angels & the thing *goes* with tremendous energy & life. *Fanny Moglio*[3] figures largely all through to Carice's intense amusement. I am *not* bringing the score as Richter wants it: it can be bound later – I don't want to alter a note except one or two false ones.

Don't bother me about conceit again – I haven't any except that I always resent any familiarity from outsiders & I *do* stand up for the *dignity* of our art – not profession

Ever deary Moss

with love

Yours

Edward.

I hope the letter on the other side, if only you had the luck to read it first gave you a very proper & deserved fit.

The reputation which Elgar was now enjoying in Germany is illustrated by the fact that it was being suggested that he should go to Essen in October, where they would like the Symphony, and that Weingartner was also making proposals.

Craeg Lea,

Malvern.

March 25, [19]04.

My dear Jaeger:

Thanks for your note concerning the pts etc of 'In the South" which I daresay will reach me during the day: you shall hear, bless you, if they don't.

I wrote to Mr Alfred [Littleton] yesterday & will you bring to his notice the possibility of German performances of the Overture. I received several letters more or less chiding & angry because somebody suggested that the future Symphony might be produced at *Essen*!

Weingartner sent word through his friend Ettling that *he* wd. gladly produce it – if he had the first performance, in Berlin & Munich – I understand he would do this with the Overture. Anyhow, he (and

---

[1] twice underlined

[2] the passage at figure [20] in the score

[3] Elgar was amused at the name of the Italian village Moglio, prefaced it with 'Fanny,' invented a fitting tune which he sang to Carice and worked into the Overture (orch. score, fig. 4?).

Ettling) will be in London soon & you can settle that: I suppose no introduction *cd* be better possibly. So don't go suggesting it in Deutschland to other folk until Weingartner has been to London.

As to the Essen concert before I can say anything about going & leaving all terms out of the question for the moment, can you tell me what time in the year they want me – what orchestra etc. they place at my disposal & what rehearsals.

In great haste
Yours ever
Edward E.

Steinbach *may* want the Overture first.

Craeg Lea,
Malvern.
Ap 1: [19]04.

My dear Moss:

I am sending all the parts of 'In the South' (& should like to send this pen also out of my sight – it has just gone wrong!) you are a pig of many kinds – I thought I cd. keep all the stuff for a month or two!

Good boy! come & drown, burn & scarify everybody – I truly *am* worried by letters out of all belief. Oh! that letter U in Banner of S. George – cannot something be done? it is as clear (to me) as daylight, but a lady writes (*professionally*[1]) "I am preparing an orch: to take (somewhere) & the conductor wishes to take at letter U the minims dotted – as in the previous bars: I think, & *have rehearsed the orchestra* (!!!!) to play at U the dotted minims in the time of the preceding★ crotchets(!)"
Think of that.
Ask West about it.
★ As the dotted minim goes at about M.M. 84 you see the minims at letter U will come out (according to this lady) at M.M. *252*. I shd. like to see that orchestra after playing it at that speed. I wd. set up an undertaker's business in the locality.

I cannot say anything about Essen: I am *not* keen to go: the Symphony cannot be done there anyhow.

I am up to my eyes in work & a shrimp has had a baby in my tank & between times I have to nurse them in a teaspoon! It all takes time.

Yours ever
Ed. Elgar

P.S. Proof of Ger: libretto goes to 1, Berners Street. I hope you are at home (your pretty home – so glad I've seen it) having a rest.

[1] twice underlined

Craeg Lea,
Malvern.
Ap 6 [19]04.

My dear Jaggs:
Very sorry to hear of the children & hope it will soon be better. These things *will* come & generally at the most inopportune times.

Proofs enclosed – I think Mr Alfred knows all about the continuation of the *Apostles*[1].

Just going out – tired of life.

Yours ever
Ed:

[*on Novello & Co.'s writing paper* 1, *Berners St. W.*]

Ap 9 [190]4

My dear Jaguar:
I have my two tickets for the circle – they are waiting for *you* at Langham Hotel : please use them.*

I am unhappy.

Yours ever
Edward

* this is a brute of a pen.

On 13 April Elgar heard of his election to the Athenaeum. He went to Birmingham to rehearse The Apostles *for the performance on the next day.*

Craeg Lea,
Malvern.
Ap: 14: [19]04.

My dear Jaeger:
The orchl. rehearsal was very good & only one error in the score which is also very good considering the complications.

Mr Kreuz (Emil)[2], who you know is a first rate musician, asks me if I am settled with an arranger for p.F. – of course *I* am not & I think if

---

[1] i.e. *The Kingdom*: Miss Burley refers to Elgar's consideration of this project while in Italy. 'On one of our walks . . . we suddenly met Dr. Armitage Robinson [Dean of Westminster Abbey 1902–1911], a fine handsome figure with a leonine head. Without any introduction he waved his hand indicating the blue Mediterranean sparkling in the sunshine below. It was the beginning of a delightful friendship. The Dean was a fine Biblical scholar and was often appealed to by Elgar, who was then writing *The Apostles* [what was to be *The Kingdom* was thought of then as a second part] and studying the Scriptures very carefully.'

[2] Kreuz (1867–1932), born in Germany but educated at the Royal College of Music, London, was a viola player in the Hallé Orchestra from 1903, also a composer.

there's anything to do he might have a chance: anyhow I should be sure to like his work if the firm (I am telling him to apply to the firm) wd. like him to do anything. I was going to write to West only he's away, thus:—

Dr Sinclair points out that a passage like this

is confusing on acct of the pause for 2nd Clar coming where it is: I think so too & the 2nd. Clar. rest shd be omitted & the passage printed 1⁰ & stems down. – I have not copied it exactly but this is the sort of thing he means. Tell Mr Pointer for future scores of the Brit[1] English school! Sinclair wants to keep the score he is using today for a space with a view to suggesting some organ arrangements. May that be?

Yours ever
Ed: Elgar:*

* Wisdom approacheth.

AⴲHNAION

From Jaeger to Elgar, 10 April 1904:

'... Oh, I say! poor Hehemann[2] is quite upset because he can't trace in the Full Score of the Apostles the Passion motif of which I speak in the Analysis.[3] He means at 20 (see Vocal Score page 15). You will remember that you told me to put a B sharp into the chord to show the theme. But alas and woe is me, in the Full Score the Clarinet has the Angel theme right enough, but that B sharp to complete the Passion (suggestion) appears only in the *lower octave* with Bassoon. I thought you would have given that B sharp to the second Clarinet or an Oboe or something else that's *nice* and *Elgarish* (synonymous terms, you know!) Won't you, before the parts are *finally printed*? Please drop me a card that I may put Hehemann out of his agony of suspense. He has nearly finished his Apostel "Führer".'

[1] deleted
[2] conductor at Essen, see p. 284
[3] see *Analysis*, p. 11

Craeg Lea,
Malvern.
Ap 16 1904.

Dear Jaguar:

No I can't alter the bit at 20. Quite unnecessary – the *harmony*
suggests the passion theme coming in quite enough & your quotation
(I haven't a copy!) will shew what it arrives at: it's all right & intended
& conformable! So tell dear Mr Hehemann to go on with his *Führer*
& not be *furious*.

Yours ever
Ed. E.

The Apostles was a fine performance at Birmingham

The Athenaeum,
Ap 22 1904.

My dear Jaguar:

Thanks for your letter with the par. I have revised it & returned it to
Mr A.H.L.

No time for more. I strenuously tried to get in Macpherson's Ps: in
the Leeds Choral Union Gerontius programme: tell me if you hear if
it *is* included. I hope so. Curiously, I have had a letter from C.M. just
when I was talking his Ps. in to people.

Yours ever
Edward.

*On 10 May Jaeger inquired whether Elgar knew what had happened to
the glockenspiel part of* In the South, *which had been missing since the
performance at Covent Garden. The full score of the orchestrated version of*
The Snow *was also mislaid. 'Is Muriel Foster singing at Köln? I see she
is singing in Gerontius at Cincinnati on the 13th inst. How she will
get back from there & to Cologne by the 21st Heaven only knows.'* In
*the same letter Jaeger says that he has refused an invitation from another
publisher to write a book about Elgar.*

Langham Hotel
London
Wedy night
[18 May 1904]

My dear J.

I came up unexpectedly last night & have been busy all day or I
would have come in. I am hoping to call at No. 1 about 12 o'clock
tomorrow. I don't remember anything of Glock etc. *or* the proof of

Snow: my wife has read your letter & will reply to it (she has just sent it on here).

I don't know *anything* about Köln – except they've asked me to go: I am quite tired of being supposed to 'Bless" performances of my things which are not 'coached' by me or my advice is asked when it is too late to make any change: but if I *must* go I must – only I don't want to go at all.

In great haste
Yours ever
Ed Elgar

My teeth are the cause of my unhappy visit!

On 19 May the Elgars went to Köln. At a rehearsal on the next day Steinbach introduced Elgar to the chorus. On the day following, the soloists not turning up to an appointed rehearsal, Elgar showed his displeasure and 'wd not come up and be seen – agitation of the Steinbachs' (Mrs. Elgar, Diary entry). The performance on 22 May, however, was 'gorgeous' and the two succeeding days were happily dedicated to eating and drinking. From Köln the Elgars went on to Düsseldorf to see Buths, returning to England in time for a Mansion House Dinner on 30 May and for a meeting with Hedley, the artist, on 31 May, to see his bust of Elgar.

Craeg Lea,
Malvern
June 3 [19]04

My dear Jagpot:

I shd. think the enclosed ought to definitely settle the point: I shd have preferred

but anything that is understood will do.

We arrived home last night & I am in a whirlwind of epistolary tomfoolery which will take me a month to clear. If a lucid moment comes I'll try & write some sense.

I've made a sweet looking blister on my face! tried Menthol for the pain (toothache) &, as that did not work, made a compress of eau de

Cologne which has persuaded the skin to come off in reams. Will you make an offer for it to bind the Apostles in?

Yours ever

Edward

Craeg Lea,

Malvern.

Monday [13 June 1904]

Dearie Jag:

Don't forget I want to see parts of score & PF. of 'in the South' & shall just have time to revise 'em before moving – we have been very busy making arrangements & shall flit soon. At the Mount (bei Carice) they have German measles so we may miss our joy while this slight ailment is in progress. Love to you – you old sinner: when do you take holiday?

Frank Damrosch[1] came here to see me & it was a great pleasure to see him

Yours ever

E.

The Editor of The Troubadour *asked Jaeger what decoration Elgar had been wearing when Weingartner conducted* Gerontius *at Queen's Hall on 9 April.*[2] *'Perhaps', wrote Jaeger, 'you have got the Garter or the Star of India after all! One never knows. It would just be like an original cuss like you to wear the Garter as your chest protector' (21 June). On 21 June Elgar received an honorary Mus. D. at Durham and on 22 June was informed by A. J. Balfour, the Prime Minister, that he was to be knighted.*

Craeg Lea,

Malvern.

June 22 1904

My dear Moss:

Don't be a fool! I wore *no* decoration at Queen's Hall or any other time. Just back from Durham.

Much love,

Yrs ever

Edward

I mean I wore *nothing* except my clothes. I never do.

---

[1] Frank Damrosch (1859–1937), brother of Walter (see p. 283), who was appointed Director of the Institute of Musical Art in New York in 1904.

[2] A performance sponsored by Professor Johann Kruse (1859–1927). The Sheffield Choir was accompanied by an orchestra mostly of Philharmonic players.

[*typewritten*]

> Plas Gwyn,
> Hereford.
> July 11th 1904.

My dear Jaggs:—

I have at length found time to look through all the stuff & send it back with my blessing; observe the following words of weight.

1) One harp part will do with the addition of the marks "a 2."—"1⁰ 8va" etc. It shd however be "1ma" I suppose & not "1mo." eh? All the tempi marks want to be added to the parts as they now appear in the skoughrre.[1]

As to the pinoa that shd have been PIANO arrgts[;] the solo will do if one or two little things I have marked are put right: as to the duet, I tried it thro' with Atkins and find it too full in the heavy parts, a great deal of the quiet parts come out very well but it's not piano music by any means, fo for which, Praises be! albeit I and the Publishers will starve over in consequence.

We are far from settled yet but it is very lovely here and thi [*sic*] weather magnificent, you must come soon.[2]

Our love to you in which Troyte, who is heey [*sic*] joins mildly.

> Yours ever
> Edward.

> Hereford.
> July 26 1904

Dear Jaggs:

I hear via Ettling that Weingartner will do *Alassio*[3] in Berlin & Munich.

I hope the 'stuff' will soon now be thro' the press.

I sent back the M.S. Duet arrgt and the proof of Solo. Oh! the weariness of these arrgts.

> Your ever
> very dismal
> Edward

[1] of *In the South*, proofs having been sent on 15 June
[2] Jaeger visited the Elgars in September (see p. 247).
[3] *In the South*

'Spur.

a knight.

Plas Gwyn,
Hereford.
July 30 [19]04.

My dear Jagpot!
   I send back the title in anr. cover. I haven't written because every-thing is dull & goes slowly: & I am tried very much liverwise & am wofully short of money. I really think I must take some violin pupils again: only, as I have not touched it for so long, I should have to begin once more with elementary ones! Such is life & I hate, loathe & detest it.
   Write & tell us how you all are & where you go for your holiday. Don't forget Steinbach has the Overture down early for Köln. I wish you wd. write to him about it & tell him the 'stuff' will be ready soon.
Yours ever
Edward

Plas Gwyn,
Hereford.
Augt 6 1904.

Dear Jagernaut:
   I could not write yesterday – was away. You will perhaps be seeing

some arrgts of the *Canto Popolare* which ought to be of some use: the keys chosen are more suitable I think than the original: the piano solo is always the trouble & I'm not sure if my arrgt will do – it *looks* better, & there is more in it than Schmid's – see pp 16–18 of his arrgt. piano solo.

It's all very well to talk to me about doing Sextetts & Symphonies & all the things I *want* to do, but tell me what & who is going to keep a roof over our heads? nobody thinks of that.

Yrs ever
Edwd.

I note all you say about U.S.A. & wait to hear more from the fountain-head – I have talked to Mr A.H.L. about it by pen I mean.

Plas Gwyn,
Hereford.
Aug. 7: 1904

My dear Jaeger:

Here's the proof for which thanks: but let me see another please.

Yes: go on with the Vio. & p. arrgt & send me *two* proofs, *one to keep for orchestratn.* & I will send a score in no time. The piano arrangemt. troubles me – see how it goes. If it does not 'go' I could use Schmid pp 16–18 as a *basis* but it's rather bald.

In great haste
Ever yours
Edward the Elgar.

From Jaeger to Elgar, 9 August 1904:

'Many thanks for your letter. I fear me that Symphony will never be published! Oh dear! what a disappointment. If I had money I'd buy it of you at a good price. Perhaps some art-loving millionaire will come along & give you a fat commission & pay cash down, who knows? Anyhow, I am awfully sorry that you, of all composers living, should now even be troubled with money difficulties. It's too damnable for words.

. . . Dear old Sanford is in town as nice as ever. He has a wonderful upright Steinway piano for you. . . . Don't rub him the wrong way. He is a good fellow at heart & means you well. Would do *anything* for you in fact.'

Plas Gwyn,
Hereford.
Augt. 10: 1904

My dear Jaeger:

Here's the M.S. – Pointer's suggestions are all thankfully adopted.

August Manns

Hans Richter

Richard Strauss

Fritz Steinbach

Notable Elgar enthusiasts

AUGUST JOHANNES JAEGER : 1860-1909.
(*Photograph by E. T. Holding.*)

A. J. Jaeger

Don't worry about me, 'cos after all my troubles are not really my own. The sickening part of it all is that to make anything (tangible) I have still to do all the work: when you think that the Variations have brought me in about eight pounds (!) you will see how easy & beautiful it is to sit down & write great & glorious works for old mossheads. I have quite the artistic feeling I hope, but I have no ambition & no conceit (yet) & there is, apart from these last, absolutely *no* inducement to write out fair the big stuff.

I hope to see Prof. Sanford before he leaves England. Give him my kind regards. I wrote to him (Paris address) a few weeks ago: his letter came during our scramble & waited for some time.

Glad to hear of your stick which must be a sight to see.

Mr Wilson (Pittsburgh) & a Mr Hamilton[1] were here yesterday *en route* for New York.

I should come & see you but can't afford it!

Yours ever
E.E.

Plas Gwyn,
Hereford.
Augt 11: 1904

My dear Jagbird:

I return the revises with all questions answered like a good boy.

I have heard from Prof. Sanford, a delightful letter about tobacco & *the* piano: I hope I may see him & have telegraphed this a.m. I am terrified at accepting the piano.

In great haste
Yrs ever
Edd.

On 12 August Jaeger sent Elgar a copy of his programme note on In the South, *to be played at the forthcoming Gloucester Festival.* 'That Battle Scene (I'm sure it's a battle scene) gave me "beans". I couldn't get the hang of it, (the meaning, I mean). . . .' *cf.* Letters of Edward Elgar, *p. 118.*

Plas Gwyn,
Hereford.
Augt 13 [19]04.

My dear A.J.J.

Many, many thanks. I return remainder of full skowre. Also titles etc of the song.

---

[1] *Lady Elgar:* 'E in very bad spirits, not out till afternoon when 2 Americans Mr. Wilson & Mr. Hamilton came. took them down to the river. Lovely evening – saw large fish & kingfisher' (Diary entry, 9 August).

Also – your admirable analysis of the Overture. I think it's all right: I've knocked out the *Sirs* & an adjective. Perhaps the Ex: shd. come from the PF. copy as being more understood but please yourself.

I do not think I should put that about Strauss at the beginning – not necessary –. S. puts music in a very low position when he suggests it must hang on some commonplace absurdity for it's very life. More of this some other time. The Battle scene is all right, only it's very short & not worthy of so much description. All thanks to Madame for the lovely writing. Oh! if we could scrawl *fast* like unto that.

I have found some lovely nooks here, you will have to walk.

Much love, yours ever

Edward.

Plas Gwyn,

Hereford.

Augt 23 [19]04

Augustus darling:

Only a hurried line.

By all means, put Gerontius in the Oratorio list[1] – there's no word invented yet to describe it.

Yes – Leeds shd. pay a guinea[2] altho' they are mean enough to get it for nix – but don't be had.

No, I don't want to see Spanish Serenade[3] – the scoring is all right, if young England could turn out as *neat* a piece of work as that – there wd. be some hope for it!

So glad you are coming to Glo'ster; my wife is writing. Glad the Overture works into your innards: I *love* it: it's alive! I am better but jolly down.

Yours ever

in haste

Ed Elgar

At the end of September, being immersed in The Kingdom *at that time, Elgar went up to London for the rehearsals for the Leeds Festival. He went to Leeds on 3 October,* In the South *being played two days later.*

Plas Gwyn,

Hereford.

Sep 28 1904

My dear Jagpotte:

Just home from *London*: I went to G.W. Hotel & only had a few

[1] in Novello's Catalogue

[2] for the use of the programme note on *In the South*

[3] Score and parts were being now engraved.

mins. in town: rehearsal this a.m. at ten & then fled! I say! *what*[1] a row
we made! Gosh! The real Romans[2] were not in it! Glad to hear all your
news – Apostles at *Norwich Fest* – Also glad you are going to Ramsden[3].
He is a brick though a very odd one *sometimes* to *some* people – not to
people he believes in bless him.

Proofs shall be returned very quickly.

Yours ever
Edward

[*typewritten*]

Plas Gwyn,
Hereford.
29/9/1904

Dear Aged & Gray:—

In grt haste I send back the prfs of the Canter popolare. Note that
ye slight variations fr. ye origal are intentional for private purposes.

Note that I have phrased ye clart prat [*sic*]

Note well that I have NOT done the Violin & Cello: I have indicated,
in the vio part the bowing as it is in the score; NOW would your dear
wife complete it & make it nice for people to play? Do ask her; she
knows how I want it to sound & I shd be very grateful. Supposing she
will graciously do this, the bowing must go in for cello also – &—mark
ye— into the accompt likewise. I think all is clear now except that Mrs
Jaeger may take revenge on me for my many grievous insults to the
capering Moss (Which is Orgustus) & refuse to touch the mercenary
page. Well, if so, tell me.

You shd have been at the R.C.M. to hear the Alassio—you cd not
only hear but fe feel also; it's a jolly fine orchestra.

Yours ever, Pospectively,

Edward the "( )-;*':%/$-\frac{1}{4}!\frac{11}{2}+\frac{3}{4}=$ £

[*handwritten*]

Those [physical] exercises have done me no end of good. Why not ask
Atkins to make an easy *organ* arrgt. now?

Plas Gwyn,
Hereford.
Saty [8 October 1904]

My dear Jaggs.

Just home & hasten to send some of the accumulated rubbish.

Thanks very many to your dear wife: the '*editing*'[4] is *excellent*: look

---

[1] twice underlined
[2] The 'Roman' section of *In the South* is detailed in *Elgar O.M.*, p. 286.
[3] ? Archibald Ramsden
[4] of the *Canto popolare*. Mrs. Jaeger had added some fingering to the violin part.

only at p. 3 Vn.pt. you are already in III pos. & the figures seem redundant or one may have been omitted which wd. take us back to I pos. – otherwise all is most clear & good. You had better put "Edited by Isabella Jaeger" on the Violin part. *Do* ask Mr A.H.L. for this. If you like I would ask Squire to do the Cello & Hobday the Viola & Draper[1] the Clarinet: but let me know what you think – anyhow I return all the stuff now.

Thanks for your letter which I will reply to later. I am awfully busy. I can't stop to talk of Leeds. Walford Davies was good.

Yours ever
Ed Elgar

Of course *give* Gran[ville] Ban[tock] the Sheikh the score & charge to me.

During this period Elgar was inundated with proofs. Not only were arrangements being made of his 'popular' pieces, but something like a collected edition was in progress. On 24 September Jaeger had written to his 'dear Sir Knight, yclept Edward ye wizard of Plas Gwyn' *as follows:* 'I'm sure it will give you *some* little pleasure (tho', forsooth, there be little enough left, I fear me, to bring a thrill of pleasure to *your* pampered soul) (pampered soul is good!) that we are now *engraving* the *full* Scores of Caractacus, King Olaf, Banner, Light of Life, Black Knight. The complete works of the Master will soon be an accomplished FACK! Anything that yet remains will also be done. Geidel is doing the Car. Olaf & Black Knight & Brause the remaining. Proofs of Car. will commence to reach us next week I hope. They have undertaken to engrave 1000 pages of Elgar score in 4 weeks!'

During the next few weeks Elgar was much exercised over the offer of the newly founded Chair of Music in Birmingham University, which he finally accepted on 26 November.

Plas Gwyn,
Hereford.
Oct 10, 1904

Private somewhat
My dear Jäger:
Many thanks for your note with the proofs. Yes: I wanted Bantock to have the score 'In the South' costing *him* nothing. Richter should have one too.

I procured from Mr Smith (your agent at Leeds during the Festival) a copy for *Mr Fricker*[2] who is preparing Gerontius: I gave it to him. Would you ask the firm to let me have a *full score* of Gerontius as

---

[1] for Squire, Hobday, and Draper see pp. 289, 284, and 283
[2] see p. 284

reasonably as they can because I want to give it to Mr Benton[1] who
has prepared so many of my things including York Minster performance & is doing (Leeds Choral Union) Geron. & the Apostles. Also,
in view of the work done by Mr Noble of York, in clearing the way
for the performance & perhaps future deeds in the Minster, I think he
should have a score also from me – or from the firm. If further music
on a large scale is given in York, it will largely depend on Mr N. Will
you bring this before Mr A.H.L. I think he's away.

Yours

Ed: Elgar

I have not said anything except to you about the Organ arrgt.* so go
ahead as you please.

* Canto popolare

[*typewritten*]   Plas Gwyn,
                                                        Hereford.
                                                        13/10/1904.

My dear Jaeger:—
    Your letter, dated 11th, received this a.m. & for it thanks. I am in a
wild hurry & so take this odd means of writing! As to the fingering, or
rathir phrasig [*sic*] of the 'cello, viola & clarinet arrgts, I think the artists
wd. probably do the little required for nothing if I say to them that you
will put 'edited by Blank' on the copies: this is what I asked you I
think; anyhow it's what I want to know; I should not propose any
"fee".
    Now, as to the proposed presentation scores: never mind the royalty,
you commercial old moss, but send them to me and I will forward
them; I wanted to know if Mr Alfred approved of the idea: I gathir
from your lette that he does: Benton should have Gerontius &
Richter "In the South": I said "a" score for Mr Noble because I
dont know what he has or has not. This I will find out if the firm
approves as aforesaid: I only wanted to suggest that a man who had
done so much & is understood to be trying all he can for the future
might be pleased at some little recognition;* do you see?

Good-bye,

Yours in hste

E.E.

[*handwritten*]
* & I don't like to give away scores to anybody without the firm's
appro[val] I mean
    Oh! dear how difficult it is to write

[1] see p. 281

In a letter of 28 October Jaeger amplified an observation which he had apparently made concerning a translation of Gerontius *into French. This was done by J. d'Offoël, who was well thought of on account of his translations of the works of Wagner. There was in view a performance of* Gerontius *in Brussels which, conducted by Sylvain Dupuis, took place on 26 March 1905 (see* Mus. T., *May 1905, p. 314). Jaeger's letter also makes this suggestion, after Elgar had demurred about extracting sections from* The Black Knight *and making them into an independent orchestral work:*

'I hope you can write the [London] Symphony Orchestra a short new work. Why not a *brilliant* quick String Scherzo, or something for those fine strings only? a real bring down the house *torrent* of a thing such as Bach could write (remember that Cologne Brandenburg concerto?) A five minutes' work wd do it. It wouldn't take you away from your big work for long. You might even write a *modern Fugue* for strings, or *strings & organ*! That would sell like cakes.'

The Introduction and Allegro, *incorporating material noted in Wales in 1901, was completed on 13 February 1905 (see letter of 26 January 1905, p. 248).*

Plas Gwyn,
Hereford.
Oct 27: 1904

My dear Jäger:

I have had a chill & find a heap to do – four letters from you unanswered among other crimes of omission.

1. Full sc. Apostles, p. 99 Bar 3. Bassoon notes *are correct*. (*a nice buzz!*)

2. Dr Sinclair wd. like to do some small thing at his Choral concert: so I asked about the parts of 'Canto popolare'. Now, wd. the firm allow it to be done: he wd. want Strings 4.4.3.4. & one each wind etc. I enclose the firm's letter – if he could have these parts or rather if *I* cd. have them in a fortnight it wd. do: but yes or no please by return on acct of printing programme.

3. I don't think the Black Knight arrgt. will do – at least not for the Symp. Orch.

4. I had no idea a French traduction was afoot![1] Who is M. d'Öffel or whatever name he bears: we will look it thro' & return it very soon: for the present I will only say I wish I had as good an opinion of myself as he has of his own Ego. He must drop the rhymes in French: assonances in that vile & beastly *conversational* language limit the literary beast much.

4[2].) Antique cymbals: Schroeder gets the noise I want by placing a bell

[1] but cf. p. 114

[2] *sic*

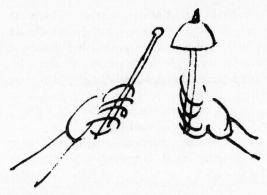

on the end of a
stick & hitting
it with another

stick: I fear if a *pair* of cymbals is employed which wd. be correct –
the ordinary player wd not be able to make them 'ring' in time.

(Harking back – is there any hurry about that French translation? the
one person *I* shd. like to see it is Mrs Edward Speyer & she is in Italy
for a long time – I will of course *mark* a selection in B.K. for possible
future use.)

Steinbach told me 'In the South' was down for *Dec 6*. But I am en-
quiring if any new arrgt has been made. Sorry to hear of your flu &
hope you are better.

In greatest haste
Yours ever
Edward Elgar.

Plas Gwyn,
Hereford.
Nov 3 1904.

My dear Jaggs:

In greatest haste.

I saw Sinclair's arrangement, he played it to me, of Prelude Pt II
Apostles & I think it excellent & it sounded well.

I send back all proofs, only keeping *first proofs Viola & C. & B.* of
small orch. – the 2nd proofs were not in the parcel, but I suppose they'll
come on.

Thanks for your note re novelty for the Sym. concert. I can't settle
on any idea! The weather is too lovely! warm & lunch out-of-doors
last Saturday in the hot sun!

What a climate.

Your exercise cure has done *wonders:* I take *no* physic now – a most
xtrordy thing! Atkins & I are going to give you a testimonial.

I am to conduct Carac: for him at Worcester next week. I suppose
the score will not be ready in any rough form – but if he has a Dodd
score[1] I shall manage. How well it looks in print. I feel that those
Editors' names shd be in the same type as the instruments they edit.
see my note on the Viola part: it wd look all right larger – don't you
think?

Yours ever

Edward Elgar

I wrote to Pitt some days ago & have not heard. I conclude he's away.
I am sending the French 'Gerontius' to Mr Schuster & you will receive
it, with 'notes', in a day or two.

Plas Gwyn,

Hereford

Friday [18(?) November 1904]

My dear Jäger

You are a funny deary. You send me a translation to look at; I send
one set of suggestions & ask a well-read-French friend to look at it.
You then write me today that it has been shewn to *4* more people
& then say *I* must not expect too much & want all their ideas incorporated.[2]

Dear boy: *I* don't want any.

When Mr. Alfred is satisfied so am I. The few suggestions in type
made here seem after all, to be the main points & may or may not be
'alterable'.

Percy Pitt says it is good on the whole with a few weak spots:
anyone with an ear can see e.g. that Marie cannot take the place of
Vierge etc. etc.

So go along. I return the sheaf of suggestions. I am not well.

Yours ever

Ed Elgar

On 28 November Elgar left again for Germany as Volbach was conducting
The Apostles *at Mainz on 30 November ('It was said there had never
been such a triumph in Mainz',* Lady Elgar, Diary entry*) and Steinbach*
In the South *in* Köln *on 6 December. The Apostles *was also given in
Rotterdam on 2 December. Elgar again visited Buths before returning home.
On 11 December Volbach arrived in England and Elgar accompanied him to
the Stanfords, the Stuart Wortleys, and the Royal College of Music, where he
conducted his choral work* Raffael. *On 15 December Steinbach was also in*

---

[1] i.e. handwritten

[2] 'Mr. L.F.S., Mr. Edwards, Mr. Shedlock &, I believe, Mr. A.H.L.' Jaeger,
16 November 1904

*London to conduct the London Symphony Orchestra. Elgar was particularly
excited by the performance of Brahms's Fourth Symphony. To complete the
circle of German acquaintances then in London there was Strauss, with whom
Elgar dined on 18 December.*

Dom Hotel, Köln.
Dec 8. 1904

My dear Jaeger:

I must send you one line from the Rhine: we have talked of you
much & wished for you here & in Düsseldorf: we were paying a
short visit to Buths yesterday: much rain.

I will tell you of the performances when we meet. At Mainz the
real effect of the shepherds

outside was beautiful & quite justifies my 'stage direction'. The Judas at
Rotterdam was the best we have yet had – in fact I could scarcely
wish for anything better!

Love to you all
Yrs ever
Ed E

Just starting for Bruxelles.

P.T.O.

I fear I forgot to tell you that *Tree* in Caractacus was really *fine* – I
think very highly of him.[1]

[on *Athenaeum writing paper*]   [2]22 Old Queen St. S.W.
Dec 16 1904

My dear Moss:

I cannot tell you how grieved we are to hear of the illnesses in your
house, we can only hope you are all improving & will soon be all right
again.

I was looking forward to much talk with you over past schemes,
present schemes &, above all, *future* ideas.

Well, this must wait until we meet.

[1] Charles Tree sang in *Caractacus* on 9 November.

[2] added by E. to the printed address

Dear old Volbach, Steinbach, auch, send all sorts of messages to you –
Volbach, whose ideas of the size of London are very vague, about 5.30
one evening, expressed a desire to pay you a little visit: I had reluctantly to tell him it was not possible to get to you, & back to Westminster to dress, dine & be at R.C.M. at eight.

Now my love to you all & send word how you are going on.

Yours ever
Edward

The concert yesterday was divine.[1]

Plas Gwyn,
Hereford.
Dec 28 1904

My dear Moss:

I am glad you are about again & mercifully the weather here looks
better & it is warmer. May these improvements reach you.

No: this cymbal is of no use: I thought we settled all this once
before! Schroeder uses a little bell in C, perched on the end of a stick,
thus,

and strikes it with a little drum stick (wood) – this
gives a clear note & 'mixes up' with the other percussion & *suggests* the
right sort of sound – ask him. It really is not of much importance.

Yes, it is dreary about poor Johnstone[2], one of the best fellows & *the*
best critic we had.

No time for more now: I am up to my eyes in work, not music,
alas!

Yours ever
Edward

Please send 'In Moonlight' in F. I shd think to Mr Cary Elwes[3]. I
haven't his address.

[1] London Symphony Orchestra, conducted by Steinbach, the principal work
being Brahms's Fourth Symphony

[2] referring to the death of Arthur Johnstone (1861–1905), of the *Manchester
Guardian*

[3] Gervase Cary Elwes, see p. 284

1905

By the beginning of the year Jaeger was a very sick man, and on 1 January
he wrote to say that he must go to Switzerland. His worries over finances
were partly eased by the liberality of his firm. But he was otherwise troubled.
'I worry', he wrote to Elgar,' 'over your *muse*, for I fear greatly we shall
get less & less out of you. This is the danger of success artistic & social!
(especially social of course). I grieve over it & so do all those who most
sincerely love & admire you. We know you *must live* but England
ruins all *artists*.' Jaeger left London on 11 January and went to Davos.
Meanwhile Elgar busied himself intermittently with the Introduction and
Allegro, *which was finished on 13 February.*

> Plas Gwyn,
> Hereford.
> Jan 3 1905
> [1904 *written in error*]

My dear Jaeger:

I – we are truly distressed to receive your sad-toned letter & trust
things are shaping to make your peremptory journey *possible* &, as far
as may be, comfortable. I feel sure the firm will do all possible for you.
This is no comfort & indeed, it is impossible to say anything under the
circumstances that does not appear foolish or at least jejune.

I have no doubt pure air out of London will set you up: Elsie Buths is
at Davos & our friends the Jebb Scotts in Egypt on the same errand.

My love to you old boy, & send me word what is going on.

Our kindest regards to Mrs Jaeger

> Yours ever in frantic haste
> Edward Elgar

On 19 January Jaeger wrote from Davos: '. . . when I was at Plas Gwyn
last September I suggested your writing something *specially* for Buths'
Lower Rhine Festival in May. You then said he (B.) would want
nothing. I said d—d nonsense. Now I have been to see Buths, while he

was away conducting a rehearsal, I had a long chat with Mrs. B. She told me that the Apostles being impossible after Köln (B. also said that) they must do without you but, when I asked whether an orchestral work specially written would be welcome, Mrs. B. said she felt *quite sure* B. & the Committee would jump at it. But it must be a Uraufführung, see? First production anywhere. Now, seeing what B. has done for your fame, I think you ought to see whether you can't do something. But it must be of your *Best* entre nous, because you will be matched with Mahler whose 3rd Symphony[1] with Chorus will form an important part of the Fest. most likely. (*This is a secret at present*). Of course you may have nothing ready. In that case never mind! I feel sure you won't mind my suggesting such a thing.'

In none of his extant letters does Elgar refer to this suggestion.

[*postcard*]

Plas Gwyn,
Hereford.
Jan 21: 1905.

My dear Moss:

Very glad to receive your address: don't worry about the doctor's reports here & there, but just roll round & get fat & well. I cannot write a letter at this moment because I am full of *business* (alas!) Here we are in the depth of winter, ground covered with frozen snow; fog abounding & frost very severe: my balcony is alive with countless birds of all sorts. Carice & my niece feed them too well perhaps. I have no news musical or otherwise. We all send our love & hope to write soon with accounts of anything interesting – if anything interesting ever turns up again, which I doubt.

Much love
yours ever affectly
Edward Elgar

Thanks also for the view.

[*postcard*]

Plas Gwyn,
Hereford.
26/1/[19]05

Dear Moss: I'm doing that string thing in time for the Sym. orch. concert. Intro: & Allegro – no *working-out* part but a devil of a fugue instead. G major & the sd. divvel in G minor.

[1] In fact it was the 2nd symphony (C minor) that was performed; and the Festival took place from 11 to 13 June.

with all sorts of japes & counterpoint. I will write soon.

yours ever affectly

Edward.

On 6 February the Elgars went to Oxford where, on the next day, Edward was created Mus. D. (h.c.), in honour of which 'Sir H. Parry made a fine oration' (Lady Elgar, Diary entry). On the evening of 8 February there was a concert at which the London Symphony Orchestra played the Variations.

Plas Gwyn,
Hereford.
Feb 16 1905.

My dear Jagpot:

At last I feel I can write a few lines: I hope you are much better & feel that resignation to a monotonous existence for a time is doing you a world of good.

Now: I wrote to S.S. Sanford & I hear from him – a most kind & affectionately worded letter – & you must let him do all he wishes to do – in case that is that he wishes to do more. This I beg you for all our sakes: I did not offer to send you anything because I think you know that anything I have is yours!

I have finished the string thing & it's all right; of course it will take you sometime to get used to it, but it will sound really wholesome & bring out much tone from the strings. There are all sorts of wild ideas afloat as to my conducting but at present all is sub rosa.

The weather has been better lately & makes it possible to get out between work but I miss my golf sadly – the Links here are too far away. We had a nice time at Oxford when the degree was conferred. Parry was in great form – there was a dinner & concert. The London Symphony Orchestra played the Variations better than ever; it is a jolly fine orchestra.

Steinbach has been again in London: I think you wd enjoy his readings – so strong & so *tender*. The critics made fools of themselves as usual: he played the boisterous Brandenburg String Concerto: some of 'em said Bach requires more *delicate* treatment; so he does in delicate movements. How is it that they always try to say the *idiotic* thing?

I make my inaugural address in Birmingham on March 16th, but cannot say much to the point: but in time I shall be able to speak out on many points.

Do you do much reading? if so what? If you did not see it, you might try 'The Forerunner' by Merojowski – fine but long. Send a p.c. sometimes, never mind a long letter. I must now conclude as I have long business letters to write & light wanes.

Yours ever
Edward

I dedicate the String thing to Sanford, bless him!

At this juncture Elgar's letters become more infrequent, Lady Elgar undertaking more of his correspondence. He himself was not really well and his never too distant melancholia was increased by the bad weather which put an end, for the time being, to his bicycle rides. This, said Lady Elgar, was his only recreation. However, inspired by Talbot Hughes, who had been painting his portrait, Elgar bought a box of paints, 'and paints strange symbolical pictures à la Boecklin[1] . . . He certainly has a power of representing a scene from his imagination, & one that he has done of a river with sombre trees on the bank & a boat crossing is very suggestive' (*Letter to Jaeger, 1 March 1905*).

On 26 March Lady Elgar wrote to Jaeger apologizing for the long delay since their last letter. Of the concert at Queen's Hall, at which both the Introduction and Allegro *and* Pomp and Circumstance no. 3 *were given a first performance she wrote as follows:*

'The Concert on the 8th was really splendid. E. conducted superbly & the Orch. is gorgeous & play splendidly for E. *Grania* was more than beautiful & poetic, the Variations delightful & the new String piece quite fascinating. Many people think it the finest thing he has written, the 4t. comes in with so beautiful an effect, the peroration towards the end *is* fine. The new March is *thrilling* – the most pacific friends were ready to fight! The critics – some of them – of course were frightened at it, but happily the audiences judge for themselves.' *On 16 March Elgar delivered his first Professorial lecture at Birmingham, an undertaking which had filled him with concern and thus contributed to his general debility.*

---

[1] Arnold Böcklin (1827-1901), a 'literary' painter, celebrated for the vitality of his colouring, and his interpretation of German bourgeois taste in painting in the 1880s. None of Elgar's attempts has survived.

None the less 'E. spoke splendidly at Birm. & looked very nice in gown & hood – Had a great reception.' *(Diary Entry)*

The subject of the inaugural lecture was A Future for English Music *(see Elgar O.M. p. 127 et seq.).*

[*postcard*]

Plas Gwyn,
Hereford.
3/4[19]05

My dear Jaggs:

Thanks for yours. I have been very unwell but am better now. Glad to hear of your progress & shall write soon. It really makes me disgusted with English musical life to see the way everybody (except Kalisch who heard me speak) misquotes me! I set a high ideal for the younger men & said incidentally that three of them had tried to uphold *serious art* in this country at the festivals: I did not say a word as to the value of the music neither did I put them *above* any other men who did not have a festival chance last year.

Love to you.
Edward.

On 29 May, preparing to leave for America where the Elgars were to be the guests of S. S. Sanford at Yale, Elgar added a note to the end of a letter to Jaeger from Lady Elgar:

My dear Jaeger:

I am so sorry not to write fully but I have really nothing to *tell* you: I wish you all good & a very happy return home. We shall meet on our return from the good S.S.S.

Yours ever
E.E.

Hereford
June 6 1905

My dear Jaeger:

Thanks a many for your letters. I'm so glad you are having your nasal business thoroughly done & wish you the best of things. I will deliver all your messages to S.S.S. & he will be delighted to hear of you. Let us hear how you get on; *his* address will be ours until July 11. (about).

What an extraordinary professor your doctor must be – he is rightly called Mahmoud but I hope he really does know what he is talking about. but we must not be too hard on doctors it seems. Jebb Scott has been suffering for years & has undergone many operations, but *this* year they have suddenly discovered that they have been at the wrong place all along & have *now* attacked the root of the evil – he's doing finely but it was a much more severe business than yours – such comfort you'll say.

I don't hear anything of music now or rather of *music* I hear much, of musicians, little: they are always quarrelling. Saw Pitt the other day & he's all right. Brewer is now a Canterbury doctor & all the others angry & he delighted: but you will hear all when you return. I have no news of myself as I have for ever lost interest in that person – he ceased to exist on a certain day when his friends interfered & insisted on his ——

It is very sad.

Good luck to you.

Yours ever

Edward Elgar.

On 28 June Elgar was made a Mus.D. (h.c.) at Yale University, and was invited to return to America during the next year to conduct at the Cincinnati Festival. On the way home he was mostly unwell.

Hereford

Tuesday [*postmark* 18 July 1905]

My dear Moss:

One line to say we arrived safely yesterday & are both well: this is to bring you all our love & good wishes: send a p.c. to say how you are & what sort of a journey you had: I was tired out with the heat too much to be pleasant but our kindest of hosts made everything lovely

Yours always

Ed:

[*letter-card*]

Sunday night

[*postmark* Hereford, 24 July 1905]

Dear Jaggs:

Many thanks for your letter: so glad to hear all about you. I have no moment to spare to say anything coherent. There is a *trunk* full of letters accumulated during the six weeks we were away. I will write soon

Yours ever

Ed Elgar.

Plas Gwyn,
Hereford
Augt 6 1905

My dear Moss:

Kirke White[1] isn't much of a poet but the idea is good. I have the poems somewhere in the house, an old book of my dear mother's (as usual) I don't think I can do anything with it – the two last lines in your copy had better be omitted.

I send you an old proof of No III p. & c., if it's not what you want tell me.

I know nothing about Apostles pt. 2 or any analysis: if it is ever finished I imagined you might take on the analysis *if* properly re-compensed: my life now is one incessant answering of letters & music is fading away.

Love to you all
Yours ever
Edward

Plas Gwyn,
Hereford.
Augt 24: [19]05

My dear Moss:

Glad to hear from you: keep up your spirits, you old dear, & all will be well. Thank you for telling me about yourself.

Look here: Can't you come to Worcester for a day or two – they are going to give me the 'freedom of the city' on Wedy – then there's the string piece & Apostles etc. etc. We can find you a bed. & the fare won't cost you anything I'll see.

You will receive – the firm will – a new part-song – my best bit of landscape so far in that line. You won't make anything of it on the P.F. – Morecambe is the place to hear it.

Much love
Yours ever
Ed E

In a letter of 25 August, the first to have survived since that of 19 January, Jaeger says that he cannot come to Worcester for the Festival. Since his left lung is not healed it is likely that he will have to go away again in the autumn. . . .

'I say, you are being honoured past all belief & beyond all precedent.

[1] Henry Kirke White (1785–1806), whose *Clifton Grove . . . with other Poems* appeared in 1803 and attracted the attention of Southey, who contributed a biographical notice to White's *Remains* (published in 1807).

I suppose there never has been a case of a composer receiving the Freedom of his native city? . . .

We i.e. Novello are now in communication with Leipzig re a performance of the Apostles there, & with Crefeld re Gerontius, (the Crefeld conductor, Prof. Müller-Reuter is said to be A 1). Siloti[1] wants us to promise him the first performance of your apocryphal Symphony, but I had to explain that we cannot promise anything for a country whose laws do not protect our Performing Rights. Anyone who would be clever enough to obtain score & parts (say through Leipzig) *before* Siloti could forestall him without our being able to prevent him. But what of the Symphony? I daresay it is *still* in the clouds, or in your brainbox. I wish I could lift the veil surrounding that much talked of & long expected Symphony.

. . . I have seen a good deal of J. Holbrooke lately . . . And now, through your help, he will get a commission for B'ham.'[2]

Four days later Jaeger wrote again to commend the just completed Evening Scene, *which, he said, reminded him of Schubert* (Der Leiermann) *and of Hermann Goetz:* 'altogether a perfect gem of a picture'.

After the Three Choirs Festival and the conferment of the Freedom of the City of Worcester Elgar went on a Mediterranean cruise (see Letters of Edward Elgar, *pp. 146–162). Immediately on his return he went to a Norwich Festival rehearsal of* The Apostles. *On 17 November Lady Elgar wrote to Jaeger, now on the point of departure for Switzerland again. At this time Elgar was on tour with the London Symphony Orchestra.* 'I was', *wrote Lady Elgar,* 'at Birmingham the 1st night [13 November] of the Tour. It was simply magnificent. I wish you could have heard the Brahms Symphony[3]. It recd. the *most* beautiful & poetic reading & as for "In the South" it was like *magic* web of lovely sound – I never heard it as it really was intended to sound, like that before – even at very good performances.'

A month later, Jaeger still being at Lausanne, Lady Elgar referred to the Birmingham Lectures, which were causing their author much worry and their critics a good deal of food for thought. Mostly, however, they found this unpalatable. 'I wish,' *wrote Lady Elgar on 14 December,* 'you cd. have heard them, you wd. have enjoyed them. They have been so dreadfully misquoted in such a misleading way. What he says is far over the reporters' heads. They cannot follow him in the least, & all the *beautiful*

---

[1] see *Elgar O.M.*, pp. 107–8

[2] *The Bells*, performed at the Birmingham Festival of 1906

[3] Brahms III: when Brodsky heard Elgar's interpretation at Manchester on 15 November he 'came in weeping saying oh if Brahms cd. have heard yr. rendering' (Lady Elgar, Diary entry).

parts are left out.[1] Yesterday was perfectly delightful. The audience
did thoroughly enjoy it & were in a suppressed state of clapping all
the time. The reports give *no idea* of what his Lectures are. Now he is
turning to music again which is a great joy.'

The music to which he turned was that of The Kingdom.

---

[1] Lady Elgar does the *Birmingham Post* an injustice. In the reports the lectures
come vividly to life. And how well they read. In the last lecture of the year Elgar
set out with the intention of answering certain questions that had been raised,
but he could not refrain from putting out new, and in some quarters provocative,
ideas, asking 'young men to draw their inspiration from their own country and
their own literature, and, in spite of what many would say, from their own
climate', and 'advocating again the provision of cheap concerts of high-class
music for the people, remarking that the people's concert now was very often
frivolous and squalid music, which the lovers of high-class music would take
infinite pains to avoid. The English working men were intelligent, and should
be educated to enjoy the best music.'

1906

Hereford.
Jan 26 1906.

Heart Friend:

I have been very evil in not writing to you but I had not the heart to do so. *To-day* we hear from Mrs Jaeger that you are seeing the proofs of my new thing[1]: I did not dare to suggest that you *should* see them & I dare not send my own sheets, so – I could not write. I am so delighted that the firm send the stuff on to you. So far it is the best thing I've done *I know*: remember it's not piano music & won't sound well on a tin kettle.

We are so really glad about your skating & know it must be a pleasure & a great help in many ways for health as well as recreation.

I was delighted to see Bell's works which he kindly sent to me: & I have done what I can in the way of recommendation but people *are* so *difficile*. I must now go on with my work but I have been *bursting* to write to you for a long time.

A dove is born★ here to-day[2] any omen, think you?

Much love in which all join

Ever yours
Edward.

[*marginal note*]
★ hatched I mean

Lady Elgar to Jaeger, 17 March 1906:

'I think yr. surroundings must have depressed you when you wrote – It is curious that that chorus [*O ye Priests*] did not fire you, it works up all who have heard it to a great pitch of excitement – & I think you might have given E. some credit for his fine literary taste & poetic feeling in his selection of words – If you cannot feel the Sacerdotalism

---

[1] *The Kingdom*

[2] According to the *Diary* the dove was hatched on 24 January, and named 'Bellerophon' by Elgar.

of any Church, there is the eternal priestdom of elect souls in all ages, who have stood above the lower minds & dragged them up; to those who believe by religion, & to others by art, literature & pure & noble character & aspirations. So instead of 'Matthias' meaning nothing to us, it is the type of everything wh. can still infuse heroism, self-sacrifice & great thoughts into all who are not dead to such things.

Wait to judge of the new work, & especially to *remark* to anyone on it till you have heard E. play it – all those who have, & all those have been real musicians think it the most original & greatest thing he has done . . . He is better I am thankful to say but the strain of the work is very great for him & makes him very easily worried – He wd. send his especial love I know, did he know I was writing. . . .'

March 26 1906

Dearie Moss:

Many thanks for your p.c.

Your remarks about those *two* bars in the Intro. were quite right & they were *never intended* to go in – they are altered now. It is easy (!) enough to write a melody – except the last two bars: I am sure it is the difficulty of avoiding a 'barn-door' ending that has kept the modern school from symmetrical melody. Meyerbeer is, of course, notorious for bad endings & Mendelssohn is almost as bad – or quite as bad in another way.

'Happy & blest', & fine opening ends

Wagner (Lohengrin) comes perilously near a bad end I think

– lovely – but how
about this?

Well: this is not to excuse my own infantile attempts & ineptitude but to show you what I feel about 'tunes' & you, with unerring instinct, put your finger on two bars which I put in my sketch to remind me of my design – length etc. The bars are better now, but I have taken 'jolly good' care not to make 'em more interesting than the real tune.

We start on Ap. 6, & I need not say, dear old man, how I hope to find you fit & well when we return: all good wishes are yours you know.

Yours ever
Edward.

[*postcard*]

Plas Gwyn, Hereford

I cannot tell you how sad your news has made us: I hope & pray all may soon be brighter. In the hurry of departure I can say no more. C.H.H.P[arry] is an angel as ever, God bless him! If you *do* want anything you know all that's mine is yours. so go ahead.

Ap 2 [19]06   Love to you, yours ever
Edwd. E.

Lady Elgar wrote to Jaeger from New York on 11 May, hoping that he was better and, perhaps, at home again. 'You will like to hear the Festival was a most satisfying success & E.'s works made the most *profound* impression. . . . Do you know *1200* people stood on the Gerontius night in the Hall – It was a wonderful sight.'

While he was in America Elgar heard of the death of his father. Having reached home towards the end of May, he was again unwell, and was ordered by his doctor to take a holiday. On 22 June Lady Elgar wrote from New Radnor: 'I know you will like to have a line to say E. is much better today & has been working hard & I hear a lovely *tune* – I do trust he will keep well now. It has been a dreadfully worrying time & he has worried so much over it [*The Kingdom*] so it is better not to write about it to him. . . .' *Three days later Elgar slipped on wet stones, hurt his knee, and was in considerable pain for a day or two.*

Plas Gwyn,
Hereford.

July 3 1906

My dear Nim:

I am better but cannot bend my knee yet!

Thanks for the copy stitched up: your suggestion on p. 97[1] will *not* do as the syllable 'Je' is so unimportant, but, my brave boy, on pp. 99 & 100, I gladly accept your emendation & we will have B♭ for "these" p. 99 & C♮ for "so" on p. 100. P.110, the cue shd. be marked Cell*i*.

In haste

Yours ever

Edward.

(the lame & blind)

I have 4 prs of spectacles now!

Plas Gwyn,
Hereford.

July 7 [19]06

My dear Jaggs:

I shall soon finish with you, look here: I want the *two* soloists T. & B. or rather their names John & Peter to sing *with* the chorus from ⟨79⟩ to ⟨82⟩ incl. & see how you can do it without messing the plate: it's simply to add the names somewhere – see p. 130 *Apostles* for example.

In the new Baptism (*refreshing*) theme I endeavoured to show the *movement* in the orchestra but I shall have to alter it as the rocking in the R.H. suggests Humperdinck – there's nothing in the harmony or outline so it's soon done. It's curious because there's *nothing* in my

---

[1] see *The Kingdom*, vocal score

orchestra arrangement which is like H. only I tried to make it *feel* like the s. quavers.

I'll carve it all right. I expect it's engraved now so send it along. That *surprise* or rather quiet astonishment theme is all right, eh?

I can bend my knee etwas but cannot do this yet.

[letter-card]

[postmark, Hereford, 9 July 1906]

My dearest Nim.

Only one line to say how very very sorry we are to hear of the boy's illness and its attendant worries for Mrs Jaeger & you. We can only hope that it will be the usual slight infantile trouble & be soon over.

Love, E.

Plas Gwyn,
Hereford.
July 20, 1906

My dear Jaggs:

Here are some *few* pages which end a page so I send 'em.

I am delighted to get your cheery card saying that the soliloquy is

good. I will look to your good suggestions when I receive the proof.
Hope all is well at home now. So hot here!

Yours ever

Edward

Please send a wire acknowledging the arrival of the score – *if you get it*!!
It's rather a 'tall' bit★ perpend.

★ bit of scoring I mean

Plas Gwyn,

Hereford.

Saturday [21 July 1906]

My dear Nim:

I hope the boy, bless him! is going on well: we are so very sorry
for your trouble – it is really desperately annoying & we can only hope
it will pass very soon.

Well: I played thro' No 9 Variation written by one Ass to the glori-
fication of another old duck: you will never be more *dearly* idealised
than that: better perhaps but not so sincere. I have been reading your
Analysis of the Apostles & very wonderful it is: I am amazed.

Now I hear with great joy that you are doing a like office for the
Kingdom. I am sending you, or rather I will send if you wish, some
commentaries on the Acts – they are not long, that is the portions necy
to the work are not long. There are sundry points I want mentioned
in the Analysis, viz:—*glossolalia*.

I am just completing the final revision of my notes & sketches: the
whole thing is intentionally less mystic than the A[postles]:—the *men*
are alive & working & the atmosphere is meant to be more direct &
simple (mixed sentence but you will gather what I mean) But we will
have a talk one day. I hope to be in town at the end of this week –
possibly – & will try & arrange to see you if it will be possible for you.

Love to you all

Yours ever

Edward Elgar

On 23 July 'E had nearly finished the composing of his beautiful
work' (*Lady Elgar, Diary entry*), *and the full score was coming along fast.
On 26 July he was in London and conferred with Jaeger over the* Analysis.

July 23 [19]06

My dear Moss:

We *are* so glad to hear you are about again & that Hans is going on all right.

I'll be sure to see you when I come – on Thursday belike.

I will not go into the points you name now – only one thing strikes me as being *plain* & you want it plainer: look at ⏐III⏐ bar after we start ♩ = 58[;] between ⏐II4⏐ & ⏐II8⏐ there is a *stringendo* which brings us, at II8 to double as quick as we started, viz – 𝅗𝅥 = 58 – at ⏐I20⏐ ♩ = 58 again so there's *no* change of time really. I will add, at ⏐I20⏐ ♩ = 𝅗𝅥 of the preceding.

It was really the only way to write it.

Ever yours
Ed.

I am sending you a book.

[*on University of Birmingham writing paper*]

July 24 [19]06

My dear Nim:

Here's a book you will find some useful things in it. You need not worry your pagan head with more than the first four chapters, & some of the final notes.

As to naming the themes we'll see to it. You will see there is no theme for *The Kingdom* – the Kingdom includes everything.

The work deals only with the Church in Jerusalem – you might hint that perhaps a further section is contemplated (it's partly written!) dealing with the church of the Gentiles. All else when we meet.

Glad the boy is better.

Yours ever & one day
Edward

Langham Hotel,
London
Saturday a.m.
[28 July 1906]

Authentic Moss:

The weather was so uncertain that I came back & am on my way home, so please send any proofs etc. (today & onwards) to Plâs Gwyn. Will you ask Mr. Pointer to see that the myrmidons of the Woolly

Lamb[1] (on whom blessings!) do not muddle the turns in the orch. parts:
as thus:—

This is a 'nonsense' passage but it shews what I mean: the two soli
will be at the same desk so that the turn is impossible.

Something (I think pubd. *not* by you), had to be engraved over
again from a similar cause.

Verb: sap.

It *was* good to see you again & your dear, old *earnest* face. bless you!

But you cannot persuade me that it's worth while to write music.

Oh! Send me today without fail (A. Ward says 'there ain't no such
word as *fale*') a copy of the Lord's Prayer section as supplied to Birmingham to Authentic Mossheads &, apparently to everyone except

Your sorrowing
Edward

My love to all at home

Plas Gwyn,
Hereford.
Tuesday [31 July? 1906]

My dear authentic Moss.

By this post some score on receipt of which I crave a telegram.
Don't worry.

There's only *one* 'stop' in the whole work – top line page 6. This
may be better marked thus // & knock out the comma. On pp 30 & 53,
the commas only shew a sort of breath mark making the word following a little pointed: the commas shd. *not* be in the PF. part which is
continuously slurred on.

I added more of these commas at Damrosch's request & I think

[1] note by Jaeger: 'Oppenheimer, Printer's agent'

Wilson – I forget about W. though. Frank D. said it made the chorus *understand so much better.*

There is no *hush* wh. you are afraid of. Am I a fool?

No. (I'm not at all sure).

Now: how long can I keep the proof of prelude, full score: when shall I receive the wind? I want to play, or rather, get it all played through by Mr Austin & I haven't enough to make it worth while. If the parts will not be coming yet I can return the sc: pro tem.

Much love
yours ever
Edward.

Plas Gwyn
Hereford
Augt 1: 1906.

My dear Nim:

Only time for a hurried line: as to the omission I *intended* it, but, as you ask, I assume there's time for an alteration, so I send one *which had better go in by all manner of means.*

As to the libretto (proofs received) the type is like your analysis, not like the 8vo Apostles.

There are several alterations in the headings necy. You will see how the difficulty about *Italics* was overcome if you look at *Apostles* libretto: all the *ital.* words are a size larger than the corresponding roman – or the *ital.* names are smaller – I can't, with my worn out old eyes, see which it is.

I have received the Arrest & it's not bad apparently. Glad you like it: I adopt, dear godfather, your suggestions.

Thankfully
Yours ever
Edward

P.T.O.

P.S. I return Mr Maclean's letter: *I have nothing to do with it!* Many people have written to me (including Zavertal[1]) about it but I know nothing. I will of course do as you wish if I get the chance.

---

[1] Ladislas Zavertal (1849–1942), conductor, of Czech origin, but naturalized British citizen in 1896, who retired to Italy in 1906.

Plas Gwyn,
Hereford.
Augt 7: 1906

My dear Moss:

This is a music pen.

Herewith pp 117–168, full score
please send a wire!

Also a few pages of proof, V. sc. also libretto. the caps, (in place of Italic) will *not* do. – try the *larger* size italic for the text. I shewed it to Mr Alfred yesterday & he said you might try that way as in the Apostles.

I forgot to say that

A) Bars 1,2, line 1 page 141 V. sc.

B)   „   1,2, line 2   „   „

are from old Hebrew tunes.

(A) "'Al Elleh"

Hymn of Weeping

(B) "Hamabdil"

Hymn of Parting.

You see, *parting* & *weeping* are in the scene.

See pp 8, 29, of the Augener book which I used for the Morning psalm in the Apostles

In haste
Yours ever
Edward

(I scored 70 pages in the week)

Jaeger, again being far from well, said on 15 August (Diary entry) that he could not finish the Analysis: *two days later, however, he promised that he would.*

Plas Gwyn,
Hereford.
Augt 19 1906

My dearie Moss:

I have been unable to steal a minute to write.

I *am so glad* you are going on with the Analysis & hope you have an easier time with it. When can you come down?

I am getting on all right with the score.

Much love from us all to you all

Yours ever
Edward.

Plas Gwyn,
Hereford
Wedy [12 September 1906]

My dearie Jaggs:

Thanks for your letter to which I can only send a hurried line: ½ of the Analysis has come & you shall not be bothered with it.

I am glad you are 'placed' amongst *nice* English sea & shore. Blessings on you.

I am torn in pieces this week by people.

I will not tell you of the festival[1]: the old effect of the building is grand as ever.

I will not go into your private affairs now: I only say do not worry yourself but do all you can to get better & don't tell us we can't understand or sympathise because, of course, we know that already: You old Moss.

Love from all
Yours ever
Edward.

[September 1906]

My dear Jaggs:

What a drastic cure! *How* I should like to join in it: we would skip together in fine form. dear old boy, I hope you are getting on well: it seems very lonely with you away & all the good Americans gone home. I have not heard from Sanford since his party left here after the Hereford Festival.

Love to you now & always

yours ever
Edward

On 26 September Elgar went to Aberdeen where he received the degree of LL.D. (h.c.). C. S. Terry, then Professor of Modern History there, wrote an anthem in honour of the occasion. On 28 September there was a rehearsal of The Kingdom *in Birmingham.*

[*postcard*]

[*postmark* Birmingham 29 Sept 1906]
on train

Hope you are allright have been unable to write

Love
EE.
LL.D. Aberdeen

[1] Of Elgar's works there were given at Hereford during this week *The Apostles*, the *Introduction and Allegro* (which he conducted) and *Gerontius*. Elgar did not hear the last, staying at home in order to work.

Plas Gwyn,
Hereford
Sept. 30, 1906.

My dear Jaeger:

I only recd. your letter this a.m. We came from Birmingham on Saturday for a quiet rest.

I do hope you will have a comfortable journey & that all will go well. I need not say how sorry we are that you have to go away again: As to the music, never mind. I am quite tired of the musical world & want room for energy – the musical world is too small for me.

I forget all about the rehearsals already!

Send us a p.c. & let us hear all about you.

Much love in awful haste

Yours ever

Ed. E.

The first performance of The Kingdom *took place at Birmingham on 3 October. The* Prelude *would appear to have been played as an organ piece by Sinclair at the Commemoration of St. Michael's College, Tenbury, some days previously* (History of St. Michael's College, *p. 55*).

[*postcard*]

Plas Gwyn,
Hereford
Oct 18 [19]06

My dear J.

How & where are you? We have been very quiet since Birmingham: you never send a word as to yourself. The weather is ever dark & gloomy, & we are preparing for winter. Good luck to you we all send love

Yrs ever

Ed E.

'Dark and gloomy': *this describes Elgar's condition at the end of this year. As usual the first performance of a work found him both physically and emotionally exhausted. He released himself from his University obligations and at the beginning of December went to Llandrindod Wells, hoping that in the New Year he might go to Italy.*

1907-1908

The Elgars stayed in Italy until the end of February, and on 2 March Edward sailed to New York, on the Germania *from Liverpool. During an extended tour of the United States he conducted* The Apostles *and* The Kingdom *in New York, and the* Variations *in Pittsburgh, where he collected another honorary degree. Back in England at the end of April he went to Morecambe and then settled down at home to write two single and two double chants for Novello, the part-song* How calmly the evening, *and the fourth* Pomp and Circumstance March. *Jaeger once again was trying to restore his now rapidly diminishing strength, this time in Germany.*

Plas Gwyn,
Hereford,
May 28 1907

My dear Moss:

I have been wofully busy & have scarcely been 'at home' yet. I do hope you are feeling satisfied – as satisfied as may be possible under the circumstances – with your new surroundings. I forget where *Westfalen* is but I am going to look at the map presently: curiously there was long ago an old family here, of German extraction I think named *Westfaling,* so spelt & there is a Westfaling street in this city. S.S.S[anford]. is in Paris safely bless him & I hope he may have a peaceful & restful time: he has been really ill during last winter & an angel to many as usual.

I had a mixed time in America – mostly very pleasant but the unpleasant times were jokable, so all passed well.

We are altogether enjoying the summer when the weather will let us: some days hot & then very cold as is today. There is really no news: all goes steadily on: I shall be fifty next week so they tell me, but I don't know it. I have my pipe & the bicycle & a heavenly country to ride in – so an end. I take no interest whatever in music now & just 'edit' a few old boyish M.S.S. – music is off.

We all send love & best of wishes to you, let us hear soon how you are taking to the new spot.

Yours ever

Edward

[*on reverse of paper monogrammed C.A.E. with note from Lady Elgar*]

[June 1907]

My dearest Nimrod:

how I did make 'you' sound in Chicago! A fine orchestra (100) & they knew (via dear old Theodore Thomas) *everything* of mine back-wards: I shed a tear over it: Now I'm busy & must not use my eyes much so I am doing trifles: poor things but mine own boyish thoughts. I wax old but not infirm. I wish you would send better news of yourself but we hope for that next time.

All love to you

Yours ever

Edward

The first pt of the 4th march is good: the middle *rot* but pleasing to march to.

On 7 June Lady Elgar wrote to Jaeger:

'. . . Edward's head has been full of music ever since his return & he has been continually sketching & playing. He has sent Messrs. N. 2 lovely motetts & the other evening wrote a lovely pt. song, & is just waiting for permission for the words wh. I trust he may soon receive. & now he is orchestrating another Pomp & Circumstance March a *splendid* one. one to rouse every spark of martial fire . . .'

So far as composition was concerned during the later summer months Elgar devoted himself to the melodies from his old 'Shed Books', and produced The Wand of Youth *suites. On 27 June, however, Lady Elgar had noted that he was* 'playing [a] great beautiful tune' (*Diary entry*), *which probably refers to the opening of the First Symphony.*

Plas Gwyn,

Hereford.

Augt 24: 1907

My dear Moss:

I was delighted to see the postmark on your letter & overjoyed to hear that you had arrived. I hope the temporary ailment resultant from the journey & this awful climate is passing rapidly away. I am not writing at length now because I am just back from the sea & had on Friday to rush to town: back yesterday. I fear I have no musical news for you: my eyes are not really workable & I have done only some ancient trifles this summer & I seem to have forgotten all about music: you know I have no ambition & so there's an end.

Now, dear Moss, this is only to bring you our love & best wishes: I shall hope to *see* you soon.

Best regards from us all to Mrs. Jaeger

Yours ever

Edward

After going to Queen's Hall to hear the first performance of the new Pomp and Circumstance March *on 24 August Elgar finished* The Wand of Youth Suite No. 1 *and played it to Henry Wood. Then came the Gloucester Festival, and next the Leeds Festival, where, on 11 October,* The Kingdom *was performed. Other works given were Parry's symphonic poem,* A Vision of Life, *and Vaughan Williams's* Toward the Unknown Region. *Meanwhile Elgar was considering his Violin Concerto and a 'gorgeous new tune' for the symphony.*

> Queen's Hotel,
> Leeds
> Tuesday
> [8 October 1907]

My dear Nim:

I have thought about you so very much during these festival times. I say! that 'Vision' of Parry's is *fine stuff* & the poem is literature: you *must* hear it some day.

I hope you are better: I heard of you via that dear good woman Mrs. Worthington[1] & wanted to climb up to you but could not.

This is only to bring my love – I've really nothing to say

Yours ever

Edward

> Plas Gwyn,
> Hereford.
> Oct 25 1907

My very dear Nim:

I have today asked Messrs. Novello to transfer all rights & royalties in the Analyses of Gerontius, Kingdom & Apostles to you from the last making up of the accounts. I am very much 'wanted' by my poor relations, just now more than ever, so I apologise to you for not making the transaction retrospective: this I wished to do but I *cannot*. So forgive your friend & please accept the little I can do.

[1] see *Elgar O.M.* p. 146 and *passim*

I hope you are going on well & when I pass through London on my way to economize 'in the South' I hope I may see you

Love

Yours ever

Edward Elgar

50 Lancaster Gate,[1]

[London] W.

Wedy [30 October 1907]

My dearest Jag.

All right! many thanks for your letter about those analyses – but you are a dear good chap – *but* E.E. is going to have his own little way for the first time in his life

Love

Edward

On 5 November the Elgars left England for Italy, where they had taken a house, 38 Via Gregoriana P. 3, in Rome.

On 3 February Lady Elgar wrote to Jaeger. Her news of Edward was somewhat gloomy, for he had been laid up with 'a strong touch of influenza, you know how wretched & depressing that is . . . Before he was ill E. had his head full of lovely new tunes. I hope he will soon be set up again, & busy again.' *That Jaeger was preparing an article on his part-songs stimulated Elgar to the following letter.*

Rome

Ap 26 1908

[1905 *written in error*]

My dearest Nimrod:

Your very welcome p.c. has just arrived & I hasten to send the reply you ask for. I was delighted to receive your last jolly long letter & should have written in answer to that but – my hand *jumps* when I write as you will see from this letter & I avoid writing as much as I can – sort of cramp & rheumatism mixed. I am *so* glad you are writing some notes & reviews & that you take pleasure in it.

It seems odd to think of anything of mine being worth writing about – I mean I remember my *first partsong* in 1890 or thereabouts 'My Love dwelt in a Northern Land'[.] Now a stock piece for superior *poetic* choirs: *then* it was said to be crude, ill-written for the voices, laid out without knowledge of the capabilities of the human voice &c. &c!! How funny it all is! Now I have made a sort of name by writing some big things & can only get *commissions* to write rot – ah! ha! I must *talk* to you some day about my avoiding work on great things – I have

[1] Alfred Littleton's house

too many people *now* alas! (& the clog gets heavier every day) to allow
me to think of anything I would wish to do: it is painful but it is the
only reward I get: I say this because I saw a portion of the letter you
sent to Mrs. W[orthington]. – More of this when we meet.

Now: all you said more or less represents what I meant. I do not
think I have overdone the marks (of expression[1]): you see nothing
emotional is ever performed in strict time & it takes conductors *years*
(literally) to find out a reading: you have only to think of the way people
play Brahms (symphonies or anything) now & compare it with the
want of reading they obtained even ten years ago. I have only put sort
of *emotional* marks for the conductor to do the best he can with. I wish
you could have heard the *Morecambe choir under Howson* sing four or
five years ago: you wd then fully appreciate what I have tried to do.
Now as to the stuff. No 1 is of course written as it is for *convenience* –
As to 'Owls' – it is only a fantasy & means nothing. It is in wood [*sic*]
at night evidently & the recurring "Nothing" is only an *owlish* sound.
One word as to my treatment of the words, not only in this Op. but
always. I hold that *short* syllables may be sustained occasionally for the
sake of effect just as an actor does. There is one dear good man against
whom I wd. not *think anything* but the greatest admiration & that is
Parry. But he almost if not quite annoys me in the way he sets the
words which swarm in our English – two syllables, both short, the
first accented e.g. petal. Set in an ordinary way a poem sounds like
reading a newspaper paragraph. I remember insisting on doing a poem
of Tennyson (Lotos Eaters![2]) by P. I liked it & studied it with the
chorus for months & had great difficulty in getting them to *take* to it:
they did it very well. After the concert a very well educated lady –
musically & artistically, in fact cultured in every way, said to me "We
have done our best to please & I am sorry you insisted: I shall never
read the poem again with any enjoyment". This of course simply on
account of the *driven* accents. Occasionally an Actor says "*Murrr*—der!"
instead of "Murder" & why should not we? You will note also that I
threw over from the first the convention of commonplace part-music –
you know the sort I mean – where every idea requiring force is put to a
high, intolerably high note for every voice: I often mark a *low* note
to be sung loudly: naturally I *know* what the effect will be but that
the poor dears cannot force it out beyond the other, maybe *well-lying*
parts: yet only the other day, one of your best chorus-masters said *I*
know nothing of writing for the voice *or* choral effect – asked why, he
pointed to a ff on a C for Sopranos: this sort of thing is annoying as it

---

[1] added in pencil by Jaeger
[2] also added by Jaeger. This was a W.P.S. performance, 10 May 1902.

shews what sort of idiots we write for. If the clown had an ounce of artistic sense he wd. have seen that the note was to help the contraltos & to lead into a *diminuendo* impossible to obtain in any other way.

As to the words: you will find they read all right. I omitted "Be" in Alto, No. 3. p.9 on purpose: – it gives force to the E♭ *Through*. You must remember that a modern partsong is to be listened to & not read. If you *hear* anyone of these, the words flow right on correctly. I added '*Can*" on the last p. to oblige McN[aught]'s idea of a better ff – which was a good thought. All else you have seen. I cannot find your letter & must rush out now.

You are an old goooose to think (Mrs W.'s letter) that I was annoyed: I am only somewhat heartbroken: I cannot afford to get a *quiet* studio where I might have worked & my whole winter has been wasted for the want of a few more pounds: it seems odd that any rapscallion of a painter can find a place for his 'genius' to work in when a poor devil like me who after all *has* done something shd. find himself in a hell of noise & no possible escape! I resent it bitterly but can do nothing. It is just the same now at Hereford, noise has developed in the neighbourhood – I dodged it doing the Kingdom at great expense by going to Wales, but I can't do it again: my lovely works do not pay the rent of a studio!

Much love to you & great rejoicing that you are having a change.

Yours ever
E.E.

P.S. Sgambati (dear man) has some wonderful things – given him by Liszt the first copy of the score Siegfried Idyll sent by Wagner to Liszt in Rome with a little writing on the title. Also the *first* exemplar of *Faust* Berlioz sent by B to Liszt! & above all (1868) the full score Meistersinger sent by W. to L. with words & the title "De profundis clamavi!" at the top a date etc. below & *Richard*. How wonderful to see & touch.

The Elgars returned to England in mid-May. At first Edward remained depressed, not least of all because bicycling was becoming so much less of a pleasure because of the advent of the motor-car (Diary entry, 1 June).

Plas Gwyn,
Hereford.
June 3 1908

My dear Moss:

I was glad to receive yours of May 26th. & to know that you had been west & had some fresh air: here it is very lovely but too suffocatingly *stuffy*: I can't write – there are too many other composers singing their own traditional compositions loudly on every bush. I am sorry your article is put off. I wish the M[usical]. T[imes]. could lead instead of follow. I am glad you are able to write & feel 'good' about it: I look forward with interest to your 'stuff '.

I can only write sadly about myself – I have done some good work in my life & now I can only get orders (which will keep my people in necessaries) for rot of kinds & I *must* do it. I have no intention of completing my oratorio cycle or whatever it is – I am not allowed to beg a dispensation of a benevolent providence who objects to the world being saved or purified or improved by a mere musician. Of course I have the thing – the biggest of all sketched – but I cannot afford for the sake of others to waste any time on it. Alas!

Well?: I am well & strong except my eyes & must be thankful to be allowed to breathe somebody else's air I suppose & walk on somebody else's roads – but I am not thankful at all.

What an object lesson is poor dear Madam Albani: one of the best of women. She has sung to these delightful English their own *oratorios* & sacred things for years. – her husband loses all their money – she has to advertise for pupils! Now look at a battered old w—e like Melba & Co: – !!! My beloved countrymen and women wd. & will subscribe anything to help her if necessary – it makes my blood boil – where is providence? *Nothing*[1]

Goodbye
Yours ever
Ed Elgar

Nikisch's variations were odd. but they never muddle you & you sound well. Bless you!

Jaeger's article, alas!, was refused publication, he not agreeing to its curtailment. But Lady Elgar wrote on 12 June, and 15 June, expressing her great appreciation of Jaeger's powers as a devoted interpreter of Edward's ideas. 'Such an interpreter', she said, 'is a necessity between the genius and the outer world. . . .' 'Edward', she continued on 12 June, 'is so absorbed in some work (I trust you will hear some day) that I know you will understand the delay in his reply to your letter.'

Plas Gwyn,
Hereford.
June 13 1908

My dearest Moss:
Here is your royalty on the "analytical notes of "The Apostles" &

[1] twice underlined

"The Kingdom": Mr. Clayton sends me a *separate* cheque to keep it *separate* & – you *must* have it. So shut up & swallow it.

I can't answer your letter at this moment. I can't say I have anything more *important* to do but it must be done & done now. Oh! such a tune

Yours ever

Edward

On 15 June Lady Elgar ended her letter to Jaeger: 'E. sends his love, you have heard from him by now, & he wants to say to you the "Sym. is A 1". It is *gorgeous*, steeped in beauty. He is quite absorbed in it.'

On 3 September Jaeger wrote to Elgar saying that he had, for the first time for many months, just heard some of his music. 'Do,' he wrote, 'let us have that third oratorio directly you have completed your symphony. You owe it to us who *do* appreciate your genius fully & to whom your music *is* an inspiration and a moving power & the "most beautiful of God's revelations" (Goethe). If we are only a hundred or thousand to-day, be sure that we shall number *all* genuine music lovers in days to come. Your works are too near, too original, too great to be appreciated by the average amateur or musician straight away. Be happy that you have made so many converts in so few years. And fear no rival!' ...

To a subsequent letter (missing) Elgar replied as follows:

Plas Gwyn,
Hereford.
Sep 19: 1908

My dear Jaggs:

We *did* want you at Worcester & were a learned party.

I loved having your letter & all you said about rehearsal was cheering.

As to the symphony – the general key is A♭ – the signature of one flat means nothing. it is convenient for the players. The first movement is in 'form' 1st & 2nd. principal themes with much episodical matter but I have – (without [definite *deleted*] intention to be peculiar but a natural feeling) – thrown over all key relationship as formerly prac-tised *: the movement has its 2nd. theme on its 2nd presentation in A♭ & as I said, the movement ends in that key.

You will find many subtle *enharmonic* relationships I think & the widest *looking* divergencies are often closest relationships

This is a sort of *plagal* (?) relationship of which I appear to be fond (although I didn't know it) – most folks run through *dominant* modulations if that expression is allowable & I think some of my twists are defensible on *sub*-dominant grounds. All this is beside the point because I *feel* & don't invent – I can't even invent an explanation *no excuse is offered* – although when a dear old Mosshead asks I try to be good: after all I am only an amateur composer – if that means I compose for the love of it – I certainly *am* an amateur letter-writer for I only write for the love of Nimrod

Whose I am ever
E E.

★ I am not silly enough to think (or wish) that I have *invented* anything: see Beethoven's late Quartetts passim.

Plas Gwyn,
Hereford.
Nov 11: 1908

My dear Jaggs:
   I am truly grieved you shd be so worried & can only hope you are better now: I am sorry also that my work is to miss your ever helpful introduction. but I cannot think of my loss when you are ill, bless you!
   You will perhaps be amused – I hear that the "new Sulphuretted Hydrogen machine designed by Sir Edward Elgar" is to be manufactured & called the 'Elgar S.H. Apparatus'!! I will not offer to send

you my invention you would soon tire of it although a nice toy.

I have my proofs of the Sym to finish & some diagrams of the machine to *draw* & send to the makers by this post so goodbye

Love

Yours ever

Edward

From Jaeger to Elgar, 26 November 1908:
'My dear, great Edward,

I was allowed to come down today for the first time for a month, and I spent some happy quarter hours on your Adagio in the Symphony (P.F. arrangement).

My dear friend that is not only one of the very greatest slow movements since Beethoven, but I consider it *worthy of that master.* How original, how *pure*, noble, etc.. . . . It's the greatest thing you have done. . . . I detected one or two places, where the great adagio of the Choral Symphony was recalled to my memory. nothing in the way of a reminiscence (the Satz is *quite* your own), but just the feeling of nobility of sentiment. At 104 we are brought near Heaven. That is a lofty & inspired thought. . . .

I must go to bed, though I know that haunting adagio won't let me sleep soon'. . . .

On 4 December, one day after the première of the Symphony, under Richter in the Free Trade Hall, Manchester, and three days before the first London performance, Jaeger wrote the last extant letter to his 'dear "poor conventional chemist" '. After repeating much of the sentiments previously expressed regarding Elgar's genius and the power of the Adagio he went on:

'The Scherzo is a real joy & one of the biggest things of the kind in all symphonic literature. And that mysterious Lento with its abysmal depths of tone colour & the astounding Finale, an overpowering outburst of optimism & joie de vivre that carries one away in spite of oneself until the superb peroration crowns the whole splendid structure. . . . It's a great and masterly work & will place you higher among the world's masters than anything you have done. Ill as I am (& I feel so ill tonight that I want to go to the nearest Ry Station & throw myself under a Train to end my misery) I hope to go next Monday. I have bought a ticket & am looking forward to what I fear will be the last great . . . [*the end of the letter has been removed.*]

Jaeger, who had resigned his post at Novello's during 1908, died on 18 May 1909, at which time the Elgars were in Italy. His funeral took place

four days later at the Golders Green Crematorium, where the music was provided by Dr. Walford Davies and choristers of the Temple Church.

On 24 January 1910, a Memorial Concert was given in Queen's Hall, at which the Elgars were present. The London Symphony Orchestra, Muriel Foster, and Plunket Greene took part and the conducting was shared by Parry, Walford Davies, Coleridge-Taylor – all of whom were represented in the programme – and Richter. Richter conducted excerpts from Die Meistersinger, Brahms's Alto Rhapsody and some of the 'Enigma' Variations.

At this time Elgar was busied with the Violin Concerto, thus giving final point to a sentence which had been written in a commemorative article on Jaeger in the Spectator (25 December 1909):

'Despondent about himself, he was full of hope for others, and spent himself in smoothing their path to fame.'

BIOGRAPHICAL APPENDIX

ALBANI, EMMA (1852–1930) – a French-Canadian soprano, whose name was Lajeunesse, that of Albani being adopted after her initial success in Milan in 1870. Appearing at Covent Garden for the first time in 1872, Albani sang there consistently until 1896. She was also successful in oratorio and was a familiar figure at Three Choirs Festival until her retirement in 1911.

ATKINS, SIR IVOR ALGERNON (1869–1953) – a pupil of G. R. Sinclair, became organist of Worcester Cathedral in 1897. Atkins's association with Elgar was close; the words of his *Hymn of Faith* (1905) were arranged by Elgar and the two men collaborated in an edition of the *St. Matthew Passion* of Bach (1911). (See also *Music in the Provinces: The Elgar – Atkins Letters*, Wulstan Atkins, *Proceedings of the Royal Musical Association*, Vol. 84, pp. 27–42.)

BANTOCK, SIR GRANVILLE (1868–1946) – educated at the Royal Academy of Music, made a precarious early living by occasional writing and peripatetic conducting. In 1896 he bravely organized and conducted a concert of works by young British composers. In the following year he became musical director at the Tower, New Brighton, Cheshire, where, after changing the resident ensemble from military band to symphony orchestra, he continued to promote the interests of native music. Subsequently Bantock, whose own talent for composition was not inconsiderable, went to Birmingham, as Principal of the School of Music in the Midland Institute. From there he exerted much influence on musical affairs in general.

BARGIEL, WOLDEMAR (1828–1897) – after various academic appointments, became a Professor of the Hochschule für Musik in Berlin. Bargiel's mother was the divorced wife of Friedrich Wieck (father of Clara Schumann), but this did not prevent Bargiel, formerly a pupil of the Leipzig Conservatorium, from becoming one of Schumann's disciples in so far as composition was concerned.

BEAUMONT, HENRY – tenor singer. *fl. c.* 1880.

BELL, WILLIAM HENRY (1873–1946) – Goss Scholar of the Royal Academy of Music in 1889, and professor of harmony there from

1903 to 1912. In 1912 Bell became Principal of the South African College of Music, in Cape Town. He first attracted attention as a composer when his early orchestral works were played by Manns at the Crystal Palace, and other conductors interested in his music were Richter, Wood and Beecham. In Cape Town his works were mainly interpreted by Theophil Wendt (see p. 70 *n.1*), conductor of the Municipal Orchestra.

BENNETT, JOSEPH (1831–1911) – was music critic of the *Daily Telegraph;* author of various libretti; and programme-note writer for the Philharmonic Society, and the Monday and Saturday Popular Concerts.

BENTON, ALFRED (b. *c.* 1855), was organist of Leeds Parish Church (of which he had once been a chorister) from 1891 to 1905. He had already been appointed organist to the Leeds Festival two years earlier, and in 1895 he took over the duties of chorus-master. In that year he also became conductor of the Leeds Orchestra and of the City's Choral Union. In addition to his work in Leeds Benton conducted societies in Barnsley, Bramley, and Morley. Later he was organist of Covington Cathedral, Cincinnati, U.S.A., and before finally settling in Liverpool was for a time assistant organist at Westminster Cathedral.

BISPHAM, DAVID (1857–1921) – an American baritone singer, who became a pupil of William Shakespeare in London in 1889. Bispham enjoyed much success both in England and America in the music-dramas of Wagner, his best parts being those of Kurwenal and Beckmesser. See his *A Quaker Singer's Recollections*, London, 1920.

BLACK, ANDREW (1859–1920) – a Scottish baritone, pupil of Randegger, came into prominence at the Crystal Palace in 1887 and after the Leeds Festival of 1892 ranked among the best singers of his generation. After his performance of the part of Elijah at Birmingham in 1894 he was regarded as the best successor to Santley. In 1903 he took the part of Judas in the first performance of *The Apostles* at Birmingham. Black was, from 1893, a teacher at the Royal Manchester College of Music.

BLAIR, HUGH (1864–1932) – succeeded William Done (whose pupil he was) as organist of Worcester Cathedral in 1895. He was an able musician and conducted the Worcester Festival in 1893 and 1896, but his temperament was uneasily situated in the environment of a Cathedral City. In 1897 he left Worcester to become organist of Holy Trinity, Marylebone, London.

BREMA, MARIE (1856–1925) – mezzo-soprano singer, of German-American descent, who was at the height of her powers between

1890 and 1910. She was a conspicuous success in Wagnerian parts not only in England, but also in Germany, France, Belgium, and America. She sang the part of the Angel in the first performance of *Gerontius* in 1900. In later life Brema taught at the Royal Manchester College of Music.

BREWER, SIR ALFRED HERBERT (1865–1938) – a native of Gloucester, who succeeded Charles Lee Williams as organist of the Cathedral in 1897. He was also a composer.

BRIDGE, SIR JOHN FREDERICK (1844–1924) – organist of Manchester Cathedral (1869–1875) and of Westminster Abbey, where he held office for thirty-six years. Bridge was a professor at the Royal College of Music, conductor of the Royal Choral Society, and in 1903 Professor of Music in London University. He wrote much music and wielded a considerable influence – but not as composer.

BRODSKY, ADOLF (1851–1929) – Russian by birth, was a distinguished violinist. After being a professor in Leipzig, he came to Manchester to lead the Hallé Orchestra and to teach in the Royal College of Music. In 1903 Brodsky invited Elgar to join him on the staff of that Institution (see *Elgar O.M.* pp. 108–9).

BRUCH, MAX (1838–1920) – composer, lived in England from 1880 to 1883 and directed the Liverpool Philharmonic Society, as well as conducting concerts elsewhere in Britain.

BRUNEAU, ALFRED (1857–1934) – was one of the most progressive French composers and critics of his time. In his operas, many to libretti by Émile Zola, he introduced Wagnerian principles. *Le Rêve* was given in London in 1891, and *L'Attaque du moulin* in 1893; but the work of his that commanded most attention in London was his *Requiem* (Op. 19), sung by the Bach Choir in 1896.

BUTHS, JULIUS (1851–1920) – was musical director in Düsseldorf from 1890 to 1908, and conductor of the Lower Rhine Festival. In addition to his enthusiasm for Elgar he also promoted the interests of Delius.

BUTT, CLARA (1873–1936) – contralto, was a pupil of Daniel Rootham in Bristol. In 1892 she received much attention when she sang in London in Sullivan's *Golden Legend* and Gluck's *Orpheus*. In 1893 she was given her first Festival engagement at Hanley, in North Staffordshire. Clara Butt (D.B.E. in 1920) had an outstanding voice but dedicated too much of her talent to trivialities.

COATES, JOHN (1865–1941) – tenor singer, who sang in *Gerontius* at Worcester and Sheffield in 1902, and in *The Apostles* (1903) and *The Kingdom* (1906) at the Birmingham Festivals. Of him the *Berliner Post* said: 'John Coates, the great English tenor, belongs to the few international singers.'

COLERIDGE-TAYLOR, SAMUEL (1875–1912) – son of a West Indian doctor, distinguished himself as a student at the Royal College of Music, and gained rapid esteem through the fluent and colourful music of his *Song of Hiawatha* (1898, 1899, 1900). In his early days he owed much to Elgar's assistance.

COWARD, SIR HENRY (1849–1944) – a self-taught musician of Northern working-class extraction, who was one of the finest choir-trainers of his generation. His most notable work was done in Sheffield, and with choirs from that City and from Leeds he toured in Germany (1906 and 1910) and in various parts of the British Commonwealth.

COWEN, SIR FREDERICK (1852–1935) – British composer, born in Jamaica, who studied in Germany. He was a conductor much sought after by the larger provincial societies. His *Scandinavian Symphony* (1880) enjoyed much success in England and abroad and displayed his special skill in orchestration. Mus. D. (h.c.) with Elgar (see p. 112).

DAMROSCH, WALTER JOHANNES (1862–1950) – born in Breslau, was taken in 1871 to New York where his father undertook various engagements. Among these were the conductorships of the New York Oratorio and Symphony Societies. In 1885 Walter succeeded to these posts, continued to maintain German Opera Seasons as his father had done, and in 1902–3 was conductor of the New York Philharmonic Society. In his later years Damrosch, by his interest in children's concerts and broadcasting, did much for musical education in America.

DAVIES, BEN(JAMIN) GREY (1858–1943) – a Welsh tenor, with a dominantly lyrical quality of voice whose principal successes, after early operatic experiences, were in the concert hall.

DAVIES, SIR HENRY WALFORD (1869–1941) – organist, especially of the Temple Church and St. George's Chapel, Windsor, was a versatile musician and an outstanding personality in British music. A fluent, often charming, composer, he enjoyed some success at the provincial festivals. Davies was a pioneer of musical education through the medium of radio, was for some time Professor of Music at Aberystwyth University College, and in 1934 succeeded Elgar as Master of the King's Music.

DRAPER, CHARLES (1869–1952) – one of the best of English clarinettists, was a member of the Crystal Palace and Philharmonic Orchestras, and played at the Leeds and Three Choirs Festivals. In June 1904 he gave the first performance of Stanford's Clarinet Concerto.

ELWES, GERVASE HENRY CARY (1866–1921) – exchanged a career in the diplomatic service for one in music. A tenor, he was regarded more for his interpretative gifts than for any outstanding vocal gifts. His best performances were as the Evangelist in the *St. Matthew Passion* and as Gerontius.

ESTY, ALICE – soprano singer, prominent in Queen's Hall Concerts, *c.* 1900.

FOSTER, MYLES BIRKET (1851–1922) – son of the painter Birket Foster, was organist at various London Churches and, between 1880 and 1892, of the Foundling Hospital. He wrote much Church music, and a *History of the Philharmonic Society* (1913).

FRICKER, HERBERT AUSTIN (1868–1943) – organist and choirmaster in Leeds, where he was also City Organist and chorus master for the Triennial Festival. In 1917 he emigrated to Canada.

GERMAN, SIR EDWARD [originally Edward German Jones] (1862–1936) – was a skilful composer of light music whose aspirations did not stop there. In addition to his light operas (of which *Merrie England*, 1902, refuses to lie down) he wrote symphonies, for the Crystal Palace in 1890 and the Norwich Festival in 1893.

GILL, ALLEN – was conductor of the Alexandra Palace Choral and Orchestral Society, which gave the first London performance of *The Kingdom* in 1906. Gill helped to inaugurate the cultivation of instrumental music in English schools and conducted various amateur music-making bodies in London, and also in Nottingham.

GRAY, ALAN (1855–1935) – succeeded Stanford as organist of Trinity College, Cambridge, in 1892. Cantatas and other works of his, well composed in an academic way, were performed frequently at festivals in his native Yorkshire in the 1890's. Gray was one of the editors of the Purcell Society.

HEHEMANN, MAX (1873–1933) was the music critic of the *Essener Allgemeine Zeitung*. In 1904 he founded the *Musikalische Gesellschaft* in Essen which he directed for three years. Hehemann issued a German edition of Grove's *Beethoven and his Nine Symphonies* in 1906.

HENSON, MEDORA (1861–1928) – soprano singer.

HOBDAY, ALFRED CHARLES (1870–1942) – viola player, distinguished in chamber music concerts in St. James's Hall, who played in Richter's Royal Opera Orchestra, and led the viola section in the London Symphony Orchestra from its inception in 1904. Hobday played for Elgar at the Sheffield Festival of 1902.

HOLBROOKE, JOSEF (1878–1958) – a prolific, if unsuccessful composer of Romantic proclivities. For Elgar's closer connection with Holbrooke see *Elgar O.M.* pp. 120–1.

KALISCH, ALFRED (1863–1933) – son of a Jewish theologian, studied law but turned to musical criticism. He championed the cause of Richard Strauss, whose opera libretti he translated into English.

KNOWLES, CHARLES – English baritone. fl. 1890–1918.

LEMARE, EDWIN HENRY (1865–1934) – as organist of St. Margaret's, Westminster, became a prominent recitalist, with a conspicuous talent for adapting orchestral works to the organ. In 1902, following a successful recital tour in 1900, he emigrated to America. Lemare also composed much organ music.

LLOYD, CHARLES HARFORD (1849–1919) – organist of Gloucester Cathedral in succession to S. S. Wesley in 1876, of Oxford Cathedral in 1882, and Precentor of Eton College from 1892 to 1914, was a composer of mainly choral music.

LLOYD, EDWARD (1845–1927) – one of the leading tenor singers of his day, came into prominence when taking part in the *St. Matthew Passion* at the Gloucester Festival of 1871. He retired from the profession, while at the height of his reputation, in 1900, *The Dream of Gerontius* being the last major work in which he was to take part. (See portrait and leading article in *Mus. T.*, June 1899, pp. 9–15.)

LUNN, LOUISE KIRKBY (1873–1930) – a Manchester-born mezzo-soprano singer, made her debut as an operatic singer in London in Schumann's *Genoveva* in 1893. She was a fine interpreter of Wagner, taking part in performances of the Carl Rosa Company, and then at Covent Garden, and in America. In 1904 she was engaged for the Elgar Festival at Covent Garden.

McEWEN, SIR JOHN BLACKWOOD (1868–1948) – a Scotsman who succeeded Mackenzie as Principal of the Royal Academy of Music in 1924. His string quartets emerge from his considerable output as undeserving of the neglect into which they have fallen.

MACKENZIE, SIR ALEXANDER CAMPBELL (1847–1935) – a Scottish violinist and composer, was Principal of the Royal Academy of Music from 1888 to 1924. Mackenzie, who lived abroad a good deal, combined a cosmopolitan style with a feeling for Scottish national idiom, and his works are among the more rewarding of their period. Between 1892 and 1899 Mackenzie conducted the concerts of the Philharmonic Society.

McNAUGHT, WILLIAM GRAY (1849–1918) – choral conductor and teacher, became editor of the *School Music Review* (Novello) in 1892, and of *The Musical Times*, succeeding F. G. Edwards, in 1909.

MACPHERSON, CHARLES (1870–1927) – born in Edinburgh, became a Chorister of St. Paul's Cathedral, London, at the age of 9, and after holding various organ appointments, returned there as sub-organist in 1895. In 1916 he became organist in succession to Sir George Martin. Apart from church music he composed a number of instrumental works with Gaelic and Scottish associations.

MANNS, SIR AUGUST (1825–1907) – was a German bandmaster who, after taking over a wind-band at the Crystal Palace, London, in 1855, developed an orchestra and a sequence of programmes that were of great significance in the popularization of the masterpieces of orchestral literature. He was also a beneficent ally to many young English composers, of whom Elgar was one, at the end of the nineteenth century.

MESSCHAERT, JOHANNES (1857–1922) – was a Dutch baritone who sang in the Düsseldorf performance of *Gerontius* in 1902. Messchaert was also notable for his interpretation of Christ in the *St. Matthew Passion*.

MÜLLER-REUTER, THEODOR (1858–1919) – a well-known composer of choral music, who had been a pupil of Friedrich Wieck and Woldemar Bargiel, was Director of Music in Krefeld from 1893 until 1918. Müller-Reuter compiled a useful work of reference in his *Lexikon der deutschen Konzertliteratur* (1909, 1921).

NEWMAN, ERNEST (1868–1959) – was in business in Liverpool before turning to his main interest, musical criticism, as a career. He published a book on Gluck in 1895 and a study of Wagner – the preface to his great work on this composer (1933–47) – in 1899. In 1906 Newman published a small book on Elgar. He was successively on the staff of *The Manchester Guardian*, *The Birmingham Post*, *The Observer* and *The Sunday Times*. Newman was a lifelong supporter of the music of Elgar.

NOBLE, THOMAS TERTIUS (1867–1953) – studied at the Royal College of Music, and held several appointments before becoming organist of York Minster in 1898. In York he conducted a Symphony Orchestra and the Musical Society. After fourteen years there he went to New York to become organist of St. Thomas's Church, Fifth Avenue. Noble's compositions were skilfully written, and his church music is still in the standard repertoire.

PARKER, HORATIO WILLIAM (1863–1919) – trained under Rheinberger in Munich, became prominent as composer and educationalist in the United States, and in 1894 was appointed Professor of Music at Yale University. Parker's music was found attractive by English choral societies and *Hora Novissima* (Worcester 1899) was the first major American work to be performed at an important English festival. In 1900 he conducted *A Wanderer's Psalm* at Hereford and in 1902, in which year he became Mus.D. (h.c.) at Cambridge, he was again at Worcester to direct the third part of *The Legend of St. Christopher*.

PARRATT, SIR WALTER (1841–1924) – an almost legendary figure by now, was said to have been able to play Bach fugues and chess simultaneously. A Yorkshireman, Parratt showed precocious talents in youth and following his father's profession of organist eventually became organist of Magdalen College, Oxford, and then (1882) of St. George's Chapel, Windsor. In 1893 he was appointed Master of the Queen's Music – he was Elgar's immediate predecessor – and in 1908 Professor of Music at Oxford.

PARRY, SIR CHARLES HUBERT HASTINGS (1848–1918) – of a wealthy Gloucestershire family, was educated at Eton and Oxford. In the 1880's he appeared as a major English composer with a Pianoforte Concerto at the Crystal Palace, and *Prometheus Unbound* at the Gloucester Festival. Parry wrote much, and such works as *Blest Pair of Sirens*, *Songs of Farewell*, and the *English Lyrics*, were remarkable for their perceptiveness and strength. Parry exerted a strong influence on succeeding generations of English composers, especially since he was Professor of Music at Oxford (1900–1908) and Director of the Royal College of Music (1894–1918). Elgar found it hard to rid himself of the feeling that Parry had enjoyed an easy route to the top.

PITT, PERCY (1870–1932) – was educated in France and Germany; hence Elgar was ready to take his advice in respect of problems of translation. Pitt was much concerned in operatic projects after his appointment as musical adviser at Covent Garden in 1902. He was Director of Music to the British Broadcasting Company from 1922 until 1930 when he was succeeded by Adrian Boult. As a composer Pitt mainly explored his theatrical interests.

RANDEGGER, ALBERTO (1832–1911) – born in Trieste, was successful as an opera composer and director before being induced to settle in England about 1855. In addition to teaching at the Royal Academy of Music Randegger continued his operatic interests but also undertook other conducting appointments. Of these the most important was that of the Norwich Festival, which he held from 1881 to 1905.

READ, JOHN FRANCIS HOLCOMBE (1821–1901) – was born in Jamaica but educated in England. At the age of twelve he played the violin in the Royal Artillery Band, Woolwich, and in due course took lessons in composition from G. A. Macfarren. After brief service in the War Office Read joined the Stock Exchange. He maintained a lively interest in music (his list of compositions is long) and was a Vice-President and member of the committee of management of the Royal Academy of Music. In 1867 he became President and Conductor of the Walthamstow Musical Society, which he directed for 25 years. He was largely responsible for the Victoria Hall being built in Walthamstow and for the Borough gaining an enviable musical reputation. See *Walthamstow Antiquarian Society Official Publication No. 12*, 1924, (pp. 18–19), for detailed biography.

RISELEY, GEORGE (1845–1932) – inaugurated a successful series of orchestral concerts in Bristol in 1877. In that city he was also conductor of the Bristol Orpheus Society, the Bristol Society of Instrumentalists, and the Bristol Choral Society. In 1896 he conducted the Bristol Festival (held triennially until 1911), and in 1898 he became conductor of the Alexandra Palace and the Queen's Hall Choral Societies in London.

ROOY, ANTON VAN (1870–1932) – a Dutch baritone who first appeared in London as Wotan in *Die Walküre*, at Covent Garden in 1898. He took part in Wagnerian productions there and in America until 1913.

SCHÖLLHAMMER, CHARLES FREDERICK AUGUSTUS (1834–1917) – born in Germany, came to England in 1856, and taught in a private school at Worksop. In 1860, having married an Englishwoman, he went back to Germany to study at Stuttgart for two years. He then returned to England and became German master at the Wesley College in Sheffield. Later he taught also at Firth College in that city. In 1863 Schöllhammer founded a Sheffield Amateur Harmonic Society. In 1869 he became conductor of the Amateur Musical Society. Schöllhammer served on the "Executive, Selection, Chorus and Testing Committees" of the Sheffield Musical Festival (for which he wrote programme notes) from its inauguration in 1896. See W. Odom, *Hallamshire Worthies*, Sheffield 1926, p. 184.

SCOTT, CYRIL (1879–   ) – like Norman O'Neill, Roger Quilter, and Percy Grainger, studied under Knorr in Frankfurt. A gifted pianist, he became one of the most effective English composers for this medium.

SILOTI, ALEXANDER (1863–1945) – Russian by birth, became a conductor after a career as virtuoso pianist. He conducted the Moscow Philharmonic Concerts in 1901–2 and then functioned principally in St. Petersburg. He was the first Russian to be interested in Elgar's works. In 1919 Siloti emigrated and eventually settled in America.

SINCLAIR, GEORGE ROBERTSON (1862–1917) – was appointed organist of Truro Cathedral in 1881 and of Hereford Cathedral in 1889. He is commemorated in the eleventh of the *Enigma Variations*.

SOMERVELL, SIR ARTHUR (1863–1937) – was a pupil of Stanford at Cambridge and then of Friedrich Kiel and Bargiel (see above) in Berlin. A graceful composer, but of no marked individuality, Somervell occupied the important post of Inspector of Music to the Board of Education between 1901 and 1928.

SQUIRE, WILLIAM HENRY (1871–1963) – 'cellist and composer, who belonged to the orchestras of Covent Garden and the Queen's Hall (1895) and also to the London Symphony Orchestra. In later life he successfully specialized in light music. Squire played for Elgar at the Sheffield Festival of 1902.

STAINER, SIR JOHN (1840–1901) – chorister at St. Paul's Cathedral, and later undergraduate and organist at Oxford University, he succeeded Goss as organist of St. Paul's Cathedral in 1872. He was active as Principal of the National Training School for (later Royal College of) Music, Inspector to the Board of Education, President of the Musical Association, and, finally, from 1889 Professor of Music in the University of Oxford. Stainer was a prolific composer – his *Crucifixion* still maintaining its popularity in evangelical circles – and a fine scholar.

STANFORD, SIR CHARLES VILLIERS (1852–1924) – an Anglo-Irish composer with a fertile imagination, would have founded an Irish school of composers had there been foundations on which to build in Dublin, and had he not been compelled to accommodate his considerable talents to the conventions of the German style that dominated English music during his youth. Stanford was a powerful influence in English music. As Professor of Music at Cambridge (from 1887) and teacher of composition at the Royal College of Music he was eminently successful. He conducted the London Bach Choir (1885–1902) and the Leeds Festival (1901–10). Considering their respective temperaments it is surprising that Elgar and Stanford did not collide more often.

STEINBACH, FRITZ (1855–1916) – was conductor of the Meiningen Orchestra that visited England in 1902, after which he often acted as conductor of the London Symphony Orchestra. In 1902 Steinbach succeeded Wüllner (see below) as Kapellmeister and Director of the Conservatorium in Köln.

STRAUSS, RICHARD (1864–1949) – was, at the time of the Elgar-Jaeger correspondence, the most controversial figure in European music. He visited London for the first time in 1897, a year after *Till Eulenspiegel* had been played twice – by Manns, at a Crystal Palace concert – on account of its incomprehensibility. In June 1903 a Strauss Festival was presented at St. James's Hall, Strauss alternating with Mengelberg as conductor of the Concertgebouw Orchestra.

SULLIVAN, SIR ARTHUR SEYMOUR (1842–1900) – an Irishman, composed a large number of works among which his church music and comic operas (with W. S. Gilbert as librettist) were, for a time, greatly over-valued by the British people. He was a frequent conductor and appeared at most of the Festivals. Elgar was grateful to Sullivan for the early interest he showed in his work (see *Elgar O.M.* pp. 82–3).

THOMAS, THEODORE (1835–1905) – born in Germany, was taken by his parents to America in 1845. From being a violinist Thomas graduated to conducting and in 1864 began symphony concerts at Irving Hall, New York. In 1877 he conducted the New York Philharmonic Society. He also organized an orchestra in Cincinnati and in 1891 founded the Chicago Orchestra, which he directed for the rest of his life.

THOMPSON, HERBERT (1856–1945) – who, although studying law, was much influenced at Cambridge by Stanford so that in 1886 he became music critic of *The Yorkshire Post*. He occupied this post for fifty years. In addition to his journalism Thompson also wrote analytical notes, especially for the Leeds Festival.

TOURS, BERTHOLD (1838–1897) – violinist and organist, of Dutch parentage, became musical adviser and editor to Messrs. Novello in 1878. Tours wrote a good deal of music, especially for the Church of England, that was useful in its day.

VOLBACH, FRITZ (1861–1941) – became musical director in Mainz in 1892, and Professor at Münster in 1919. In 1901 a symphonic poem by Volbach was played at a Promenade Concert in London, and a year later his *Easter* was performed at the Sheffield Festival (see *Sheffield Festival Programme* and *Sheffield Telegraph*, 3 October 1902). In 1904 Volbach conducted several of his works at the Royal College of Music.

WEINGARTNER, FELIX (1863–1942) – held various posts as Kapellmeister in Germany before becoming conductor of the Kaim
Concerts in Munich in 1898. In 1907 Weingartner returned to
Austria to succeed Mahler as conductor of the Court Opera in
Vienna. He first visited London in 1898, but thereafter made frequent
visits, as also to other parts of the world. Weingartner's interpre-
tations were distinguished by a consummate musicianship, which
quality is also said to belong to his compositions.

WEST, JOHN EBENEZER (1863–1929) – a nephew of Ebenezer Prout,
joined Messrs. Novello in 1884 and was appointed musical editor
and adviser in 1897. He occupied this post until his retirement in
1929.

WILLIAMS, CHARLES LEE (1853–1935) – was organist of Llandaff
Cathedral (1876–82) and of Gloucester Cathedral (1882–97). He conducted five Festivals at Gloucester. Like many English musicians
of his period he composed a fair amount of undistinguished church
music.

WILSON, R. H. (1856–1932) – was born in Manchester where he studied
music with Frederick Bridge. In 1889 Wilson was appointed chorus-
master of the Hallé Choir, which appointment he retained until
1925. He worked with Richter and was largely responsible for the
great development of interest in choral music that took place in the
years before the First World War. Wilson was in charge of the
chorus at the Birmingham Festival on four occasions. His thorough
preparation of *Gerontius* for performance in Manchester helped to
ensure that that performance first showed the true stature of the
work to an English audience. He also prepared *The Apostles* for its
first performance in Birmingham.

'He had an immense veneration of Elgar, and used to tell some
thrilling stories of the period of devout inspiration that Elgar lived
in while he was writing his choral masterpieces' (Neville Cardus in
obituary notice, *Manchester Guardian*, 20 January 1932).

WOOD, SIR HENRY JOSEPH (1869–1944) – was engaged by Robert
Newman to conduct the Promenade Concerts in the Queen's Hall,
London, in 1895. In fifty seasons he made these concerts the most
remarkable feature of modern English popular musical culture.
Wood, whose interests were wide and uninhibited, conducted
many concerts and societies, with unflagging zest, in all parts of
Britain.

WÜLLNER, FRANZ (1832–1902) – German pianist, conductor, and composer, also became Kapellmeister in Aachen in 1858, and succeeded
von Bülow at the Court Theatre in Munich in 1869. In this capacity

he was closely involved with Wagner, whose *Das Rheingold* and *Die Walküre* he directed. From Munich Wüllner went to Dresden, and in 1884 he succeeded Ferdinand Hiller as Director of the Köln Conservatorium and of the Gürzenich Concerts in that City.

WÜLLNER, LUDWIG (1858–1938) – Son of Franz Wüllner, was both actor and singer. Although not a great singer, his dramatic gifts compensated for certain vocal deficiencies, and he made a great success of the part of Gerontius at Westminster Cathedral in 1903.

GENERAL INDEX